1988

The Uses of the Past

The Uses of the Past

Essays on Irish Culture

EDITED BY
Audrey S. Eyler
and
Robert F. Garratt

DELAWARE

Newark: University of Delaware Press
London and Toronto: Associated University Presses

Associated University Presses
440 Forsgate Drive
Cranbury, NJ 08512

Associated University Presses
25 Sicilian Avenue
London WC1A 2QH, England

Associated University Presses
2133 Royal Windsor Drive
Unit 1
Mississauga, Ontario
Canada L5J 1K5

The paper used in this publication meets the requirements
of the American National Standard for Permanence of Paper
for Printed Library Materials Z39.48-1984.

Library of Congress Cataloging-in-Publication Data

The Uses of the past.

Selected papers presented at the conference held in
Tacoma, Washington, Apr. 24–27, 1985, sponsored by
American Conference for Irish Studies.
Includes bibliographies.
1. Ireland—Civilization—Congresses.   2. English
literature—Irish authors—History and criticism—
Congresses.   3. History in literature—Congresses.
I. Eyler, Audrey S., 1943–   .   II. Garratt, Robert F.
III. American Conference for Irish Studies.
DA933.2.U83   1988   820'.9'358   86-40601
ISBN 0-87413-326-2 (alk. paper)

PRINTED IN THE UNITED STATES OF AMERICA

Contents

Preface

For over one hundred years, as Ireland has struggled toward a modern sense of cultural and political identity, artists, writers, and scholars have played no small part in the discussion and delineation of the elements of national consciousness. At every stage of the evolution from the Celtic Revival to the present concern over Ulster, those studying and writing about contemporary Ireland have found it necessary to reach back into history to understand the present. The presence of the past in contemporary life is more evident in Ireland than in many other modern nations both because modern Irish culture insists upon recalling its ancient heritage in literature, art, and music and because the contemporary Irish political climate often evokes particular historical events. The persistence of history in recent politics and cultural development dramatically demonstrates the tenacious grip of the past upon the contemporary Irish imagination. This historical sense seems inextricably bound to a crisis of identity, the logical result of living in a bifurcated society in which Gaelic and British elements struggle to authenticate themselves within their respective traditions. Both elements of Irish society, propelled by the confusion of differing political and cultural realities, look to the past to validate a sense of community and identity.

Ireland's historical imagination is evident not only in the political events of the past twenty-five years, when the past has often been repeated or invoked by those who attempted to shape those events, but also in cultural movements, as when, at the turn of the century, writers like William Butler Yeats were ideologically attracted to heritage and tradition in their efforts to create a national literature. These deliberate uses of the past have been the focus of recent Irish commentary in *The Crane Bag* and the *Field Day* pamphlets, and of current North American scholarship on Ireland. Such work inspired and shaped the 1985 meeting of the American Committee for Irish Studies (it has since been renamed the "American Conference for Irish Studies," or ACIS) held in Tacoma, Washington, 24–27 April, on the campuses of Pacific Lutheran University and the University of Puget Sound. Papers were gathered from artists and scholars in Irish studies, representing history, literature, film, folklore, anthropology, music, political science, and economics, as well as other disciplines. All participants were asked to address the importance of history and a sense of the past in understanding political and cultural identity. The essays in this collection were nominated from more than fifty papers presented at the Tacoma conference.

Thomas Flanagan and Richard Murphy present a dialogue on the importance of history to the Irish literary imagination. Both writers address the presence of the past in their works—Flanagan's novel *The Year of the French* and Murphy's narrative poem "The Battle of Aughrim"—by admitting its inevitability; in Flanagan's words, "History doesn't get into literature; it can never be kept out." Declan Kiberd offers a revisionist version of the legacy of the Irish Literary Revival, in which the Yeatsian view of history produces a contemporary impotence in Irish politics. Kiberd argues for a "revolutionary" alternative to a political rebellion and a literary revival in which history goes on "repeating itself, reduced to a narrative stutter tending toward infinity," the authoritarian hero "dying for nothing beyond his own gesture of heroism."

"Women in Irish Writing" was the deliberately ample title for a double session in which Bonnie Kime Scott was a responding participant. Although we have included none of the papers to which she refers in her essay, her generalizations are in themselves provocative and instructive, as she relates the Irish literature under discussion to various feminist frameworks. Looking at the history of critics and publishers in Irish literature, Scott admits that they "have not ignored women writers to the extent that their colleagues in British and American studies did for generations."

Hazard Adams shows the importance of Yeats and Joyce to contemporary literary theory, implying that great writers first challenge and then stimulate critical theory and practice. Yeats and Joyce anticipate deconstructionist thought by expressing the "infinite degree of readings" possible in modern culture. Yeats, Adams contends, offers his collected poems as an antithetical book to "face the terror of history." Joyce, in *Finnegans Wake*, engages in an infinite play of language that defies the fixing of any single reference, opting instead for a wider sense of *"about-ness"*—about original sin, Anna Livia Plurabelle, Ireland, family, love, procreation, Parnell, nature, the social world, history.

David Lloyd explores the very personal past in Clarence Mangan's work; in the larger monograph of which this essay is part, he suggests an analogous pattern in Irish nationalism. And in his essay describing patterns in *Cré na Cille (Churchyard Clay)*, Robert Tracy places Ó Cadhain's work, "the most important novel ever written in Irish," in its European, Irish, and English literary context. Like *The Waste Land*, that collection of historical and literary "fragments . . . shored against . . . ruins," *Church-*

yard Clay portrays with great vitality through the conversations of the dead "the collapse or eclipse of European culture."

Contesting the idea of class as a significant cause of peasant faction fighting of the early nineteenth century, James Donnelly provides a strong picture of a traditional Irish violence. We have, in fact, presentations of quarreling at numerous levels and in varied times—the infighting among Cosgrave's party in Maryann Valiulis's study of the Cumann na nGaedheal, the Gaelic League's "uneasy alliance" with Celtic Renaissance writers in Philip O'Leary's paper, and the struggles charted by Padraig O'Malley between the Social Democratic and Labour Party and Sinn Fein for Nationalist party leadership in the North, between the traditional nationalists and the radical socialists within Sinn Fein, and between the Irish Republican Army and the Irish National Liberation Army for military leadership. These divisions are, of course, a microcosm of the deeper divisions that permeate Ireland, North and South, divisions that exist not only between nationalist and unionist, but between unionist and unionist, nationalist and nationalist: divisions that make Ireland today, in the haunting words of Seamus Heaney, "an island of comfortless noises."

In contrast, folklorist Margaret Steiner demonstrates a balancing of rural prejudice and neighborliness through joking, courtesy, and pride of place. Here is community coexisting with faction; here is a noise of some comfort.

It is not the editors' naive intention to offer any single solution to Ireland's problems. Indeed, the selections in this volume recognize the deep complexity in Irish culture. Yet, in the ongoing discussion and analysis of that complexity, interdisciplinary scholars and artists of the ACIS offer another comforting sound.

Our thanks are recorded here to our colleagues in the ACIS, especially its Executive Board, the chairs of our conference sessions, and the 1985 conference participants; to Zack Bowen for his help; to our respective universities for their support; and to Megan Benton for her technical expertise.

Audrey S. Eyler
Robert F. Garratt

The Uses of the Past

1

Contrasting Fables in The Year of the French

Thomas Flanagan

Our general subject is how history gets into literature, with the ways in which history and literature traffic together. There is one general objection that could be made to the topic itself, one that we should not forget. There is no way in which history can ever be kept out of any kind of literature, even when that literature is being its most private and its most precise. Any poem, any shaped narrative, is the writer's response to circumstance, to the present, and any present carries within itself the sense of some past, if not of the past itself. And this would be true if for no other reason than that literature is shaped from words, and words—language—are rooted in several kinds of history. But this is not our immediate subject, which has to do with literary works that seek to recover, for whatever reasons, a past, or a version of the past, or a vision of the past, and nearly always of some specific past. And yet we could suggest works that would seem to have as a generating impulse simply "a sense of the past," to use Henry James's terms. A sense of the past: such an impulse is itself historically determined, a creation of the first romantic generations.

The term "historical novel" is one that I have always resisted, even before I became a historical novelist. But I do not resist it any more strongly than I do such other terms as "the social novel," "the psychological novel," or "the stream of consciousness novel." Such terms do, in fact, point toward generic distinctions that are genuine, although they do so at a cost. Nevertheless, there are differences among modes, and with the instance of the historical novel, I would suggest this difference by an anecdote.

It is somewhere recorded that Henry James at a party was told by his dinner partner of a dramatic occurrence that had involved acquaintances of hers. She told him about it briefly and casually. James was absorbed

13

and excited. "There's a marvelous story in that," he said, with a quizzical delight. She, in turn, delighted by the chance to be of service to an artist, said at once that she knew much more about the case than that; she knew all the details. James raised his hands at once to silence her. "No, no," he said, "not a word more."

Everyone who has ever written a story of any kind will likely know what James meant and why he acted as he did. But that is exactly what a historical novelist would not or, at least, should not do. A historical novelist would want to know more.

There is a multitude of facts known about the Mayo Rising of 1798 that I did not use in my novel about it. One of them is extraordinary. The French General Humbert lingered poised in Castlebar for a week, perhaps because he was hoping for reinforcements from France, perhaps because he was hoping for a more impressive local rally than he had received. He used this week to organize his so-called Republic of Connaught, appoint civil officials, and so forth. But he also organized, or caused to be organized, a grand ball and banquet attended, according to the various accounts, by many prominent persons of Mayo. There is no doubt that this so-called ball took place, but no one has left an account of it. And it beggars my imagination. When I was writing *The Year of the French* I would have welcomed, even in the terrifying form of a graveyard specter, a dinner partner who had attended it, the daughter perhaps of some half-mounted squireen from Crossmolina, whose escort for the evening had been Brigadier Sarrizen. Given the absence of particulars, such a revenant might be essential.

Lacking particulars, I did not feel my imagination could create the scene, and it is not in *The Year of the French*. (The producers of the television miniseries felt no such scruples. But not with felicitous results.) The historical novelist or the poet, when engaging the historical past, stands in a complex relationship to it. He or she is under an obligation, a comingled aesthetic and moral obligation, to render the past as it truly was, yet knows that the truth of the past is unrecoverable.

Writers have complex relationships not only toward the past but also toward readers. Simple readers assume that historical novels are "true," and for them the past is a series of brightly colored tapestries whose ontological status is unchallengeable. Even more sophisticated readers who know that novels, however wise, are fiction, often assume that the great nineteenth-century histories by Carlyle, Froude, Parkman, Prescott, and Taine are "true" rather than visions of the past imposed by those historians upon recalcitrant materials, shaped inevitably by the choice of represented incident, by language, by tone, and by expository and rhetorical strategies. The realization of this in our own time has led to the virtual abandonment by historians of narrative history, as though narrative is of itself a commitment to a kind of fiction. In consequence, historiography today is somewhat more accurate and infinitely more tiresome.

"What is truth?" wondered Pilate, and went to work on his novel. My own impulse was not primarily to tell the truth about the Mayo Rising, but rather to use what I took to be that truth as the substance from which a novel could be shaped. As such fictions go, I think it is quite faithful to what we believe to be the "facts." But I did take a number of liberties as the following examples describe and explain.

Part 1 of *The Year of the French* opens with the title "From *An Impartial Narrative of What Passed at Killala in the Summer of 1798*, by Arthur Vincent Broome, M. A. (Oxon.)" The internal title is italicized to suggest a book published a few years later, anonymously. The author was in fact Joseph Stock, the Anglican bishop of Killala. It was in his episcopal palace that Humbert set up his headquarters, and after Humbert moved south it remained headquarters for the garrison of French rebels, with Stock and his family housed on the second floor in crowded safety. The Stocks were not released from their captivity until the town was recaptured for the Crown by General Trent. Stock is, of course, the original Arthur Vincent Broome.

Now if I had simply fictionalized Stock, giving him another name, one could hardly have objected to so trivial a departure from records. But I went beyond this. I wanted a first-person witness to the Killala event but did not want someone so grand as a bishop. I therefore ruthlessly abolished the Diocese of Killala some thirty or forty years before the Mayo Rising with a vigor that might have impressed Gladstone and certainly would have impressed McHale. But more than this I made Broome an Englishman of a certain type, whereas Stock was a member of a distinguished Irish family, some of the distinction earned by his own reputation as a mathematician of rigor and ingenuity. One or two readers of the novel assumed that I didn't know about Bishop Stock and had given Broome a narrative with the same title by some fluke. But I took yet another step. Stock calls his narrative "impartial" and, in fact, it truly is so, more so at least certainly than the Rev. George Story's in Richard Murphy's poem "The Battle of Aughrim." Stock's is a curious kind of impartiality though. He seems to be impartial because he dislikes every-one connected with the events of which he writes—the rebels were louts, the Orangemen were bigoted bumpkins, the yeomen were incom-petent, the Frenchmen were boastful and ignorant of the terrain, the peasants were in general ignorant. There is something to warrant each of these prejudices. But Bishop Stock's narrative characterizes him, it seems to me, as a sensible, rather waspish fellow, who by grotesque accident has been drawn into a ludicrous episode on the ragged edge of

Europe. I wanted for Broome, however, that other mode of impartiality, which issues from warmth rather than ice. I created a character very much unlike that which I take to have been Bishop Stock's—fussy, generous, ridiculous, loveable, overly fond perhaps, as he himself admits, of civility and buttered toast. I wanted him, perhaps too obviously, to be one particular kind of registering consciousness.

Obviously Bishop Stock and Mr. Broome see very different rebellions, even though they report the same event. Compare, for example, the relationships of Ferdy O'Donnell, the rebel captain in Killala, with the actual Bishop Stock and with the imaginary Arthur Broome. Stock sees O'Donnell as a peasant, ignorant and wrathful but touched with a bit of nobility, who detests random violence and is, in some measure, to be credited with saving the lives of the Protestant prisoners in Killala. The man whom Broome sees is similar; how could he not be, for almost everything I know about Ferdy O'Donnell comes from Stock's narrative. But I made him more accessible. I wanted a strange friendship, but a genuine friendship, to spring up between Broome and O'Donnell. Who reports of O'Donnell more accurately, Stock or Broome? I'd be presumptuous, indeed, to argue that he was seen more clearly by my fictional creation than he was by an eyewitness who seems to have been shrewd, practical, and, on the whole, unwarped by partisanship.

But here my novel asks the basic question of all fiction: what if? What if Ferdy O'Donnell had not been seen by a Stock but by a Broome, a magnanimous Englishman seeking with whatever indifference to success to understand this alien and rebellious people? I was led, step by insensible step, out of history and into fiction, which is where novelists, historical or otherwise, properly belong, like poets and playwrights.

One of the great, if unacknowledged, American literary critics, it has long seemed to me, was the late Samuel Goldwyn. He did not like historical films and produced them only with reluctance. As he put it, "I don't like those movies where they write with feathers." He pointed out that nearly every movie he made about the American Civil War, good, bad, or indifferent, had made money, but virtually every movie about the American Revolution had flopped. Goldwyn doesn't offer any explanation for this. His critical style was very much like that of T. S. Eliot— bold shafts of illumination with the explanatory tasks left to disciples. The explanation in this instance seems to me that the Civil War occupies a place within Americans' psychic history that is both central and deep. It resonates for us at all levels, whether of the highest art or the most popular. It has also (especially at the popular level) great iconographic energy. So also, one would suppose, should the war of the Revolution, which, after all, is our foundation myth, our *Aeneid*, our *Book of Invasions;* it should have, but in fact it does not. At one time it did, of course; it inspired the men who fought the Civil War on both sides. But the final proof is in the box office receipts: Gettysburg pays, Saratoga does not.

There are many reasons for this but one of them, and perhaps not the least, is that George Washington wrote with a feather. So too, I believe, did Lincoln, although steel pens were by then in common use. The point is that the Revolution was a more "feathery" war, in the Goldwynian sense; each of us has a limited reach into the past. One's sense of history has its central nerve, its spinal cord, situated where the present feels joined to the past, and this sense of jointure grows every day fainter.

A few years ago an Irish historian suggested to me that in the seventeenth century it was the wars of Cromwell upon which Irish history pivoted. He was quite right, of course. Or perhaps Irish history has had three pivots, Kinsale, Drogheda (letting Drogheda stand for the Cromwellian Wars) and Aughrim. Not certainly that grotesque tussel in Mayo—and not really the United Irish Movement. He was quite right but also irrelevant. What is important for any writer is what grasps the imagination.

Yeats numbered these dates differently. They are his four bells, as he calls them—the flight of the Earls, the Battle of the Boyne, the coming of French influence among our peasants (he says somewhat inscrutably) and the beginning of our own age. "My historical knowledge, such as it is," he says, "begins with the second bell." He clarifies what he means by his own historical knowledge by asking whether his great-great-grandmother, the Huguenot Marie Voisin, felt a vindictive triumph, or rather remembered that her friend Archbishop King had long been a loyal servant of James II. Yeats then speaks of the Huguenot artists and weavers who designed the tapestries of the Boyne and Derry for the House of Lords.[1] I cannot vouch for Yeats's great-great-grandmother; in genealogical matters he was a historical novelist manqué. But his meaning is clear. By historical knowledge he means that imaginative reach, nourished upon particularity, that defines for him the actualizable past. And, in truth, beyond the time of Murphy's Aughrim we sense that we are in a dark abyss of bogs and mists and uncertainties.

Murphy, in his fine poem, gives an affectionate portrait of Sarsfield, as Sarsfield came to exist in the imagination of one part of post-Aughrim Ireland—"In Restoration wig, with German sword," cavalier, "horseman of the white cockcade."[2]

Beyond Sarsfield in that earlier century, the century of the first bell, rests a comparable figure in the post-historical imagination, Hugh O'Neill, the Earl of Tyrone, recreated for us and shown in Sean O'Faolain's biography, which has as its frontispiece a doubtful portrait ("putative" is O'Faolain's term), but it is all we know of Hugh O'Neill: an old man's head, thick-bearded, indistinct, drifting off into darkness, into surface imperfections that in the reproduction resemble stars. We reach as far back into the past as luck enables us, as we are enabled by chance, urgency, and curiosity; if we are fortunate, as we are when we read Murphy's poem or O'Faolain's biography, we can make out of the past a part of our continuing present.

NOTES

1. W. B. Yeats, *The Variorum Edition of the Poems of W. B. Yeats,* ed. Peter Alt and Russell K. Alspach (New York: Macmillan, 1957), 832–35.

2. Richard Murphy, "The Battle of Aughrim," in *High Island* (New York: Harper & Row, 1974), 72–73.

2

The Use of History in Poetry

RICHARD MURPHY

A general always hoped, in the past wars when there were pitched battles, to be able to choose the ground on which he fought. But here I find myself in a chapel (almost giving a sermon), a Protestant church, and talking on the subject of history and poetry because in the sixties I wrote a poem called "The Battle of Aughrim." Aughrim had been a watershed, a black line drawn across history, separating old and new. As the character Dennis Browne comments in Thomas Flanagan's *Year of the French*, "After Aughrim we all had to find our way in a new world."[1]

The village of Aughrim lies in the center of Ireland, the navel of the country. My connection with it was accidental at first. I happened to drive through it on my way to and from Dublin when I was living in Connemara, and always, going through the village (I knew little or nothing about the battle then), I felt an ominous sense of something terrible's having taken place there. That was the germ of what became a long sequence of poems—not an epic, because nowadays, certainly in this century, the epic has been taken over by the historical novel—but a way of coming at certain events in our past that have shaped the country we live in today.

In *The Year of the French*, the landlord George Moore refers to some passing herdsmen as men who lived and died below history. Of course that could be true in 1798, but today historians are most interested in what went on in the minds of the people who lived "below history." I tried to bring some of them into my poem, which became, rather than a narrative of events that took place on 12 July 1691, an equation of all the forces that met and decided those people's fate and the future of the country at that time and place. So the poem is a complex equation of people, ideas, myths, legends, facts—all mixed up. My eventual problem in writing this poem was how to put these pieces together, because I believed in allowing an organic growth of its parts rather than imposing a rigid pattern on them.

I was also trying to occupy ground midway between history on the one hand, and music, on the other. There is an explicit historical sense that I hope at no point the poem reaches, yet I think an assumed sense of history is essential to a poet. On the other hand was the music provided for the poem by Sean O'Riada, whom I met in London in 1962 when he came to a reading I was giving there. He introduced me to the traditional music of Ireland. (I met his musicians; he gave me the theme tunes that were combined with the poem in its first performance broadcast by the BBC in 1968.)

The poem itself took me five years to write. The following short piece expresses the way history invaded my imagination as I faced my project.

"History"

One morning of arrested growth
An army list roll-called the sound
Of perished names, but I found no breath
In dog-eared inventories of death.

Touch unearths military history.
Sifting clay on a mound, I find
Bones and bullets fingering my mind:
The past is happening today.

The battle cause, a hand grenade
Lobbed in a playground, the king's viciousness
With slaves succumbing to his rod and kiss,
Has a beginning in my blood.

Small as the audience for poetry is, I don't think we could write at all unless we were certain of having a definite audience in mind, some people who will read the works. In the 1960s narrative poetry was unfashionable and there was almost no audience for it at all, particularly for a long, long poem. But the BBC offered a medium in sound—radio— and the combination of music and poetry gave this poem quite a large audience, something like fifty thousand listeners.

But why write a history poem at all? The problems are immense. The greatest problem is dealing with material that is so far away that you have to work up the feeling to find any real connection with the past. It's easier, perhaps, in Ireland than it is in America; I had very strong family reasons, personal ones, for dealing with the Battle of Aughrim because I had ancestors who fought on opposite sides in that battle. I believe Ireland is a country in which many people are thus divided. And in assembling the bits and pieces I was as much concerned with what people in Ireland thought happened in the past as what actually did.

I think a lot of history is really about what people believed took place, not always about what did. The art of history is of immense value in correcting those myths about the past, the errors of judgment that have biased people's minds. Another reason for writing the poem, apart from family connection, was one that increased with force as I continued to work through the sixties and the war in Vietnam developed. The Battle of Aughrim too was fought by major powers, England against France, on the soil of a poor colonial territory. I was recently reminded of it by a remark made by Caspar Weinberger, U.S. Secretary of Defense, in connection with a more recent struggle. He said, I believe, that he was defending California when he fought in New Guinea, that it was better to defend California there than in Oregon. That is precisely what William of Orange was doing in Ireland and what Louis XIV was doing when he sent the Marquis of St. Ruth with the small token force to Aughrim.

The Rev. Arthur Vincent Broome in *The Year of the French* remarks that while we cannot learn anything from history, we may perhaps learn something from historians. I think the dangers with writing a historical poem are in being dogmatic, and in being political. One cannot write any poem that is not political in some sense, in my opinion, but there is a special danger with a set piece like a battle, where you know what has happened in the past, that the poem itself can become programmatic. In "The Battle of Aughrim," for example, I was harsher, I think, on the Protestant side because I was reared on that side and because I was living at the time in a small fishing village on the west coast of Ireland with Catholic friends. For instance, one section, set in the house of a Cromwellian ancestor of mine on the eve of the battle, is called "Planter":

Seven candles in silver sticks,
Water on an oval table,
The painted warts of Cromwell
Framed in a sullen gold.
There was ice on the axe
When it hacked the king's head.
Moths drown in the dripping wax.

Slow sigh of the garden yews
Forty years planted.
May the God of battle
Give us this day our land
And the papists be trampled.
Softly my daughter plays
Sefauchi's Farewell.

Dark night with no moon to guard
Roads from the rapparees,
Food at a famine price,
Cattle raided, corn trod,
And the servants against us
With our own guns and swords.
Stress a hymn to peace.

Quiet music and claret cups,
Forty acres of green crops
Keep far from battle
My guest, with a thousand troops
Following his clan-call,
Red-mouthed O'Donnell.
I bought him: the traitor sleeps.

To whom will the land belong
This time tomorrow night?
I am loyal to fields I have sown
And the king reason elected:
Not to a wine-blotted birth-mark
Of prophecy, but hard work
Deepening the soil for seed.

Countering that, this picture of "Rapparees" is based mainly on Macaulay:

Out of the earth, out of the air, out of the water
And slinking nearer the fire, in groups they gather:
Once he looked like a bird, but now a beggar.

This fish rainbows out of a pool: "Give me bread!"
He fins along the lake-shore with the starved.
Green eyes glow in the night from clumps of weed.

The water is still. A rock or the nose of an otter
Jars the surface. Whistle of rushes or bird?
It steers to the bank, it lands as a pikeman armed.

With flint and bundles of straw a limestone hall
Is gutted, a noble family charred in its sleep,
And they gloat by moonlight on a mound of rubble.

The highway trees are gibbets where seventeen rot
Who were caught last week in a cattle raid.
The beasts are lowing. "Listen!" "Stifle the guard!"

In a pinewood thickness an earthed-over charcoal fire
Forges them guns. They melt lead stripped from a steeple
For ball. At the whirr of a snipe each can disappear

Terrified as a bird in a gorse-bush fire,
To delve like a mole or mingle like a nightjar
Into the earth, into the air, into the water.

The music of Sean O'Riada, which accompanied the original broadcast of this poem, stirs me deeply as a true voice of the suffering people of Ireland at the time of Aughrim, particularly his "Limerick's Lamentation" and "The White Cockade." Yet O'Riada's music is one-sided in a way that I did not wish my poem to be, and to balance that when it came to the recording, we involved Englishman Henry Purcell as well.

I believe that the best, the most important, history in all poetry is in the words themselves, the history that is latent in all the words we use. To a poet that is the most important history—the etymology of words. And when history is assumed into the body of the poem and becomes another sense of it, as when it is assumed in the words themselves, then it is of more value than writing poems about history.

NOTES

1. Thomas Flanagan, *The Year of the French* (New York: Pocket Books, 1980), 540.

2. Richard Murphy, "The Battle of Aughrim," in *High Island* (New York: Harper & Row, 1974), 52. Subsequent quotations are from this edition, cited parenthetically by page number in the text.

3

The War against the Past

DECLAN KIBERD

> The best women, like the best nations, have no history.
> —George Eliot

> The greatest sin a man can commit against his race is to
> bring the work of the dead to nothing. . . . We all hope that
> Ireland's battle is drawing to an end, but we must live as
> though it were to go on endlessly. We must pass into the
> future the great moral qualities that give men the strength to
> fight. . . . It may be that it depends upon writers and poets
> such as us to call into life the phantom armies of the future.
> —W. B. Yeats

Just after the triumphant production of his play *Cathleen ni Houlihan* in 1902, W. B. Yeats wrote the above words. Like so many nationalists before and since, Yeats there seemed to extol the notion of the fight as a self-sustaining tradition, rather than the more humane idea of the culture fought for. It is the mark of many conservative thinkers to see in sacrifice not the highest price a man may pay to assert his self, but an end in its own right. Even more sinister is Yeats's implied view of the Irish revival not as a restoration of personal freedoms but as bleak revenger's tragedy, in the course of which this generation will get even with England on behalf of Ireland's patriot dead.

This fatalistic view of history leaves little room for the autonomy of the person. In his dramatization of the Deirdre legend, Yeats showed how slender are the resources of individual protagonists when pitted against the destiny embodied by the chorus. The play *Deirdre* opens with the first musician declaring:

I have a story right, my wanderers,
That has so mixed with fable in our songs,
That all seemed fabulous.[1]

At first it seems as though the tale already has its final form, needing
only to be narrated. The second musician yearns for that sense of an
ending that will ensure her significance as a professional teller:

> The tale were well enough
> Had it a finish . . .
>
> (113)

But Fergus, the king's man, insists that history is still open. Deirdre and
her lover Naisi *have* been forgiven, despite the terrible prophecy. Each
time the first musician reopens her story on the appointed line—"There
is a room in Conchubar's house, and there" (115)—and just as often
Fergus brutally cuts off the fated tale, asserting the rights of the individual to curve, or even break, the line of history. Yet even he too stumbles,
almost against his better judgment, into piecing together the missing
elements of the plot that he is so keen to abort. He recalls an ancient tale
of how Lugaidh Redstripe and his wife played at chess on the night of
their death. He conjures up a ghost from the very past that he seeks to
escape:

> I can remember now, a tale of treachery,
> A broken promise and a journey's end—
> But it were best forgot.
>
> (117)

Yet he remains oblivious of the fact that Deirdre and Naisi seem about to
reenact that half-remembered story. Half-remembered, and for that very
reason wholly to be repeated.

At this point in Yeats's play, the men are all agreed that ancient tales
are the appropriate concern of terrified and superstitious women, while
men alone have the courage to "meet all things with an equal mind"
(118). They have not reckoned with Deirdre, however—a woman who
has already decided that she is both musician and tragic protagonist,
both rebel and poet recording and extolling her rebellious act. It has
often been remarked that whereas the men in the play are still intent on
sorting out their relations to one another, Deirdre alone realizes that the
only crucial task remaining is to establish a fitting relationship with the
chorus:[2]

> But I have one [she boasts]
> To make the stories of the world but nothing.
>
> (121)

There will still be moments when Deirdre is tempted to tamper with the
fatal tale, as when she threatens to destroy the beauty that so dazzles

and inflames the king; but, on that occasion, Naisi dutifully takes up the chorus line:

> Leave the gods' handiwork unblotched, and wait
> For their decision; our decision is past. . . .
>
> (123)

Inevitably Fergus, the congenital interrupter, is himself interrupted by the king's message, which heralds death for Naisi and the betrayal of Fergus's precious trust. There is nothing left for the lovers but to put a brave face on things, so that the long-remembering harpers will have matter for their song. As they plunge to inevitable death, the phantom armies of the future will derive comfort from the inspiring story of how Deirdre and Naisi composed themselves in the face of the grave. Naisi nerves himself for his plunge into history by casting himself in a role from the ancient costume-drama of Lugaidh Redstripe:

> What do they say?
> That Lugaidh Redstripe and that wife of his
> Sat at their chess-board, waiting for their end.
>
> (124–25)

Deirdre is torn by conflicting impulses, between the desire for "a good end to the long cloudy day" (125), which further affiliates her to the musicians who voice this need, and, on the other hand, a growing awareness of the dangers of playing like that "cold woman" (125) of the old story. Whenever one of the lovers loses relish for the assigned role, the other coaches the offending partner in the stratagems of performance. Naisi advises; "It is your move, take up your man again . . ." (126), just as Deirdre had coached the chorus to "make no sad music" (125). Curiously, it is at the moments when the characters seem most resigned to the plot that the musicians grow restless with their assigned parts. The more Deirdre appropriates herself to the chorus, the more the musicians empathize with the characters caught in the web of events. The first musician effectively makes available the knife with which Deirdre will kill herself. She doesn't exactly give it, for Deirdre snatches it, but the impression is nevertheless created that, for all their human sympathy, the musicians need a shaped story and have a vested interest in giving history a shove. The first musician says:

> You have taken it,
> I did not give it you; but there are times
> When such a thing is all the friend one has.
>
> (127)

By this stage, both Deirdre and Naisi have resigned themselves to their roles in history, which are likened to a net that entraps the tragic hero; the more he struggles to free himself, the more enmeshed he becomes. In her own mind Deirdre has already passed beyond life, and she loiters only to ask the singing women what words they will find to praise her and Naisi. Like Hamlet breathing his last words to Horatio, she gives the first musician a bracelet and prophesies that many welcoming doors will be opened to her

> . . . because you are wearing this
> To show that you have Deirdre's story right.

> (127)

It is almost as if she decides to die, less a martyr to the king than to the literary tradition, which will derive sustenance from the tale of her death and inspire future lovers, as the tale of Lugaidh Redstripe inspired this pair, to repeat the deed, never as farce, but always as tragedy.

Many of the classic elements of the authoritarian personality are latent in Yeats's tragic protagonist—particularly the courage to suffer the decrees of destiny without complaint, but not the courage of trying to stop pain or, at least, to reduce it. "Not to change fate, but to submit to it, is the heroism of the authoritarian character," says Erich Fromm in *The Fear of Freedom*. Fromm extends his analysis by showing that such a character worships the past, believing that what has been will eternally be. "To wish or work for something that has not yet been before is crime or madness. The miracle of creation—and creation is always a miracle—is outside his range of emotional experience."[3] It is, of course, hard for any man to love that which does not exist, and yet it is the very nature of true love to effect such a miraculous creation. A passing Samaritan, when faced with the broken flesh and bones of another's past, offers tenderness not really to the ravaged body so much as to the full person who this very act of kindness will bring into being. It was for this reason that Simone Weil wrote that "creative attention means really giving our attention to that which does not exist."[4] What is true of individuals may also be true of the love one gives to a nation, so that a real patriotism would base itself not on the broken bones and accumulated grudges of the national past, but on an utterly open future. A true hero would thus be one who imagines future virtues, which would be admirable precisely because others could not conceive of them. In a land where the word *past* is interchangeable with the word *guilt*, the idea of an uncertain future has a liberating force, as much because it is uncertain as because it is the future. The theologians of liberation have, indeed, seen such heroism as the duty of every Christian person. Rudolf Bultmann has gone so far as to redefine the sinner as the one who fears the future and desperately tries to forestall its coming.[5] Such a person—and Yeats was one—sees history not as the story of a people creating itself, but as a series of meetings with remarkable people, who turn out to be remarkable not for any individual qualities but simply and solely for their ability to submit, ostentatiously, to the approved patterns of the past.

Colonialism had denied the Irish personality the right to know itself. It was not surprising that those who suffered in consequence from a tenuous sense of selfhood should have prostrated themselves before apparently charismatic leaders. Unable to be self-sufficient, the colonized race nursed feelings of hatred for the authority that had so humiliated it. The way out of this crisis was to idealize some ordinary man as a superepitome of the history that was overtaking them all. Fromm's description of this process in Germany can be translated, with only a little straining, into Irish terms. The idealization of the new leader harmlessly drained off the accumulated feelings of hatred, while the glamour surrounding the "uncrowned king" converted the humiliation into intelligent obedience.[6] Hence, Yeats viewed nineteenth-century Irish history as the story of O'Connell and Parnell.

Unfortunately, the Yeatsian view of history inserted itself into the school textbooks. As an analysis it is, of course, not really historical at all, based as it is on a rupture of chronology by the endless repetition of familiar crises, with no hope of a resolution. It is in just such a context that the fight becomes more important than the thing fought for, and "history" is deemed history only if it exactly repeats itself. New leaders may climb to power, but only if they have a gift for verbal repetition. In *Life Against Death*, Norman O. Brown points out that "under the condition of repression, the repetition-compulsion establishes a fixation to the past, which alienates the neurotic from the present and commits him to the unconscious quest for the past in the future. Thus neurosis exhibits the quest for novelty, but underlying it, at the level of the instincts, is the compulsion to repeat."[7] There could hardly be a more fitting description than this of the psychology of literary revivalism, or of its effect in reducing history to a narrative stutter tending toward infinity, in the manner of Christy Mahon telling his story six times since the dawning of the day, before leaving the stage to repeat his short, sharp, meaningless encounter in every other Mayo parish.

INTERNAL COLONIALISM

The situation is tragic rather than ludicrous because, even after the colonizer has gone, the obsessive pathology of repetitiousness remains, visible in the career of Eamon de Valera, the new Yeatsian leader. The paralysis that Frantz Fanon detected in certain newly independent African states also gripped "independent" Ireland:

> The leader pacifies the people . . . unable really to open the future. . . . We see him endlessly reassessing the history of the struggle for liberation. The leader, because he refuses to break up the national bourgeoisie, asks the people to fall back into the past—and to become drunk on remembrance.[8]

This is doubtless the kind of thing that Conor Cruise O'Brien had in mind when he accused his countrymen of seeming intent on commemorating themselves to death. It is instructive, in this context, to contrast the behavior of the Irish electorate in the 1930s and 1940s—which consistently reelected ex-gunmen who talked repeatedly about past gunplay—with that of their counterparts in Britain, who unsentimentally disposed of Winston Churchill after World War Two lest his once-valued martial rhetoric come between them and a welfare state.

The Irish leader, on the other hand, was as lacking in a sense of self as the public that supported him. Revivalist leaders—and there are many in the world today—have no comprehensive program. They desire not to lead but to occupy the position of leader. It is this very emptiness that gives them their charm, allowing them to reflect back to their followers whatever it is that the followers want to see. Karl Marx spotted such a figure on the world stage in the middle of the nineteenth century and wrote an essay about him entitled "The Eighteenth Brumaire of Louis Bonaparte." Marx regarded him as a comic buffoon who "can no longer take world history for a comedy and so must take his comedy for world history."[9] So, in the Irish parallel, the boy from Bruree must be the subject of endless radio broadcasts that remind listeners of his rise from humble country cottage dweller to shaper of a nation. That the nation is *not* being shaped is what this self-mythologizing is designed to occlude—just as the Yeatsian hero dies for nothing beyond his own gesture of heroism, fights for nothing beyond the notion of the fight, and lives for nothing beyond his own place in literature. Confronted with each crisis of statecraft or economics, the new leader, like Deirdre and Naisi in the play, can do little but repeat the tale of his own apotheosis. The classic political career in "independent" Ireland thus becomes a farcical repetition of Yeats's own progress, which began with a youth intent on reshaping an entire nation and ended with a besieged and weary old man merely defending an archaic sensibility. In such a culture, persons are judged on what they are—or more precisely on what they say they are—rather than on what they do. No wonder, therefore, that de Valera is best remembered for his sole witticism—that in most countries it doesn't matter what you say, so long as you do the right thing, but in Ireland it doesn't matter what you do, so long as you find the right formula of words.

It need not necessarily have been so. To restore to history the openness it once had, one has only to reread James Connolly's warning that the worship of the past was really an idealization of the mediocrity of the present:

> In Ireland . . . we have ever seized upon mediocrities and made them our leaders; invested them in our minds with all the qualities we idealized, and then when we discovered that our leaders were not heroes but only common mortals, mediocrities, we abused them, or killed them, for failing to be any better than God made them. Their failure dragged us down along with them. . . . Our real geniuses and inspired apostles we never recognized, nor did we honour them. We killed them by neglect, or stoned them whilst they lived, and then went in reverent procession to their graves when they were dead. . . .[10]

That passage remarkably parallels P. H. Pearse's famous retraction of his attacks on J. M. Synge. In *An Claidheamh Soluis*, 21 November 1908, Pearse wrote: "In our sentiments and tastes, we are often too extreme. We worship our poets and politicians for a time, as if they were gods, and when we discover them to be human we stone them. Some writers of the Abbey may have sinned against our deepest sentiments, but the good they have done outweighs all their shortcomings."[11] By 1913 Pearse had come to identify very strongly with Synge in his martyr's role and to regret that he was no longer around to dramatize the events of the Dublin Lock-Out. Stirring indeed were those events: in that year the average circulation of Larkin's socialist paper the *Irish Worker* peaked at ninety thousand copies, while the nationalist paper *Sinn Fein* was selling two thousand.

THE SEARCH FOR AN ABUSABLE PAST

It is significant that Pearse should have endorsed not only Synge plays but, by implication, their antiheroic vision as well just when he regarded the people as its own messiah. For no better critique of the authoritarian heroism of Yeats's *Deirdre* has ever been offered than Synge's last play on the same theme, *Deirdre of the Sorrows*. His Fergus, betrayed by the king at the end, throws his sword into the lovers' grave in symbolic repudiation of the bankrupt aristocratic code. Here the place of the chorus is taken by the old woman Lavarcham, but she interprets her assigned role with far greater flexibility than did Yeats's musicians. Although she does, on occasion, invoke the coercive power of the plot to influence the other protagonists, this is done not to propel the ancient prophecy but rather to save the lovers from themselves, as when she warns Naisi against violating the king's prerogative: "That'll be a story to tell . . . that Naisi is a tippler and stealer. . . ."[12] Throughout the play, what distinguishes Lavarcham is her submission to her part as recounting chorus, *along with* her insistence that the malign destiny need not be fulfilled. Most observers note how Synge humanized his characters, treating them as fallible mortals rather than as stiff Yeatsian royalty, but few remark on how he also humanized his chorus. Here the lovers return from Scotland, not under *geasa* (ritual obligation), but because of the more human fear of old age in Alban. Lavarcham is as unimpressed by this more homely reasoning as she was by the claims of the fated prophecy. "There's little hurt getting old," she warns Deirdre, "saving when you're looking back, the way I'm looking this day, and seeing the young you have a love for breaking up their hearts with folly." (235). Deirdre, however, incorrigibly Yeatsian, is anxious to hear Lavarcham tell stories of past queens Maeve and Nessa and is already a connoisseur of her own literary performance in the same tradition, posing fatally for posterity: "and a story will be told forever" (229). Lavarcham's more pragmatic impulse is to ask—like a certain Anglo-Irish joker—what has posterity ever done for us; but the self-dramatizing Deirdre suffers the last infirmity of the romantic mind, the belief that all nature is in reckless collusion with her mood. The little moon, she thinks, will be lonely when she is gone, as lonely as the woods of Cuan. It is part of Synge's realism that he can let the Celtic nature poets have their eloquent say, only to mock such self-delusion in the final lines of the play, in which Lavarcham questions those very notions of pathetic fallacy that helped to nerve Deirdre on the way to her death: "Deirdre is dead, and Naisi is dead; and if the oaks and stars could die for sorrow, it's a dark sky and a hard and naked earth we'd have this night in Emain" (268). But the oaks and stars disobligingly survive our deaths and that is the loneliest discovery of all, as Synge once remarked.

Those lines are a wonderfully ambiguous conclusion, for in them Lavarcham discharges the traditional role of telling the tale to its finish while sustaining her reservations about its romantic predestination. In many respects Lavarcham is Synge's most complex creation for, like all his heroes and heroines, she can provide the imaginative appeal of a good story, while also retaining a healthy respect for those elements of human experience that resist imaginative transformation. As he got older and wiser, Synge's interest in the recalcitrant elements grew, until he seemed to find in their imperviousness to literature the basis for a strange kind of hope. It is that part of the person that refuses the surrender to the prescribed patterns of the past that truly excited Synge, just as it was soon to animate the similarly antiheroic James Joyce.

In one respect, the burdens borne by Joyce's Mr. Bloom are immeasurably lightened by the fact that he is not even aware that his wanderings around Dublin reenact the voyages of Odysseus. Yet reenact them he does and, in a deeper sense, his very unawareness may seem to indicate an even ruder curtailment of his freedom. If, as Engels said, freedom is the *conscious* recognition of necessity, then most definitely Leopold Bloom is unfree—his whole existence is an inauthentic rehash of someone else's. His very being is a literary revival, for his life is lived in inverted commas or, as the structuralists would say, perverted commas. There are crucial moments in *Ulysses* when the Homeric plot seems a great deal more real than the tenuous and uncertain self on which it is imposed. Bloom thus partakes of the same unauthenticity as an Irish Renaissance staged in manifest quotation marks, as a revival of various revivals. Yet to say this is to say little enough, for what delights us in Bloom are not his mindless concurrences with the past but rather, as Hugh Kenner first argued, those moments when history repeats itself with telling human variations, as in the immortal Dublin witticism, "the same, only different."[13] In such a context the repetitions no longer seem purely constricting, but give to the differences savour and meaning. The very unpretentiousness of Bloom, his utter innocence of the parallels between himself and the ancient Greek hero, adds not only to the poignancy of Joyce's character, but also to the final likeness. It repeats Homer's most telling point—that heroism is never conscious of itself as such. It is in this light that we are forced to reread Yeats's plays and to concede that, far from being a heroine, his Deirdre is merely a Celtic Hedda Gabler who was caught in a plot that prevented her from becoming herself. Like Ibsen's fatal woman, she kills herself when she discovers that her role leaves her with no self to kill. Ireland was to do much the same in 1922, as we shall presently see.

By far the most brilliant retelling of the Deirdre legend in recent times is Brian Friel's *The Faith Healer,* a play whose protagonists, like its critics, are as unaware as Bloom that they are reenacting an ancient legend.[14] Yet Friel's plot tells of a well-brought up girl who is destined for a noble calling in the north of Ireland but spirited away to Scotland by an attractive but weak young man, to the great dismay of her elderly guardian. In Scotland, and also in Wales, the lovers live well enough for many years, supported by their manager Teddy, who performs the same role as Naoise's brothers in Synge's play. Ultimately, however, this nomadic life is felt to be stressful and, not without foreboding, they return to Ireland only to find no sense of homecoming. In both Synge's and Friel's versions the characters delight in listing the names of places loved and lost, but Friel's heroine lives on for a year of misery before her suicide, in keeping with the Old Irish version of the legend.

Constrained by a time-honored plot, the characters, like the author Friel, improvise what little freedoms they can. They each face the audience in soliloquy and tell discrepant versions of the old tale, altering the story with a twist that gratifies their vanities. Like the artist-healer, they remould their shattered lives to some private standard of excellence, just as Friel has remoulded the story to his current artistic needs. In *The Anxiety of Influence* Harold Bloom suggested that every major artist is a kind of Francis Hardy, creatively distorting and misreading a work from the past to clear some imaginative space for himself in the present and avoid being smothered by past masters.[15] In similar fashion, James Connolly creatively misinterpreted the landholding systems of Gaelic Ireland to pave the way for the communist systems of his ideal future. If the artist—and in his reading of history Connolly was nothing if not an artist—fully understands his ancient model, then he will be overwhelmed by it, as Yeats was by the official version of Deirdre. On the other hand, what Harold Bloom calls the "strong artist" will imperfectly assimilate the past model and be thereby saved by the mistake. So, for Friel and Synge as for Joyce, the same can also be the new. By a somewhat similar process, Pearse summoned Cuchulain to his side in the General Post Office (GPO) of 1916, but only to validate his dream of a welfare state; while Joyce smuggled the most subversive narrative of the century into polite society, having first gift-wrapped it in the likeness of one of Europe's oldest tales.[16]

To explain this maneuver, the Spanish philosopher Ortega Y Gasset used the beautiful metaphor of the step backward taken by the bullfighter before delivering the mortal thrust. Ortega believed that the man of antiquity "searched the past for a pattern into which he might slip as into a diving-bell, and being thus at once disguised and protected might rush upon his present problem." Thomas Mann saluted this attitude as, quite literally, festal, a constant making present of the past as in an anniversary.[17] There is, however, another view. All too often the fighter of Irish bulls takes one step back only to be impaled on the horns of the past and never recovers to deliver the mortal blow. Such a maneuver leads not to personal liberation but to tragedies of mistaken identity, such as one finds in a modern Ireland whose people have never had the opportunity to become themselves. After the Easter Rebellion, they abandoned the Irish Renaissance as a search for personal freedom and turned it into a Yeatsian tragedy; they made it an attempt to vindicate "the work of the past" (in Yeats's terms) rather than one to forge the "uncreated conscience of the race" (in Joyce's definition). All of a sudden the national stage was filled with the ghosts of dead men insisting that the living simplify and abandon their daily lives, to the point of becoming agents of the dead. History, as Marx explained in "The Eighteenth Brumaire," became a nightmare in the minds of the living, a phrase that would reecho in the opening pages of Joyce's masterpiece. The revolutionaries had sought to create themselves out of nothing; those who remained were reduced to revivalists, seeking mere revenge.

The national dilemma was dramatized by the career of Shakespeare's Hamlet, as writers as diverse as Yeats, Joyce, and, more recent, Heaney have testified.[18] Yeats's Hamlet was a deployer of masks, Joyce's became his own father, and Heaney's stands by graves dithering and blathering. But the full implications of the parallels have never been traced. At the age of thirty, after a protracted education as courtier, soldier, and scholar, Hamlet was about to come into his own when he met a ghost and, henceforth, could never become himself. Although the role of revenger was one to which he was ill-suited and ill-disposed, once the ghost had seized the center stage Hamlet was destined to fill it. Hamlet becomes in consequence, as Yeats noted, a character obsessed with role-playing.[19] He coaches Polonius and the players in the art of acting, tells the queen to assume those virtues she doesn't have, and punctures the thin disguises of Osric, Rosencrantz, Guildenstern, and the usurping king. His gift for mimicry is unbounded but, in the end, it is his tragedy to be able to discover and play virtually every part except his own. Like Yeats's Deirdre—also something of an expert in stratagems of performance—to know his deed he has to postpone and finally cancel the moment when he might know himself. By act 5 he reappears among the graves, not really as the mature man sought by Joyce, but more as a kind of ghost come back from the dead—much as Pearse, Connolly, and the other dead men eternally return, their words simplified and insisting that those who follow simplify themselves too. In a radical reinterpretation of the theme, Harold Rosenberg has shown how Hamlet wiped away all trivial fond records of his own half-constructed past and abandoned himself to a merely historical role.[20] Having hovered precariously in the first four acts between an assigned role and a putative self, he finally surrenders to the ur-Hamlet, the preordained revenger's plot. The living man capitulates to the dead. To murder the false king, he must first abort his scarcely born self. Yet that is not all; as Rosenberg argues, the dilemma of the man-actor remains:

> On the stage which is the world the plot is written by nobody and no one can denote himself truly. . . . The drama in which the living man attempted in vain to seize his life as particular to himself concludes by proclaiming the utter irony of human existence, as Fortinbras orders a

soldier's burial for Hamlet, not for what he did but for what he might have done.[21]

In similar procession, Pearse and Connolly pass into Irish iconography attired forever in that most inappropriate garb, the military uniform. Even the ghosts of our fathers are thus simplified before they are allowed to terrify and haunt us, clanking around in their unwieldy and incongruous armor.

ESCAPE FROM FREEDOM

The rebellion of 1916, and the Irish Revival that surrounded it, may have led people into a similar tragedy of mistaken identity. The question to be asked is not how the socialist Connolly could have thrown in his lot with the nationalist Pearse, but rather how two such complex and radical thinkers, intent on instituting "the people" as its own messiah, could have so dreadfully mistaken their historic moment. In "The Eighteenth Brumaire" Marx had already warned about the lamentable tendency of ghosts to appear on the eve of revolutions. So the men of 1789 nerved themselves for the unthinkable by casting themselves as resurrected Romans. As Caesar had worn the mask of Alexander, and Alexander of Miltiades, so the rebels of 1916, without the irony of a Pearse or a Connolly, donned the mask of Cuchulain. The whole of history had been a story of mistaken identity said Marx, staged as a bizarre costume drama in which the protagonists could never be themselves. Even the radicals of recent times, just when they seemed on the point of creating themselves out of nothing but their own desires, had relapsed into the farce of revivalism:

> An entire people, which had imagined that by means of a revolution it had imparted to itself an accelerated power of motion, suddenly finds itself set back into a defunct epoch and, in order that no doubt as to the relapse may be possible, the old dates rise again, the old chronology, the old names, the old edicts, which had long become a subject of antiquarian erudition, and the old minions of the law, who had seemed long decayed.[22]

History becomes a farce without events, where "nothing happens" not just twice but indefinitely, "wearing with constant repetition of the same tensions, the same relaxations."[23] The ancient plot takes over, much as the individuals are suppressed by the emphatic chorus in Yeats's play. However, Marx had no doubt that when a real revolution finally came, the people would not mistake themselves for historical actors but would wear their own clothes.

This was exactly the point made by Sean O'Casey when he opposed Captain Jack White's introduction of military uniforms into the Irish citizen army. He argued that formal costumes would simply set up Connolly's men as highly visible targets for the opposing army. In the opening acts of *The Plough and the Stars*, the rebels and their supporters strut in the most outlandish historical uniforms, complete with ostrich plumes, evoking a mixture of awe and contempt among the tenement-dwellers, but when the fighting nears its end the rebels are pathetically anxious to shrug off their incriminating clothing and seek shelter in the anonymity of proletarian dress and tenement life. One of the escaping rebels threatens to shoot the "slum lice" if they continue to loot shops. In using that phrase to characterize the people in whose name he has helped to lead the rebellion, the officer confirms the suspicion that there is yet another tragedy of irrelevance.

It is well known that colonialism always makes its subjects seem theatrical so that even their gestures of revolt seem "literary" rather than "real." Hence the theatricality of the 1916 rebellion, led by poets and playwrights who brandished ceremonial swords, sported kilts, and played the bagpipes during a guerilla confrontation at a potently symbolic time of the year, invoking sacrifice, renewal, and resurrection. But the more poignant the gesture is in literary terms, the more tragic is its irrelevance to human needs. For example, the rebels of 1916, as elsewhere in Europe that year, seem to have affected every form of dress except their own. In his essay "The Suit and the Photograph," John Berger marvelled at the crumpled and ill-fitting suits worn by most laborers, peasants, and craftsmen at the time. Such workers did not lack the skill to choose good cloth or the knowledge of how to wear it, but the suits were designed for the sedentary administrators of a ruling class. The vigorous actions of the laborers merely spoiled the suits, which were clearly inappropriate for the lives they led. A clear example of class hegemony, the suits worn by Dubliners on the barricades at Talbot Street in 1916 showed their acceptance of cultural norms that had nothing to do with their daily experience, and condemned them "to being always, and recognizably to the classes above them, second-rate, clumsy, uncouth, defensive."[24]

Even less appropriate, more archaic forms of costume were worn by some rebel leaders inside the GPO, most notoriously the kilt. They mistakenly believed that kilts had been worn by Irish chieftains and their pipers as they marched into battle; the aristocratic connotations pleased the more snobbish elements among the revivalists. In fact, the ancient Irish wore hip-hugging trousers long before the English (and were reviled for it), but they never wore kilts, which offer few defenses against the insinuating moisture of the Irish climate. Indeed, it has recently been shown that the kilt, far from being an ancient Highland dress in Scotland, was invented by an English Quaker industrialist in the early 1700s and "was bestowed by him on the Highlanders not in order to preserve their traditional way of life but to ease its transformation: to bring them out of their heather and into the factory."[25]

Many other "ancient traditions" of the Irish Revival turn out, on inspection, to be cases of instant archaeology. History becomes a form of science fiction by which people can pretend to find in the endlessly malleable past whatever they secretly desire in the golden future. So "Gaelic" football was invented in the 1880s as a consciously wrought antidote to soccer. Such ploys were at once a rejection of Englishness and a craven surrender to the imperialist English notion of an antithesis between all things English and Irish. So, if the English had hockey, the Irish must have hurling; if the English wore trousers, the Irish wore kilts; if John Bull spoke English, Paddy spoke Irish, and so forth. This slot-rolling mechanism was derided in recent decades by Seán de Fréine as "the ingenious device of national parallelism," whereby for every English action there must be an equal and opposite Irish reaction. De Fréine acidly noted the failure of the Irish mind to clear itself of imposed English categories: "It was felt that the Irish could not claim as theirs anything that was characteristic of England; on the other hand, not to have it could betoken inferiority."[26] Irish people were so busy being not-English that they had scarcely time to think of what it might mean to be Irish. They forgot who they were or might be in their hysterical desire not to be taken for something else. J. M. Synge laughed at the knee-jerk nationalism of a Gaelic League that could define itself only according to English categories. "With their eyes glued on John Bull's navel," he mocked, "they are afraid to be Europeans for fear the huckster across the street might call them English."[27]

If any hucksters had had the temerity to hurl such an insult, they would probably have been right. The IRA created its military structure with the help of manuals stolen from the British army, while the nationalist courts deliberately aped the legal rituals of the power they fought. Even today something of that trend persists as IRA funerals, shown on British (but not fully on Irish) television, exactly parallel the obsequies for English soldiers killed in the north of Ireland. Indeed, at the height of the revival, the very worst excesses of imperialism seemed to have built a replica of themselves in Irish brains. So Arthur Griffith, a founder of Sinn Fein, could call for a stronger Irish industry, lest Ireland never "be placed in a position to influence the cultivation and progress of less-advanced nations and to form colonies of its own."[28] It was small wonder that the political and legal institutions in the far-from-Free State were slavish imitations of English models. One cannot avoid suspecting that the new leaders, having no clear sense of selfhood, were bending over backwards to win the approval of those English authorities whom they had just ejected. Nowhere is this more obvious than in Yeats's hopeless rehabilitation of the modes of Irish deference. The English had deemed the Irish backward, superstitious, and uncivilized, but Yeats urged the Irish for "backward" to read "healthily rooted in tradition," for "superstitious" to read "religious," and for "uncivilized" to read "instinctive." Thus the racist slur was sanitized and worn with pride.[29] The deepest insults could now be happily internalized in the postcolonial mind. Irish people could postpone indefinitely the moment of self-identification. Instead they could spend their lives acting out assigned roles that might not be their own, but had the advantage of being well known.

For many years, up to 1922, the Irish had hovered, Hamlet-like, in the no man's land between a role and a self. True independence would have meant further years in hard search of that self, but instead partial freedom saw them resign themselves to a time-honored role. In *The Fear of Freedom* Erich Fromm describes this familiar capitulation: "To put it briefly, the individual adopts entirely the kind of personality offered to him by cultural patterns; . . . the discrepancy between the 'I' and the world disappears. . . . This mechanism can be compared with the protective colouring some animals assume. . . . But the price paid is high; it is the loss of the self." That lost self is replaced by a pseudoself (what Beckett would later call a "vice-exister"), as a result of which "thoughts can be induced from the outside and yet be subjectively experienced as one's own.[30] The costume-drama continues and a whole population goes on playing a part not its own. Independence means only that the old imperialist style of administration will be deployed by boys from Clongowes and Belvedere rather than from Eton and Ampleforth; when, in 1933, the less-colonized Tweedledum replaced the more-colonized Tweedledee, nothing changed. And in the 1940s and 1950s while England reformed her own society and created a welfare state, the Irish persisted in administering themselves through the old structures of imperialist England. The lookalikes replace the lookalikers. They are all in on the "act."

REVIVAL OR REVOLUTION?

Yet, now and then, a person will speak out on behalf of that tenuous (but never quite extinguished) Irish self, which feels demeaned and violated by all this play-acting. Like characters in a Beckett play, such people feel that others they do not know have been living their lives. Some years ago, a correspondent to the *Sunday Press* wrote:

> It is as if the Irish people are still living as an underground movement in their own country. The "shape" of Irish society and institutions fits Irish people like a badly tailored suit. We do not acknowledge the suit as our own; we do not feel at home in it, but we tolerate it as we have always tolerated everything. I never hear Irishmen talking about *our* courts, *our* garden, *our* representatives, etc.[31]

This condition gives rise to the suspicion that every Irish deed is an impersonation rather than an avowal, an "act" rather than a truly complete "action." "To say 'I' in a poem is hard for me," reports contemporary poet Eiléan Ni Chuilleanáin. This problem also agitated Yeats from start to finish, for despite repeated resolutions to "walk naked" he found it impossible to commit the ultimate revolutionary deed of speaking with his own face instead of performing through a rhetorical mask. Even the beautiful image with which he sought to dignify the executed rebels in "Easter 1916"

> . . . our part
> To murmur name upon name
> As a mother names her child,
> When sleep at last has come
> On limbs that had run wild[32]

manages also to trivialize the insurgents' theatrical gesture in a recognized colonialist way. In the words of that great purveyor of imperialist fictions, Captain Marryat, "what a parallel there is between a colony and her mother country and a child and its parent."[33] Yeats has infantilized the fallen rebels in much the same way as they obligingly, if unconsciously, infantilized themselves in the opening sentence of their proclamation. His poem ends by hinting that the rebels were really children, not full moral agents, and therefore forgivable—as far beyond or below the law as a black in the American South in the mid-nineteenth century.

More self-aware writers, such as Samuel Beckett, constantly monitor themselves for traces of just such an impersonation. In *The Unnamable*, the third volume of his trilogy, Beckett's narrator complains of the "vice-existers": "All these Murphys, Molloys, and Malones do not fool me. They have made me waste my time, suffer for nothing, speak of them when, in order to stop speaking, I should have spoken of me and of me alone."[34] Though this is primarily a search for the authentic language of the self, the political implications of such a program should never be underestimated. Like the Irish, Beckett's characters must constantly shake off the masks proffered by others and invent themselves *ex nihilo*, on a stage with no props to offer reassuring clues from the past as to how such a program might begin. In *Murphy* the stage-Irish mask imposed by English onlookers on "the ruins of the ruins of the broth of a boy" is manifest enough, as is his refusal to live in any zone of physical buffoon-ery when he can come alive in the pure world of the mind. By *Endgame* Clov overtly dissociates himself from centuries of play-acting, from tradi-tion and the prison-house of other people's language, in contrast to the theatricalized Hamm who "was never really there." In many respects, the war against the past is waged most insistently in the political uncon-scious of Ireland's least politicized writer. Beckett, a dramatist without any obvious tradition, writes instead about the attempt by characters without context to create one: "Yesterday. In my opinion, I was here, yesterday."[35]

The politics of impersonation are a burning issue in the work of Joyce from first to last. Stephen Daedalus complains of the foreignness of certain English words like "home," "Christ," "ale," and "master" that he cannot use "without unrest of spirit," for his soul frets in the shadow of an "acquired speech."[36] And Joyce's own fate, as Richard Poirier ob-served, was to have been able to parody all available English styles, yet achieve no finally recognizable style of his own.[37] It is now fashionable to see this escape into stylelessness as Joyce's deliberate mimicry of the spiral of modernism that "must always struggle, but never quite tri-umph, and in the end must struggle not to triumph."[38] Such a reading would find in the endless succession of styles a version of the consumer spiral, whereby each fashion must be usurped by the next at breakneck speed.[39] But it is surely a different kind of usurpation that Joyce points to here; as Stephen complains, his ancestors threw off their own language and allowed themselves to be subjugated by a pack of foreigners, leaving him to carry the debt. And carry it he does, like Flann O'Brien after him, whose restless changes of pseudonym betoken a corresponding admis-sion that he too could play many parts except his own. Both men's vaunted experiments with the English novel arise from their sense that the form does not truly fit the Irish experience that they seek to record. The English novel describes a land of stable gradations of made lives, whereas Irish writers must depict a land of instability, of lives in the making. It was their ambiguous fortune to impersonate novelist by writing books that themselves aped the form of novels, in an age that found in their self-evident sham an echo of its own. Nonetheless, that should never blind one to the underlying postcolonial strains, for it never blinded Joyce. His Stephen, usurped in the tower by the neo-colonial Mulligan who toadies to the English Gaelic revivalist, knows the exact implications of the story of Hamlet—a tale of usurpation, of player kings, and of ghosts whose injunctions press like nightmares upon the brains of the living.

What Stephen resents most is the Englishman's desire to convert him into another obliging Irish actor, a flashy Wildean phrasemaker: "A jester at the court of his master, indulged and disesteemed. . . . Why had they all chosen that part?" he asks himself.[40] Yet Haines too is forever acting—acting the part of a reasonable Englishman who can always find in history, but never his own history, the handy scapegoat. His Gaelic revivalism is not just a grotesque impersonation, but a hint from Joyce that all revivalism is just such impersonation, demanded by colonizers and their Yeatsian agents at a certain stage in the development of the colonized. As Frantz Fanon wrote in *The Wretched of the Earth*, revivalists only come onto the scene very late in the day, to collect the despised husks of a culture that even the natives have largely cast off. They exalt custom-as Yeats does in "A Prayer for My Daughter"—but only because it is always the mummification of culture. They pick, says Fanon, among shells and corpses not the protean signatures read by Stephen on Sandymount Strand but "a knowledge which has been stabilized once and for all." The revolutionary intellectual, on the other hand, "who wishes to create an authentic work of art . . . must go on until he has found the seething pot out of which the learning of the future will emerge."[41] The revivalist embraces the native culture and mummifies it, as a bulwark against the revolution announced by Joyce. Culture for the revivalist "is always something that was,"[42] but for the revolutionary it is something that will be. The revival thus becomes a valued weapon of the counter-revolution, for it sentimentalizes that backwardness that the insurgents are hoping to end. And it reveals itself as an insincere act, performed by mumming companies, rather than a purposeful action, for it is buried in the inauthenticity of quotation marks.

That inauthenticity of life among the colonized was epitomized by E. M. Forster in the famous echo from the Marabar Caves in *A Passage to India*, a noise that convinced the English liberal Fielding that "the original sound was always good—the echo always bad." In other words, English people are all right in England, but in India or any other colony they become false to themselves and induce an echoing falseness in others. Similarly, among his fellow-Indians Dr. Aziz is a reputable doctor, but when faced with an Englishman he loses his impeccable sense of evidence. Worse still, he begins to act, becoming "greasily confidential" to those English ladies whom he promises to take to "some frightfully super places."[43] At much the same time, this most civil of men becomes stagily aggressive to the English official Ronnie Heaslop. The echo set off by imperialism is always bad, especially when it has an Englishman aping the idioms of an Enid Blyton, but the worst echo of all comes from the native intellectual who confirms English hegemony by his willingness to accept and dignify the colonizer's valuation of the colonized. Forster knows, however, that there is also a resounding echo from the imperial Englishman who is impersonating himself. In *Howards End* Forster captured this staginess in a mundane scene in Simpson's Restaurant: "The guests whom it was nurturing for imperial purposes bore the outer semblance of Parson Adams and Tom Jones. Scraps of talk jarred oddly on the ear: 'Right you are. I'll cable out to Uganda this evening. . . .' "[44] This is a delightful exposure of the contradiction inherent in the myth of a primitive people overtaken by industrial and imperial power. V. S. Naipaul has offered a brilliant gloss on the scene:

> Between the possession of Uganda and the conscious possession of Tom Jones there is as little connection as there is between the stories of Kipling and the novels of his contemporary Hardy. So, at the height of their power, the British gave the impression of a people at play, a people playing at being English, playing at being English of a certain class. The reality conceals the play; the play conceals the reality.[45]

The hypocrisy of such a performance is strictly functional, but it is nothing compared to the bad faith it induces in the colonized. The English ploy is usually designed only to fool others, for at heart they know who they are, but the Indians, or Irish, end by deceiving themselves. Before the colonizers leave, they place replicas of themselves in the rebels' heads.

This process occurred in Ireland with astonishing swiftness. The middle-class civil servants and office workers who tittered in 1926 at the urban leprechauns on Sean O'Casey's stage were the same people who, fifteen years earlier, would have accused the same author of mounting Irish shenanigans on stage for the delectation of a Castle audience. Yeats had hoped that by gathering a national audience in Dublin he could express Ireland to the Irish rather than exploit it for the foreigner; but he had not reckoned with the capacity of the occupier to insinuate an entire symbology into his own and his audience's minds.

The story of how a revolution was reduced to a revival has been told many times, most often as a cautionary political tale. Maurice Goldring has shown how the myth of a rural nation played a spuriously unifying role by giving a common vocabulary to Irish people who were, in fact, deeply divided on many issues.[46] For one thing, the myth could never include the peasants themselves, whose activities in the Land League often led to attacks on the property of Anglo-Irish writers. Gaelic revivalism was, of course, a largely urban phenomenon offering a brand of self-respect to a somewhat snobbish lower middle class. Yet even within the cities class tensions could surface, as when the nationalist rebel Cathal Brugha sacked an employee for trying to form a union. As late as April 1920, however, it seemed as if the revolution might be carried through. On the fifth of the month, workers organized a general strike for one hundred republican prisoners who were fasting for political status. The neocolonial union leadership sedulously avoided committing itself, and leaving rank and file members to wage a campaign commandeering buildings, vehicles, and so on. Within twenty-four hours they had produced an organization so awesome that the government preferred to concede than to see such self-confidence develop. The *Irish Times* saw the shrewdness of this concession: "A continuation of the fight which ended yesterday might have witnessed the establishment of soviets of workmen in all parts of Ireland."[47] Certainly the previous few years had witnessed an astounding decline in deference to all forms of authority. No doubt the Great War had helped to discredit figures of authority from fathers to property owners. As David Fitzpatrick has pointed out: "The post-Rising labour movement was radical because, far from begging government or men of property to raise the labourer's status in traditional fashion, by granting him land, it arrogantly asserted that the landless worker, as chief producer of the nation's wealth, was a superior person in his own right."[48] This is an image quite at variance with the stoic and enduring Yeatsian peasant.

Though the politics of the Labour Party's subsequent strangulation by conservative nationalism are well known, the psychological aspects have been less often analyzed by Irish intellectuals, perhaps because they are so painful to contemplate. Yet, in the words of Ortega Y Gasset, "every life is a ruin among whose debris we have to discover what the person ought to have been."[49] It would be plausible to argue that the revivalists, having won the day, rewrote the history books and edited the radicals out of their narrative, which to the historians had the inevitability of a Greek tragedy. Such a conservative view of history mistakes what happened for the inevitable "given," the very terms of reality itself. It has always been a ruse of colonialism to confirm in its victims a fatalistic conviction that the world as given to them could never be changed, merely accepted.

Yet there are, it must be admitted, severe liabilities to futurology. Those who catch a whiff of the future may be so intoxicated by the smell that they cannot afterwards recall it at all. They have not the consolations of some well-plotted appointment with the past, but instead the nerve-wracking tensions of going onstage, like a Beckett character, without benefit of a script, which can itself only take form in the future. It was René Char who said that our heritage is not preceded by any testament. Pondering this notion, Hannah Arendt decided that the first who failed to remember what the treasure was like were precisely those who had possessed it and found it so strange that they did not even know how to name it. . . . The point of the matter is that the "completion," which indeed every enacted event must have in the minds of those who then are to tell the story and to convey its meaning, eluded them; and without this thinking completion after the act, without this articulation accomplished by remembrance, there simply was no story left to be told.[50]

If one tried to complete the tale not as a political fable but as a psycho-drama between fathers and sons, one might at least end the story one began, and not some other. The official ending emphasizes the Irish Revival as a tale of recovered national identity; but the story, at its outset, was to concern itself with increasing the freedom of the Irish individual.

FATHERS AND SONS—IRISH STYLE

In all societies in the throes of revolution, the relation between fathers and sons is reversed. The Irish *risorgimento* was, among other things, a revolt by angry sons against discredited fathers. The fathers had lost face, either because they had compromised with the colonizer in return for safe positions as policemen or petty clerks, or because they had retreated into a demeaning cycle of alcoholism and unemployment. The Irish father was a defeated and emasculated man, whose wife sometimes won the bread and often usurped his domestic power while the priest usurped his spiritual authority. Most fathers accepted colonialism as part of the "given" and warned their sons against revolt. This did not prevent the fathers from being enthusiastic revivalists; on the contrary, their very caution made revivalism all the more necessary as a form of cultural compensation. In *A Portrait of the Artist as a Young Man*, Simon Daedalus recalls the athletic feats of his youth and asks if his son can vault a five-barred gate. Wherever one looks in the literature of the Irish Renaissance, one finds fathers lamenting the red-blooded heroes now gone and evoking the conquests of their own pasts. Joxer and Boyler, Michael James, and Philly Cullen are all debased versions of Yeats's searched-for hero, who can only be a hero if his deed is done in the past, as the Mayomen discover in Synge's greatest play and as Yeats was finally to admit, with honest split-mindedness, in "Easter 1916."

In a colony the revolt by a son against a father is a meaningless gesture because it can have no social effect. Since the natives do not have their hands on the levers of power, such a revolt can neither refurbish nor renew social institutions. To be effective it must be extended to outright revolution, or else sink back into the curtailed squabbles of family life. The pressure and intensity of family life in a colony cannot be overestimated, for (as Albert Memmi has reported in the case of Tunisia) the family is the only social institution with which the colonized can fully identify. The law, the state apparatus, the civil service, and even the colonized church are in some senses alien. Because these social forms are repudiated by the young in a colony, they petrify, in much the same way as the language of Elizabethan and Cromwellian England petrified in Ireland. Memmi noticed disconsolately how few of his countrymen had any awareness of, much less aptitude for, government.[51] In Rousseau's terminology, such persons were subjects, not citizens. This lack of civic commitment is often adduced as the major reason why colonized peoples are among the last to awaken to national consciousness. When the sons of each generation rebelled, they soon saw the meaninglessness of their gesture and lapsed back into family life, as into "a haven in a heartless world." Yet it was a haven that, in every respect, reflected the disorder of the outside colonial world. The compromised or broken father could provide no true image of authority. In Memmi's words: "It is the impossibility of enjoying a complete social life which maintains vigour in the family and pulls the individual back to that more restricted cell which saves and smothers him."[52] All that remains is for the son, thus emasculated, to take the place of his weak and ineffectual father.

The classic texts of the Irish Renaissance read like oblique meditations on this theme. Many secondary artists, such as Pearse and Kavanagh, write about the overintense, clutching relationship between mother and son without displaying any awareness of the underlying implication that the very intensity of the mother-son relationship suggests something sinister about the Irish man, both as husband and as father. Women sought from their sons an emotional fulfillment denied them by their men, which suggests that the husbands had failed as lovers. But the women could not have achieved such parental dominance if the husbands had not also abdicated the role of father. The space vacated by the ineffectual father was occupied by the all-powerful mother, who became not just "wife and mother in one,"[53] but surrogate father as well. The primary writers of modern Ireland, the Joyces, Synges, and O'Caseys, therefore sidestepped the cliché and resolved to examine the deeper problem of the inadequate Irish male.

O'Casey is famous for his juxtapositions of industrious mothers and layabout fathers, of wronged girls and unscrupulous, sweet-talking men. In *Juno and the Paycock* Mary Boyle is left pregnant by a rascally schoolmaster and then disowned by her boyfriend of long standing. All this she can take. It is only when her father disowns her and her child that she breaks down completely: "My poor little child that'll have no father." Mrs. Boyle's rejoinder is O'Casey's epitaph on the Irish male: "It'll have what's far better. It'll have two mothers."[54]

That same indictment of Irish fatherhood echoes through the work of Joyce, who chronicles a whole series of unreliable, inadequate, or absent fathers, priests, and authority figures. The Stephen who at the start of *A Portrait* proclaimed his father "a gentleman" ends by scoffing at him as a "praiser of his own past" (241); by the start of *Ulysses* he has fled the father in search of an alternative image of authority and self-respect. "Why did you leave your father's house?" asks his savior, only to be told: "To seek misfortune" (608). At the root of Joyce's art is the belief that "paternity may be a legal fiction" (252), that fathers and sons are brought together more by genetic accident than by mutual understanding, and that most sons are compelled to rebel. "Who is the father of any son that any son should love him or he any son?" (191) asks Stephen; wryly he concludes that a father is a necessary evil, but not before he has repented of his refusal to fulfill his dying mother's wish that he pray at her bedside. As he teaches school in Dalkey, Stephen ponders his dead mother's love: "Was that then real? The only true thing in life?" (33). So the basic groundwork of *Ulysses* is identical with that of *Juno*—the truth of maternity interrogates the myth of paternity.

Similarly, Synge's plays depict a rural Ireland where enterprising males are either in jail, the grave, or America, leaving such "puny weeds" as Shawn Keogh to inherit the land. In such a place, father-slaying may be a moral necessity as well as a dire compulsion. In *The Playboy of the Western World* the frustrated young women of the area lament the banality of their confessions to Father Reilly, "going up summer and winter with nothing worthwhile to confess at all" (33), just as Pegeen condemns a father who believes so little in protecting his daughter that he abandons her for the flows of drink at Kate Cassidy's wake—an all-male affair that ends with "six men stretched out retching speechless on the holy stones" (67). What brings Pegeen and Christy together is their shared conviction that fathers are intolerable, for Christy was driven to "kill" his father, who tried to earn some extra drinking money by marrying off his hapless son to the horrendous Widow Casey. It is no surprise to learn that, although Mahon's other children have abandoned him, they are still haunted by his ghost: "and not a one of them, to this day, but would say their seven curses on him, and they rousing up to let a cough or sneeze, maybe, in the deadness of the night" (25). It is remarkable that both Synge and Joyce depicted motherless sons in their masterpieces, the better to dramatize the real roots of the problem of the Irish male as inadequate father. This tradition is taken up as well by Brian Friel in *Philadelphia, Here I Come.*

Although Joyce, Synge, and O'Casey all vividly describe the widespread disenchantment with the Irish male as father, none of them offers a convincing analysis of the causes of parental failure. And this despite the fact that a remarkable number of the foremost writers of the period either lost their fathers at an early age (Synge, O'Casey), had ineffectual fathers (Joyce, Shaw, O'Connor), or had fathers who saw themselves as gifted failures (Yeats, Wilde). The tortuous attempts by foreign critics to explain the recurring theme of weak paternity may make us glad that the artists did not similarly seek to explain away the phenomenon. One reason for the obsession is hinted at in the opening story of *Dubliners*, where Joyce depicts an orphaned boy fighting free of the oppressive aura that surrounds a dead and discredited priest. In Synge's *Playboy*, as in Joyce's story, the priest never appears onstage, as if to suggest that he is no longer an authoritative force in the people's lives. The orphaned youth and discredited priest seem paradigms of a late-Victorian culture deprived both of God and of the consolations of a received code. "If there is no God," cries out a baffled soldier in a novel of Dostoevsky, "then how can I be a captain?" Many a Victorian father may have asked the same question about his own fatherhood, just as many a Victorian son may have decided, like another of Dostoevsky's characters, that after the death of God anything—even father-murder—was possible. It is no accident that the self-invented Christy Mahon promises Pegeen Mike the illicit delights of poaching fish in Erris "when Good Friday's by" (64). Henceforth the day on which God dies will be the day on which man learns to live.

This revolt of the artistic son against an unsatisfactory father is a leitmotif that spans the literature of Europe from D. H. Lawrence to Thomas Mann in the early years of the twentieth century. The breakneck speed of change in society gave added force to the concept of "generation," and the gap that had always separated fathers and sons grew so wide as to suggest that the young and old inhabited totally different countries. For the first time in history, perhaps, writers found themselves forced to write solely for their own immediate generation—as F. Scott Fitzgerald joked, an artist speaks to today's youth, tomorrow's critics, and posterity's schoolmasters. To a modernist generation intent on "making it new," the fact of fatherhood was an encumbrance and an embarrassment. The emerging hero was self-created like Jay Gatsby, who sprang from some Platonic conception of himself, or an orphan of indeterminate background, or a slayer of fathers.

There were, however, particular colonialist pressures in Ireland that gave that revolt an added urgency. The fathers, as has been shown, were already defeated and broken men, and emigration had robbed the community of many potential innovators. In such a context Yeats's search for heroic models takes on a sinister overtone for, in a world peopled by Michael Jameses and Simon Daedaluses, the cult of the hero is more a confession of male impotence than a spur to battle. To those revivalists who might sigh "Unhappy the land that has no hero," the radicals could reply "No! Unhappy the land that *needs* a hero!"

Whenever a colony starts to crumble, these dramas are enacted as a reversal of the relations between fathers and sons. In the Algeria of *A Dying Colonialism* in the 1950s, Frantz Fanon found that as families broke into their separate elements under the new stress, the true meaning of a national revival emerged: "Each member of this family has gained in individuality what it had lost in belonging to a world of more or less confused values."[55] Women asserted their independence of fathers and husbands, often appearing more manly than their partners. This masculinization of woman may also be found in the major Irish works written in the period of national resurgence.[56] Even more telling, however, is Fanon's account of the men. At first, he says, the colonized father gives the impression of indecision and evasiveness, while even those sons who have adopted nationalist positions remain deferential in the home. With the start of the revolution in 1954 "the person is born, assumes his autonomy and becomes the creator of his own values." The father still counsels prudence but the son, in rejecting the counsel, does not reject the father. "What he would try to do on the contrary," says Fanon, "would be to convert the family. The militant would replace the son and undertake to indoctrinate the father."[57] Thus, Christy Mahon walks off the stage in control of his delighted parent, "like a gallant captain with his heathen slave" (80), in a situation that Fanon has described: "At no time do we find a really painful clash. The father stood back before the new world and followed in his son's footsteps."[58] The old-fashioned respect for the young, which Wilde feared was dying out at the start of the 1890s, would be evident again for three decades, even in the poetry of Yeats, whose denunciations of old age are a pervasive theme.

It was in this very period that Freud in Vienna developed the notion that all politics are reducible to the primal conflict between father and son. As a boy he had been reprimanded by his father for urinating in his trousers: "The boy will come to nothing!" This was, according to Freud, the source of all his subsequent ambition, as though he had decided at that moment to show his father that he *could* amount to something. Years later as a successful adult he had what he called, significantly, his "revolutionary dream," in which a strong son reprimanded a guilty father for the same offense. It was, says Carl E. Schorske, a kind of revenge.[59]

In Ireland, however, matters did not unfold as they had in Synge's play, Fanon's country, or Freud's dream. Instead the fathers had their revenge on the sons for daring to dream at all. After 1922 the shutters went up and the emigrant ships were filled not just with intellectuals but with thousands of young men and women. People started to emigrate not from poverty or the hated English law, but because the life offered to them was boring and mediocre. Those who stayed created a new myth to appease and explain their disappointment. According to this myth, the most creative and promising intellects had been lost after the executions of 1916 and subsequent hostilities to a small country that could ill afford such a reckless expenditure of its most gifted youth. Yeats, again, was the prime creator of this myth; in "Easter 1916" he explicitly mourned not just Pearse, but also MacDonagh, the "helper and friend" who "might have won fame in the end."[60] This—as with everything else—is merely an Irish version of the English myth of a lost generation of brilliant young officers cut down in their prime in the trenches of World War One. Both narratives have equally little basis in fact. It has been shown that although British losses in the officer corps were heavy, most who served came home—to become prime ministers, politicians, and civic leaders. Similarly, most of the intellectuals and radicals of the Irish Renaissance also survived the experience of war and counterrevolution. In the case of England, Robert Wohl has argued that "the myth of the missing generation provided an important self-image for the survivors" and "a means of accounting for the disappointments of the present."[61] (Thus—as Connolly had predicted, with bitter irony in this context—the worship of past heroes was really a deification of current mediocrity.) Moreover, the myth reflected the survivors' guilt at being alive at all while their comrades rotted in trenches, along with their conviction that "they had been the victims of a dirty trick played by history incarnated in the evil form of the Older Generation."[62] In Ireland, of course, these trends were reinforced by the loss of many more imaginative and energetic souls to emigration. The revivalists had won: the fathers with their heroes and ghosts from the past—the revolutionaries were snuffed out—and the sons with their hopes of self-creation in the image of an uncertain future.

REBELS OR REVOLUTIONARIES?

Yet the revenge of the fathers was barren in every respect. It represented a final surrender to colonialist modes of thought. The occupier who seemed to have gone left behind a ghost in every mind and machine. Ireland had taken two steps back only to find that after that retreat, instead of a liberating leap into the future, all movement ceased. By 1929 Daniel Corkery could describe the national consciousness as a quaking sod, neither English nor Irish nor any fruitful blend. And since then the sod has quaked and quaked.[63] A revival, which should have extended personal freedom, served only to confirm the pathology of dependency. Today the Irish Republic has the highest hospitalization rate for mental illness in the world. On census day in 1971 two out of every hundred males in the west of Ireland were in mental hospitals; even today there are four times as many patients per thousand of population in Irish as in English psychiatric hospitals. When Nancy Scheper-Hughes visited the country, she found not the fighting Irish of ancient legend but men whose reserved behavior indicated a terrible self-suppression. She found habits of verbal ambiguity that, however, well they served a Swift or a Joyce, "can provoke schizophrenia in vulnerable individuals." The personality structure of the Irish male showed feelings of masculine inadequacy and high dependency—a dependency that afflicts even the nation's leaders, most of whom now celebrate the national holiday on platforms in Pittsburgh, New York, or Birmingham. Scheper-Hughes found fathers to be marginalized in their own families, yet the sons also had no control, ceding much of the high ground to charismatic mothers.[64]

Such a depressing report might be taken as the jaundiced view of a clinical foreigner were it not for the massive corroboration by native analysts. By 1976 the chief psychiatrist of the Eastern Health Board, Ivor Browne, noted a growing belief among Irish adults, even in urban areas, that they would never take control of their own lives, government, or economy. Commenting on the ridicule that greets persons of enterprise—a ridicule that by 1986 took the form of 60 percent taxation on an income of a mere ten thousand pounds—he argued that apathy, selflessness, and loss of autonomy characterized the postcolonial personality, along with civic indifference. Urging his fellow countrymen to cast off the security of oppression, he lamented that "we are only concerned with aping our oppressors, with proving to ourselves that we are the same as they were and can use the same methods of oppression on each other.[65]

The character structure sketched by Ivor Browne is what might be termed "revivalist"—in which an individual depends on other peoples and past images to acquire the strength of self it lacks. Whether they know it or not, such persons betray symptoms of self-loathing and acquired incompetence. A Dublin psychotherapist, J. V. Kenny, finds in postcolonial Irish personalities evidence of a people who are in fact secret rebels, dragging like dead weights against authority. Because of their skills in verbal ambiguity, they can never, says Kenny, confront one another with feelings of anger or love, can never express inner needs nor appreciate them in others. Instead, each in the prison of a pseudoself turns away from reality, ignores his or her appearance, and elaborates an inner world of fantasy.[66] These findings are a stunningly exact repetition of Shaw's allegation in *John Bull's Other Island* (1904) that "An Irishman's imagination never lets him alone, never convinces him, never satisfies him; but it makes him that he can't face reality nor deal with it nor handle it nor conquer it: he can only sneer at them that do and . . . be 'agreeable to strangers.' "[67]

These problems are in large part a result of colonial oppression, but for the past sixty years the sole agents of that oppression have been the Irish themselves. Is there any hope for a change? To ask that question is to ask why Ireland has produced so many revivalist rebels and so few revolutionaries. If the country were to produce a generation of social visionaries the process would begin, as Fanon insisted, in the family. In Ireland today most psychologists still find that children with problems are mother-dominated, but they now concede that such problems can very often be attributed to the father's failure to assume full responsibility. This, indeed, is now the received international wisdom and the central argument of the best-selling book *Families and How to Survive Them*, by Robin Skynner and John Cleese. Their central theory casts much light on the Irish situation. Briefly, they argue that the father's role is central in the second year after a child's birth. The toddler needs space in which to achieve the beginnings of independence, but the mother feels a natural sadness at the prospect of a less intimate bond. The father at this point must try to compensate for this loss by reclaiming his place as a lover, as well as by fulfilling the duties of father. If he doesn't, so the theory goes, "he's not helping the mother, or the baby, to cope with their next move of stepping back from each other."[68]

Many emasculated fathers in colonial and postcolonial societies may lack the self-confidence, or hope for the future, that such a deed demands; by failing to act at the right moment they launch another generation into a further hopeless cycle. On the other hand, those fathers who *can* demonstrate that they are not under the mother's control help to cure the child of absolute dependency. By asserting his due authority over his children, the father allows them to explore their own anger until they can control it at will and learn to stand up for themselves. Even more important, the father thereby teaches the child that other people have needs too, and that we all function as members of wider and wider groups. When such fatherly authority is not asserted, the child may become a self-indulgent subversive with no respect for the configurations of the larger community—in other words, a rebel. Weak fathers lead to clutching mothers who raise rebel sons. If the father does assert himself, the child may begin the task of achieving a vision of society as a whole and the even more exhilarating challenge of framing an alternative. Irish rebels, feeding off the past, know what they are against; Irish revolutionaries, once they have learned to love the future, may yet learn what they are for.

NOTES

1. W. B. Yeats, *The Collected Plays* (New York: Macmillan, 1953), 112. Subsequent quotations are from this edition, cited parenthetically by page number in the text.

2. Peter Ure, *Yeats, the Playwright: A Commentary on Character and Design in the Major Plays* (London: Routledge and Kegan Paul, 1963), 50–54.

3. Erich Fromm, *The Fear of Freedom* (London: Methuen, 1984), 146, 148–49.

4. Simone Weil, *Waiting on God* (London: Collins Sons, 1983), 105.

5. Quoted in Ruben A. Alves, *Tomorrow's Child: Imagination, Creativity, and the Rebirth of Culture* (New York: Harper & Row, 1972), 110.

6. Fromm, *Fear of Freedom*, 142.

7. Norman O. Brown, *Life against Death: The Psychoanalytical Meaning of History* (Middletown, Conn.: Wesleyan University Press, 1959), 92.

8. Frantz Fanon, *The Wretched of the Earth*, trans. Constance Farrington (Harmondsworth, Eng.: Penguin, 1967), 135.

9. Karl Marx, "The Eighteenth Brumaire of Louis Bonaparte," in *Surveys from Exile*, ed. David Fernback (Harmondsworth: Penguin, 1973).

10. Quoted in Bernard Ransom, *Connolly's Marxism* (London: Pluto Press, 1980), 46.

11. P. H. Pearse, *An Claidheamh Soluis*, 21 November 1908.

12. J. M. Synge, *The Complete Works of John M. Synge* (New York: Random House, 1936), 226. Subsequent quotations are from this edition, cited parenthetically by page number in the text.

13. See the chapters on *Ulysses* in Hugh Kenner, *Dublin's Joyce* (Bloomington: Indiana University Press, 1956), and in Frank Kermode, *The Sense of an Ending: Studies in the Theory of Fiction* (New York: Oxford University Press, 1967), 113ff.

14. For an extended version of this analysis see Declan Kiberd, "Brian Friel's *Faith Healer*," in *Irish Writers and Society at Large*, ed. Masaru Sekine (Gerrards Cross: Colin Smythe, 1985), 106–22.

15. Harold Bloom, *The Anxiety of Influence: A Theory of Poetry* (London and New York: Oxford University Press, 1975).

16. See Declan Kiberd, "Inventing Irelands," *Crane Bag* 8 (1984): 11–26, for a fuller application of this idea.

17. Quoted in Thomas Mann, "Psychoanalysis, the Lived Myth and Fiction," in *The Modern Tradition: Backgrounds of Modern Literature*, ed. Richard Ellmann and Charles Feidelon, Jr. (New York: Oxford University Press, 1965), 677.

18. Heaney's fixation with Hamlet was taken by critics of the *Field Day/Crane Bag* enterprise as an example of how eternal students of phenomena may be immobilized by "too much consciousness of the complexity of things." In "From Explanations to Intervention," Nina Witoszek and Pat Sheeran note Hamlet's ineffectiveness and ask if the ghost has anything to say (*Crane Bag* 9 [1985]: 83–87). The present essay offers my alternative interpretation of the Hamlet tale, and a response to their critique.

19. W. B. Yeats, *Autobiographies* (London: Macmillan, 1955), 47.

20. Harold Rosenberg, *The Act and the Actor: Making the Self* (Chicago: University of Chicago Press, 1983), 74–103.

21. Ibid., 102.

22. Marx, "The Eighteenth Brumaire," 94.

23. Ibid.

24. John Berger, *About Looking* (London: Writers' and Readers' Publishing Co-op, 1980), 35.

25. Eric Hobsbawm, "Inventing Traditions," in *The Invention of Tradition,* ed. Eric Hobsbawm and Terence Ranger (New York: Cambridge University Press, 1983), 22.

26. Seán de Fréine, *The Great Silence* (Dublin: Foilseacháin Náisiúnta Teoranta, 1965), 108.

27. J. M. Synge, "Can We Go Back into Our Mother's Womb?" in *Prose,* ed. Alan Price (London: Oxford University Press, 1966), 400.

28. Quoted in Maurice Goldring, *Faith of Our Fathers: The Formation of Irish Nationalist Ideology 1890–1920* (Dublin: Repsol, 1982), 80ff.

29. On this slot-rolling mechanism see Declan Kiberd, "Anglo-Irish Attitudes," in *Ireland's Field Day* (London: Hutchinson Educ., 1985), 92ff. Also see G. J. Watson, *Irish Identity and the Literary Revival* (London: Croom Helm, 1979), 121ff.

30. Fromm, *Fear of Freedom,* 160, 161.

31. Quoted in Desmond Fennell, *The State of the Nation: Ireland since the Sixties* (Dublin: Ward River Press, 1983), 31–32.

32. W. B. Yeats, *Collected Poems* (London: Macmillian, 1951), 204.

33. Capt. Frederick Marryat, *Masterman Ready; Or, The Wreck of the Pacific* (London: Bell, 1878), 140.

34. Samuel Beckett, *Molloy; Malone Dies; The Unnamable* (London: Calder, 1959; reprint, 1976), 305.

35. Samuel Beckett, *Murphy* (London: Picador, 1973), 46.

36. James Joyce, *A Portrait of the Artist as a Young Man* (Harmondsworth: Penguin, 1969), 189.

37. Richard Poirier, *The Performing Self: Compositions and Decompositions in the Languages of Contemporary Life* (New York: Oxford University Press, 1971), 8–14.

38. Irving Howe, *Literary Modernism* (Greenwich, Conn.: Fawcett Publications, 1967), 14.

39. Seamus Deane, "Heroic Styles," in *Ireland's Field Day,* 45–58. I wish to acknowledge a wider debt to Professor Deane, whose own critical writings have been a potent source of inspiration to me, and whose solidarity as a colleague has been an eloquent reminder that even in Ireland radical intellectuals have a right to a job.

40. James Joyce, *Ulysses* (Harmondsworth: Penguin, 1969), 31. Subsequent quotations are from this edition, cited parenthetically by page number in the text.

41. Fanon, *Wretched of the Earth,* 181.

42. Patrick Kavanagh, "Memory of Brother Michael," in *Collected Poems* (London: Martin Brian and O'Keeffe, 1972), 84.

43. E. M. Forster, *A Passage to India* (Harmondsworth: Penguin, 1965), 58.

44. Quoted in V. S. Naipaul, *An Area of Darkness: An Experience of India* (London: A Deutsch, 1964), 209.

45. Ibid.

46. Goldring, *Faith of Our Fathers,* 68ff.

47. Quoted in Mike Milotte, *Communism in Modern Ireland: The Pursuit of the Workers' Republic since 1916* (Dublin: Gill and Macmillan, 1984), 30–31.

48. David Fitzpatrick, *Politics and Irish Life 1913–1921: Provincial Experience of War and Revolution* (Dublin: Gill and Macmillan, 1977), 234.

49. José Ortega y Gasset, "Pidiendo un Goethe desde dentro," in *Obras Completas* (Madrid: Revista de Occidente, 1966), 4:401.

50. Hannah Arendt, *Between Past and Future: Six Exercises in Political Thought* (London: Faber and Faber, 1961),6.

51. Albert Memmi, *The Colonizer and the Colonized*, trans, Howard Greenfeld (Boston: Beacon Press, 1967), 95–100.

52. Ibid., 101.

53. Kavanagh, "The Great Hunger," in *Collected Poems*, 36.

54. Sean O'Casey, *Three Plays* (London: Macmillan, 1970), 71.

55. Frantz Fanon, *Dying Colonialism*, trans. Haakon Chevalier (Harmondsworth: Penguin, 1970), 81.

56. See Declan Kiberd, *Men and Feminism in Modern Literature* (London: Macmillan, 1985).

57. Fanon, *Dying Colonialism*, 83, 85.

58. Ibid., 86.

59. Carl E. Schorske, *Fin-de-Siecle Vienna: Politics and Culture* (New York: Vintage Books, 1981), 191–97.

60. Yeats, *Collected Poems*, 203.

61. Robert Wohl, *The Generation of 1914* (Cambridge: Harvard University Press, 1979), 115.

62. Ibid.

63. Daniel Corkery, *Synge and Anglo-Irish Literature: A Study* (Cork: Cork University Press, 1931), chap. 1.

64. Nancy Scheper-Hughes, *Saints, Scholars, and Schizophrenics: Mental Illness in Rural Ireland* (Berkeley and Los Angeles: University of California Press, 1979), 3, 65, 111ff.

65. Ivor Browne, "Mental Health and Modern Living" (paper delivered 8 May 1976 at a seminar of the Eastern Health Board, reported in the *Irish Times*, 9 May 1976).

66. J. V. Kenny, "The Post-Colonial Personality," *Crane Bag* 9 (1985): 70–79.

67. G. B. Shaw, *The Complete Plays of Bernard Shaw* (London: Odhams, 1937), 411.

68. Robin Skynner and John Cleese, *Families and How to Survive Them* (London: Methuen, 1983), 189ff.

This essay is an extended version of a lecture given at ACIS, Tacoma, Washington, 1985. I wish to acknowledge helpful discussion of that lecture with Rob Garratt, Deirdre Bair, Vivian Mercier, Richard Murphy, and John A. Murphy.

4

Feminist Theory and Women in Irish Writing

Bonnie Kime Scott

"Women in Irish Writing" was the title used in a call for papers for the 1985 ACIS Meeting. As a respondent for the proposed panel, I thought first about the title itself. It resists a feminist formulation and may betray some misgivings about feminist theory among practitioners of Irish studies. The "women in" designation avoids specifying a generalized or theoretical "woman" for analysis as image, type, or psychoanalytical subject. The title also does not restrict participants to women writers as a category. My suspicions of caution over feminism were confirmed in the introduction to the panel, where it was explained that the title was chosen to transcend feminist interpretation and to achieve inclusiveness that "goes beyond a single way of seeing."[1] One panelist suggested that "a feminist approach obviates the reader's working his or her way to the essential humanity" of poems by an author he was considering.[2] A second had confided in an early draft, "I would rather not get entangled in definitions or issues," perhaps recognizing the complexities of current definitions of feminism, as well as some people's emotional responses to the word *feminist*.[3]

Since Irish literature and feminist critical theory are companion interests to me, I decided to use a more complex and positive view of feminism to integrate and extend the collection of subjects and approaches that the call for papers evoked. Is feminism a singular or narrowing approach, as two panel participants suggested? Or are its complexities too much to take into a simple paper on an Irish writer? In this essay, I use several feminist frameworks, and I deliberately cast this in the plural, because plural forms are definitely needed to encompass the papers and to characterize feminist theory today. These offer new ways of relating Irish literature to other literary sets: the British and American literature by male authors that has dominated the literary canon, the sets of literature developed in women's studies, including images of women and women's writing, and the "feminine" in literature—an articulation in language that is hypothetically possible for writers of both sexes. The resulting essay is introductory, and does not claim to be comprehensive of women in Irish writing or of feminist theory.

One distinct feminist tradition that panelists found useful in analyzing women in Irish writing is androgyny—a theory of the mind articulated by Virginia Woolf in *A Room of One's Own* but for which she cites Coleridge as a source. Androgyny has been heralded in a number of male authors (but not Yeats) by feminist critic Carolyn Heilbrun.[4] Conrad Balliet tentatively made the claim of androgyny for Yeats. He detected, I think correctly, a one-sidedness to Yeats's androgyny, and was himself more comfortable with men expressing female physical traits than the reverse. Yeats and Balliet are fairly typical in asserting the male need for the female principal, or *anima,* but like Carl Jung are less comfortable in finding *animus* in women. As one example of an androgynous attitude in Yeats, Balliet examined Yeats's representation of a female mind in "On Woman," citing its first stanza:

> May God be praised for woman
> That gives up all her mind,
> A man may find in no man
> A friendship of her kind
> That covers all he has brought
> As with her flesh and bone,
> Nor quarrels with a thought
> Because it is not her own.[5]

As Balliet analyzed it, the seemingly mindless accommodation in this female mind (a sexist Yeats) can also be seen as a giving up of "analytical and destructive thought processes" that ends with an androgynous "composite" (a feminist Yeats). I think that Yeats's attack on western male mental habits would be more convincing if he practiced it more directly upon male minds in his works, but agree that it exists in this poem.

In the same poem Balliet finds "an odd androgyny" in the female possession of a phallic "bone," though "flesh" is readily acceptable. In this line, Yeats has ventured into a writing of the female body—feminine writing or *écriture féminine*—a genre explored by French feminists like Hélène Cixous and Luce Irigaray.[6] When it comes to female eroticism, it is questionable whether men are sufficiently informed to write convincingly. When, for instance, in a related analysis Balliet assigns "stiffening" to the male body, I find it necessary to remind him that this quality is not limited to male arousal. Yeats's provision of a space to which male language may return does relate to *jouissance* as discussed by another French feminist, Julia Kristeva.[7]

I think that James Joyce has been more successful than Yeats in writing the female body. This is because Joyce frequently writes on mother figures, reproducing textually the desire of the child to return to the physicality of the mother. Stephen Dedalus provides an example of this in his encounter with the prostitute in *A Portrait of the Artist as a Young Man*. In this scene her lips "pressed upon his brain as upon his lips as though they were the vehicle of a vague speech; and between them he felt an unknown pressure, darker than the swoon of sin, softer than sound or odour."[8] Yeats is more apt to write of a remote, aloof, arche-typal female, to whom male physiology may seem more appropriate. In "No Second Troy" she has "beauty like a tightened bow" and is "high and solitary and most stern." But the language lacks the physical appeal of the "vague speech" Stephen encounters. Hers is "an old bellows full of angry wind," used as a negative example in Yeats's design of conventional femininity for his daughter, "A Prayer for my Daughter."[9] The limits of Yeats's writing of the female body offer a good subject for future research, especially considering the far-reaching influence of Yeats as a model for later Irish poets, particularly the women poets like McGuckian and Ni Chuilleanáin, who have studied him as a great master of their literature.

Returning to the feminist phenomenon of androgyny, we also find it in Irish fiction. It is notable in some of the male characters of Kate O'Brien's *Without My Cloak*. Though he plays the possessive patriarch, Anthony Considine is deeply touched by his first parenting experience, which is something far tenderer than any satisfaction at achieving a male dynasty—the reaction expected by his wife. Caroline Considine's nephew, Denis, and brother, Eddy, both empathize deeply with her desire for freedom, perhaps because they have strong feminine aspects: Eddy has a refined aesthetic sense and a love of flowers. Both Denis and Eddy are willing to defy the patriarchy for the sake of loved women, but only temporarily, showing the lasting power of the virile male norm.

Several of the conference's papers on women in Irish writing partici-pate in a third feminist practice that Elaine Showalter has termed "femi-nist critique."[10] This feminist approach was pioneered in the early 1970s, though it was anticipated by liberals like Virginia Woolf, Rebecca West, and notably by Kate O'Brien in the 1920s and 30s. Such critics detect and question male-biased attitudes, especially in authors' creation of charac-ters and the realistic representation of women's lives in patriarchal so-ciety. Balliet's paper on Yeats gave considerable attention to stereotyping, citing in particular bitch and witch types as degrading. A thorough consideration of stereotyping in Yeats would also take on less threatening, conventional women. The beautiful woman of "Adam's Curse," for example, is stereotypical though beautiful, as is the daughter that Yeats wants to become "a flourishing hidden tree," protected by a bridegroom's house, dispensing "magnanimities of song."[11] Yeats produces more archetypal than stereotypical women, however, and here feminist myth criticism is more to the point.

We encounter the rough boundaries between human, perhaps stereotyped, women and superhuman, archetypal women in the female protagonists of Augusta Gregory's folk histories. As with Yeats in works like "No Second Troy," our tolerance for masculine or inconsistent conduct from goddesses may be stronger than our tolerance for these qualities in women purported to be part of history. Mary Bryson located several stereotypes that Gregory triumphs over: "Nineteenth century stage cartoons of the mother-as-victim or the woman-as-bitch" are replaced with "a more multidimensional image of woman." When we come to Gregory's involvement in the sexual politics of the Irish Literary Revival, there is intriguing material for feminist critique. Bryson cited and considered as sexist Gregory's self-designation as "a woman of the house" in her dedication of *Cuchulain of Muirthemne:*

> And indeed if there was more respect for Irish things among the learned men that live in the college at Dublin where so many of these old writings are stored, this work would not have been left to a woman of the house, that has to be minding the place, and dividing her share of the food.[12]

In its context, this does not function merely as a sexist epithet. Instead it criticizes the neglect of Irish manuscripts by "the learned men that live in the college at Dublin." The remark belongs alongside Virginia Woolf's burlesque in *A Room of One's Own* of the "obsolete" dons of Oxbridge, guardians of the library with "its treasures safe locked within its breast."[13] Like Woolf, Gregory constructively assumes a declassé, outsider's, viewpoint to a territory well known to women. Being outsiders to power is also a familiar experience to the Irish, and thus a perspective of importance to Irish literature.

Yeats reenters the discussion of feminist critique in conjunction with Gregory. As a supporter of the woman writer, he seems to merit feminist approval. Yet some of his ideas about woman in Gregory's work do not stand up well to feminist critique. He was dubious when Gregory made Gormaleith too central to her drama, and skeptical that Gregory's female characters could find so much to say. In a similar spirit of restrictiveness, Yeats discouraged Margot Ruddock and Dorothy Wellesley from adopting a masculine voice in their poetry, while he was not reluctant to adopt a feminine one.[14] It seems undeniable that Yeats "used" women for his own revitalization and self-definition. While Yeats does not tend to use women as an alien "other" in the sense defined by Simone de Beauvoir, his systems in *A Vision* come closer to Jacques Lacan's definition of unreachable "other" as a paradigm for defining the self.

I have already identified Kate O'Brien as an early practitioner of feminist critique. Within her novel, O'Brien sets up a view of the Considine family as a patriarchy. In describing a family council over Denis's affair with a country girl, O'Brien notes, not so gently, "But no one was paying heed to the ladies. This was an affair for males."[15] Molly Considine is stereotypically cherished by her husband as a child-wife, but she ranks in his attention beneath his new house and his firstborn son. She escapes the chaste, angel-in-the-house, victim of childbirth stereotypes, however, through her indifference to the many children she produces and her secret though highly developed enjoyment of sex.[16] While a comparison of *Without My Cloak* to Galsworthy's *The Forsyte Saga* has been suggested, I should like to place the novel in the company of Kate Chopin's *The Awakening* and Edith Wharton's *The House of Mirth* for its sensitivity to the commodification of women in mercantile society. To her father and husband, Caroline Considine is a perambulating dress; the father focuses on the jewels men have provided: "a new emerald bracelet . . . that cost two hundred guineas if it cost a halfpenny." In a male symbolic order of progress and acquisition, the woman loses her sensitive, sensuous being, and her own set of desires. Adele Dalsimer would like O'Brien's novels to end in feminist triumph for their discontented heroines and defiant youths, but I think O'Brien was satisfied with depicting the traps erected by patriarchal Irish society. While not as utopian, this naturalistic treatment is a feminist project, and one shared by Joyce in Catholic terrain in *Dubliners*, *A Portrait*, and the early chapters of *Ulysses*.

Lady Gregory's play *Grania* allows us to critique the problem of male centering. I see Diarmuid's central concerns to be love of the father figure, Finn, and reverence for the patriarchal law of female possession. A primary motivation for Gregory's women is a denial of their decentered position. In his Amazon-like archetypal females, Yeats usually offers a powerful, solitary figure like Helen, who may serve as a destructive "other" figure, but who is also granted a primal position, created before the archangels in "The Rose of the World." Yeats also draws upon an Irish pagan tradition of an exclusively female community. Nostalgia for this lost female community is suggested in Crazy Jane and "A Crazed Girl." The more beautiful, communal Amazons resemble those of feminist utopias, women who ride under Ben Bulben, displaying "completeness of their passions won."[17] In featuring Amazonian rather than maternal archetypal women, Yeats offers a set of women who are not defined in terms of men, a goal shared by French feminist author Monique Wittig.[18]

The conference papers I was asked to respond to also pose the problem of the category of woman writer. The relevant feminist practitioners are the "gynocritics."[19] They are concerned with writing by women and work to define a historical tradition of women writers. Yeats has served as a useful touchstone in our consideration of female character and archetype, and is an undeniable male influence on women poets. He was the only man represented on the otherwise gynocentric ACIS panel. It was only passively gynocritical, however, since no effort at tracing an Irish women's tradition was made. To the contrary, Joseph Browne quoted Eavan Boland's own statement questioning the "woman writer" concept: "I would like to emphasize that I do not consider myself a woman poet." Interestingly, Boland also denies an "Irish" label—a position of some concern to practitioners of Irish studies. Her statement is not an unusual one, as is attested in Elaine Showalter's recent essay, "Women Who Write are Women."[20] Mary McCarthy, Doris Lessing, Joan Didion, Margaret Drabble, Cynthia Ozick, and Iris Murdoch have all cringed at the "women writers" designation and deny that they write primarily for women. Showalter sympathizes with the problems they protest, such as the assumption that all women writers must take up women's causes, or that they fit with the awful stereotypes of women writers offered by such authorities as Norman Mailer: "Quaintsy Goysy, tiny, too dykily psychotic, crippled, creepish, fashionable, frigid, outer-Baroque, maquillé in mannequin's whimsy, or else bright and still-born." But as earlier remarks on the characters imagined by Gregory and O'Brien might suggest, woman writers have brought something fuller to the depiction of women in literature. Gynocritics suggest that, with all the differences among individual women and women in diverse cultures, women have some experiences that have been trivialized or overlooked. Boland's *Night-feed* bears a title that is not suggestive of men's experience, even in the most devoted of fathers; the erotics of nursing are a female experience. Eiléan Ni Chuilleanáin has, like Augusta Gregory, great interest in historical Ireland and a greater interest in "a mystery of human experience." Yet "articulating [her] feminine identity"—"the female 'I' problem"—a concept that is more subtle than the sex she was born into—was, by her own analysis, critical to her development as a poet. She no longer wears the "asexual mask" of her earlier poetry. The female body—articulated sometimes in historical metaphors of plundering—is also written openly in Boland's *In Her Own Image*. Both Boland and Medbh McGuckian suggest that the woman poet has a new relation to the muse—an archetype who in male creation never writes herself. They refashion that formerly male-serving archetype in relation to the woman writer. Muse and woman poet merge in McGuckian's "Ode to a Poetess" from her femininely titled collection, *Venus in the Rain*:

> I will not write her name although I know it,
> With the never-to-be-repeated awakening
> Of a letter's morning freshness, or the wide-
> Apart windows I recall of the summers of love,
> Where my scholar's fingers bungled their role.
> Now you are in a poem of your own cold
> Making, on your second fret, your life knit
> Like a bird's when amid the singing
> Of the Sparrow Hills, you yourself could not sing.
> It is ten o'clock, I am thinking of those
> Eyes of yours as of something just alighted
> On the earth, the why that had to be in them.
> What they ask of women is less their bed,
> Or an hour between two trains, than to be almost gone,
> Like the moon that turns her pages day by day,
> Letting the sunrise weigh up, not what they have seen,
> But the light in which the garden, pressing out into
> The landscape, drew it all the more into its heart.[21]

A major enterprise of critics interested in women's writing has been to make more of it available. The authors gathered here offer several good examples. Boland, in particular, discusses other women writers, Adrienne Rich and Kate O'Brien, and publicizes their work. Ni Chuilleanáin promotes McGuckian. Gilbert and Gubar's new *Norton Anthology of Literature by Women* includes Isabella Gregory for the first time in a Norton anthology.[22] I wish that it represented Irish women poets like McGuckian, Boland, and Ni Chuilleanáin, or Kate O'Brien, whom Elaine Showalter also failed to cite in her landmark work, *A Literature of Their Own*.[23] But O'Brien has been served by two feminist publishing houses—the Irish Arlen House is publisher of her second novel *The Ante-Room*, a sequel to *Without My Cloak*. Arlen has also brought out two volumes of Boland's poetry. It is thus understandable that Boland should have written the introduction to Arlen's edition of *The Ante-Room*, an introduction very much in harmony with Adele Dalsimer's class-oriented paper. In addition, Virago Press has published two of O'Brien's later, more individualist studies, *Mary Lavelle* and *That Lady*. Interestingly, Virago has been such a success in Britain that the venerable Penguin publishing house is taking over these titles. Of the three women poets featured in this paper, however, McGuckian is most readily available today because she is published by Oxford University Press with its worldwide distribution.

I sense that critics and publishers in the field of Irish literature may not have given the highest acclaim to their women writers, but they have not ignored women writers to the extent that their colleagues in British and American studies did for generations; indeed, my colleagues in Irish studies have always brought women writers to my attention. The papers presented at ACIS in 1985 showed some casual assimilation of basic feminist frameworks. It is essential to keep the communication channels open between Irish and feminist specialists to sustain this pattern and enrich its possibilities in fully realized scholarly analysis.

NOTES

1. Jean Argoff served as organizer and introducer of the panel. The papers, all on recent writing, were "W. B. Yeats: Chauvinist/Feminist" by Conrad Balliet; "Not So Simple Folk," a study of Kate O'Brien's *Without My Cloak* by Adele Dalsimer; "Lady Gregory: The Good-Bad Heroines of the Folk History Plays" by Mary Bryson; and brief assessments of the poets Evan Boland, Eiléan Ni Chuilleanáin, and Medbh McGuckian by Joseph Browne. While each of these papers has feminist traces, only Balliet's made deliberate use of feminist theory.

2. This is Browne's remark, concerning Boland.

3. The remark was Conrad Balliet's. He did go on to provide a rudimentary definition of a feminist as "an individual who is aware of and concerned with negative effects of stereotyping, and makes some effort toward changing and improving the perception and treatment of females."

4. Virginia Woolf, *A Room of One's Own* (New York: Harcourt, Brace & World, 1963), 102–6; Carolyn Heilbrun, *Toward a Recognition of Androgyny* (New York: Knopf, 1973).

5. William Butler Yeats, *Collected Poems* (New York: Macmillan, 1956), 144.

6. For introductory selections of their works, see Elaine Marks and Isabelle de Courtivron, eds., *New French Feminism: An Anthology* (Amherst: University of Massachusetts Press, 1980).

7. See "Women's Time," trans. Alice Jardine and Harry Blake, *Signs* 7 (1981): 13–35.

8. James Joyce, *A Portrait of the Artist as a Young Man* (New York: Viking, 1964), 101.

9. Yeats, *Collected Poems*, 89, 187.

10. Elaine Showalter, "Feminist Criticism in the Wilderness," in *The New Feminist Criticism*: Essays on Women, Literature and Theory, ed. Elaine Showalter (New York: Pantheon, 1985), 243–70.

11. Yeats, *Collected Poems*, 186–87.

12. Isabella Augusta Gregory, *Cuchulain of Muirthemne* (Gerrards Cross: Colin Smythe, 1970).

13. Woolf, *Room of One's Own*, 8.

14. Balliet made this observation, based on Yeats's letters to Ruddock and Wellesley.

15. Kate O'Brien, *Without My Cloak* (New York: William Heinemann, 1932), 372.

16. Dalsimer's paper focused on a comparison of O'Brien's novel to *The Forsyte Saga*, by John Galsworthy. She did notice O'Brien's capacity for gentle irony, implying a critical vision of patriarchy, and she noted Molly's secret sexual joy.

17. Yeats, *Collected Poems*, 341.

18. Diane Griffith Crowder, "Amazons and Mothers: Monique Wittig, Hélène Cixous and Theories of Women's Writing," *Contemporary Literature* 24 (1983): 117–44.

19. Showalter, "Feminist Criticism," 247–50.

20. Elaine Showalter, "Women Who Write are Women," *The New York Times Book Review* 16 December 1984).

21. Medbh McGuckian, *Venus in the Rain* (Oxford and New York: Oxford University Press, 1984), 11–12.

22. Sandra Gilbert and Susan Gubar, eds., *The Norton Anthology of Literature by Women* (New York: Norton, 1985).

23. Elaine Showalter, *A Literature of Their Own: British Women Novelists from Bronte to Lessing* (Princeton: Princeton University Press, 1977).

5
Yeats, Joyce, and Criticism Today
HAZARD ADAMS

In the tenth chapter of *Finnegans Wake*, Shem, under the name of Dolph, instructs Shaun, under the name of Kevin, in the construction of a geometric figure that will represent the sexual delta of their mother, ALP. Shem claims for this instruction that Shaun will "see figuratleavely the whome of [his] eternal geomater."[1] He begins with a straight line, each end of which he makes the center of a circle (". . . circumscript a cyclone. Allow ter! Hoop! As round as the calf of an egg!" [294]). The line is the radius of both circles. Two triangles are obtained by making the line the base of each and the apex the upper and lower meeting points of the two circumferences:

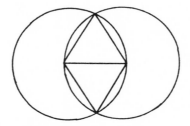

Shem identifies this figure with Solomon's seal:

He then declares that if ALP's apron be lifted her nether parts will be displayed. He observes triumphantly to Shaun, "So post that to your pape and smarket. . . . I've read your tunc's dimissage" (298). This remark refers to the earlier treatment of ALP's letter by the four old annalists and, by extension, Shaun in chapter 5. Shem's remark is, I think, a dismissal of that reading as inadequate because it is fixed and univocal. I shall return to this.

There are indications that the two circles or "gyribouts" (298) represent Shem and Shaun and that as searchers they merely reproduce themselves, that everything comes round again. It is further stated that ALP's "redtangles are all abscissan for limitsing this tendency of our Frivulteeny Sexuagesima to expense herselfs as sphere as possible, paradismic perimutter, in all directions on the bend of the unbridalled, the infinisissimalls of her facets becoming manier and manier as the calicolum of her umdescribables (one has thoughts of that eternal Rome) shrinks from schurtiness to scherts" (298–99). That is, among other things, the treatment of ALP as a triangle is a way of preventing her from being expended "as sphere as possible." The geometrical constitution of ALP by Shem prevents her possible disappearance in the direction either of the infinite, symbolized by the sphere, or of the infinitessimal. It also, of course, constricts her. The effort seems to be to hold on in interpretation to ALP's particularity, even as her universality is insisted on.

By now one has perhaps noticed that this section of the text (approximately 293–303) is full of words recalling Yeats's *A Vision*: in addition to "gyribouts" and "sphere," there are references to a great egg, Byzantium, dreaming back, shiftings, creative mind, body of fate, and mask, to say nothing of triangles, spirals, circles, and the "same" and "other," which Yeats found in the *Timaeus* of Plato. There are references to spectre, emanation, and vortex, which Yeats takes in part from Blake. The connection of Yeats's gyres to the seal of Solomon has been noticed by at least one critic.[2] Even Yeats himself is present in the word *Doubbllinnbbayyates* (303).

A passage that is clearly a parody of *A Vision* (300) is followed by Shaun's description of Shem "ownconsciously grafficking with his sinister cyclopes after trigamies and spirals' wobbles . . ." (300). In Yeats's book much is made of the effort to constitute the phenomenal world geometrically in the form of a set of interlocking gyres, spirals, or whorls, often reduced to triangles in the diagrams Yeats provides. In the revised 1937 edition, it is declared at a critical point that the ultimate unknowable reality may be symbolized (though quite inadequately) as a sphere.[3] Shem seems to be playing a knowing Yeats, author of *A Vision*; Shaun, who doesn't get it quite right, seems to be the character Yeats, who is cast by the author Yeats as recipient and sometimes the misinterpreter of instruction. If the triangle has to be constituted to keep ALP from disappearing into the beyond that the sphere symbolizes, it is merely a heuristic model. Shem claims no more for it. So are the gyres of

A Vision according to Yeats's instructors. Involved here is an understanding of limits that is an ironic understanding. The irony took some time getting through to the character Yeats: "No, we have come to give you metaphors for poetry," said his instructors after he had offered to devote his life to exposition of their system (8). Even then, it took him some time to adjust himself to the ways of their thought. The irony never quite gets through to Shaun. He is scandalized by Shem's revelation, and he would prefer to repress what he has learned.

Shem's mode of interpretation, in contrast to that of Shaun and the Four, is ironic. He knows that what the sphere symbolizes cannot be reached in interpretation, just as he knows that there are no perfect spheres in nature and that we are limited to "redtangles" and "muddy old triangular deltas." There is in such a situation always, alas, another reading: "Scholium, there are trist sigheds to everysing . . ." (299). As Margaret Solomon has observed, Shem proceeds to leave behind two-dimensional geometry, preferring three and implicitly, four or more dimensions.[4] The text of ALP is more than a simple one or two or three. It is interesting to note that Campbell and Robinson can make a plausible reading of this section of *Finnegans Wake* without ever mentioning the Yeats connection.[5] Yeats observes in *A Vision* that experience of the system is like being in a room full of mirrors, implying that there is an infinite regress of readings. One of Yeats's instructors had disliked the geometrical symbolism even though he had employed it, as he said, for Yeats's "assistance" (13). At times the instructors are irritated with Yeats, and he is reproved for vague or confused questions.

After Shem's instruction, poor Shaun is still in the dark, and Shem bursts out, "you're holy mooxed and gaping up the wrong palce as if you was seeheeing the gheist that stays forenenst, you blessed simpletop domefool!" (299). Further explanation is of some help, but Shaun still profoundly misreads the lesson's intent, because his perspective is so profoundly different. Shaun is prurient, and prurience survives best under sexual repression or what Blake called "mystery." So Shaun lashes out at Shem, predicting his damnation, hating what Shem has taught him. Shaun remains identified with his and the Four's earlier elaborate attempt to interpret ALP's letter, the "tunc's dimissage" of chapter 5, where ALP's sexuality is symbolized by the TUNC page of the Book of Kells or a repressive dream-garbling of the word *cunt.*

If Shaun is adolescent, smirking, and accusatory about sex, the Four are senile and garrulous historians, gossips, and judges. Their position is perhaps best set forth in a speech by one of their number, Matthew Gregory:

He is cured by faith who is sick of fate. The prouts who will invent a writing there ultimately is the poeta, still more learned, who discovered the raiding there originally. That's the point of eschatology our book of kills reaches for now in soandso many counterpoint words. What can't be coded can be decorded if an ear aye sieze what no eye ere grieved for. Now, the doctrine obtains, we have occasioning cause causing effects and affects occasionally recausing altereffects. Or I will let me take it upon myself to suggest to twist penman's tale posterwise. (482–83)

If they can't code it, they will "decord" it and "twist" it.

Some narrator in the book, perhaps the ultimate dreamer or the ubiquitous ass that pulls the cart of the Four, has been well aware of polysemy in the text she (if it is the ass) inhabits. ALP's letter and the delta are synecdoches of the text. As early as page 20 one reads: "So you need hardly spell me how every word will be bound over to carry three score and ten toptypsical readings throughout the book of Doublends Jined. . . ." And on page 51: "in this scherzarade of one's thousand one nightinesses that sword of certainty which would indentifide the body never falls." The Four are much more anxious about this state of affairs than the early narrator, whom perhaps we should name merely "narration"; the Four declare in frustration, "The unfacts, did we possess them, are too imprecisely few to warrant our certitude" (57). Yet their drive to understand, that is, achieve a certain certitude, on their principle of an authoritative reading, is never blunted. In Chapter 5, where we see them in action, the principal object of parody is not Yeats's book but Edward Sullivan's discussion of the Book of Kells.[6] The reading made by the Four is exceedingly confused and rambling, but it can be partially characterized by 1) its search for an authoritative allegorical meaning: "Father Michael about this red time of the white terror equals the old regime and Margaret is the social revolution while cakes mean the party funds and dear thank you signifies national gratitude" (116); 2) its claim that the literal sense will not yield a sufficient interpretation: "Yet to concentrate solely on the literal sense or even the psychological content of any document to the sore neglect of the enveloping facts themselves circumstantiating it is just as hurtful to sound sense . . ." (109); 3) its tendency to skirt around the text in garrulous discussions of its written characters, its sound, and its possible scribe; finally, 4) its expressions of moral judgment in a mood of irritation: "and the fatal droopadwindle slope of the blamed scrawl, a sure sign of imperfectible moral blindness, the toomuchness, the fartoomanyness of all those fourlegged ems: and why spell dear god with a big thick dhee (why, O why, O why?)" (122–23). In all of this behavior, especially in their rejection of literalness, the Four seem to be helpless or misguided. *Finnegans Wake* is literal with a vengeance, in the literary sense of the term. It constantly discourages univocal reading or allegorical interpretation and tends relentlessly to frustrate (while at the same time seductively inviting) the use of inter-

pretive paradigms. The principle is similar to the one apparently employed by Yeats's instructors: "A frustrator doubtless played upon my
weakness when he described a geometrical model of the soul's state after
death which could be turned upon a lathe" (13). In any case, the behavior
of the Four, always deflecting themselves from the text, is the behavior
for which the American New Critics excoriated their historicist predecessors.

The Four (and Shaun) are judges, more moralistic than aesthetic. Like
Blake's Urizen, with whom they are identified, they would establish the
law of the text if they could find a place to stand. This is not to say that
the Four are always wrong or that *Finnegans Wake* tells us interpretation is
futile, even though the great number of titles offered for ALP's
"mamafesta" suggests something like this. What the Four tell us is
usually more irrelevant than downright wrong. Even so, they occasionally say something provocative, if the reader is prepared to take it
somewhat ironically. For example: "but one who deeper thinks will
always bear in the baccbuccus of his mind that this downright there you
are and there it is is only all in his eye" (118).

In the light of all of this, one certainly thinks today of the work of
Jacques Derrida and his principle of dissemination as well as of that
movement in contemporary critical theory that has emphasized the role
of the reader. With respect, first, to the Derridean notion, one is perhaps
specifically reminded of the play implied in the activity of the muse of
the book, ALP, whose gifts are many, to all, and not always appropriate
from the point of view of any notion of decorum. Derrida's play is one of
infinite difference, in which meaning is endlessly deferred. For him
interpretation, as history has frequently conceived of it—and as the Four
conceive of it—is absurd, an act that is necessary but that cannot be
defended philosophically. The version of deconstruction practiced by the
late Paul de Man draws from a similar sense of language its seductive
unreliability with respect to meaning.

Both of these views could be regarded as responses to characteristics
of language apparently forefronted in *Finnegans Wake*. Derrida's writing
is well aware of Joyce, and his essay "Two Words for Joyce" is included in
a recent collection called *Post-Structuralist Joyce: Essays from the French.*[7]
He there mentions that *Finnegans Wake* plays in several of his works—
"The Pharmacy of Plato," "Scribble," and *La Carte postale*. He remarks
that he has not really begun to read Joyce and has therefore never dared
to write *on* him. This essay, a play with two words from *Finnegans Wake*
(258, line 12), considers among other things the problem of "translation"
generated in *Finnegans Wake* as a result of a polysemy involving more
than one language in that text. Certainly one can imagine Derrida's
theorizing in general (if that is what one calls it) as a response to Joyce's

book or perhaps as carried on while the text of Joyce looks over his shoulder. Geoffrey Hartman has linked *Finnegans Wake* and Derrida's *Glas:* "Not since *Finnegans Wake* has there been such a deliberate and curious work: less original (but what does "original" mean to Derrida?) and mosaic than the *Wake,* even flushed and overreaching, but as intriguingly wearyingly allusive."[8] One is tempted to speculate here, though to do so would not be popular in some fashionable quarters today, that critical theory and practice *always* arise in response to preceding or nearly contemporary works of literature—presuming one held the notion that there is such a thing as literature, that is, something separate from theoretical writing. There is little point in straining to make an absolute argument out of such a speculation, but I think it is obvious enough that critical theory has usually responded to the puzzlement created by a just previous literature. As fully as any writers of the century, Yeats and Joyce, arguably the greatest, pose for readers many of the problems that recent criticism has been trying to address.[9]

Contemporary theory, following recent philosophy and writers like Joyce, is linguistically rather than epistemologically or ontologically oriented; this seems on the surface at least, right as a response to *Finnegans Wake.* Certainly Joyce's book is a surface. But I think a theory that can cope in a reasonably successful way with *Finnegans Wake* must move beyond the concept of the endless play of difference or de Man's notion of unreliability. The first is not likely to say anything about the text because, though it attends to it, it does not value enough what I regard as the necessary moment of critical constitution of the text, even though one must heed its warning that such constitutions are always dangerous and ultimately in some way misleading. Derrida's own work has become less and less analytical and interpretive, more and more allusive and juxtapositional. It no longer talks about a text, because that would be, according to Derrida, to fix it. It is true, of course, that at least in his earlier work Derrida accepts the need to pass through interpretation and thus tarry with the doubleness of metaphor, and that is what deconstruction is all about; but *Glas* certainly suggests impatience with that process. He seems to have come to the point of foregoing the moment in its momentariness, when to offer a reading is valuable, though certainly not eternal or necessarily capable of being a predecessor to a "better" reading to follow. This leads us away from the possibility of conversations about a text, and it draws us, for that reason, away from each other and ultimately away from literature as an ethical force in society.

The de Manian way—and de Man does not deal with Joyce—for all its interest and the brilliance of its inventor, is inadequate because, with its tendency toward a negative theology, it is not likely to grasp the comic temper of *Finnegans Wake* and its immense inventiveness. *Finnegans Wake* is not unreliable at all except to a theory of language that refuses to accept figuration as a potentiality rather than as a constant swerve away from a meaning that can never be achieved in the first place.

With respect, second, to the presently popular emphasis in criticism on the role of the reader, Joyce's text seems certainly designed to "rouse the faculties to act," as Blake, an important predecessor, claimed art should and Stanislaus Joyce claimed his brother thought. Stanislaus tells a story about Joyce's reference to "the Nolan" in the first sentence of an early essay, "The Day of the Rabblement":

> Jim had kept the reference to "the Nolan" advisedly, overriding objections from me, his doubting Thomas. He intended that the readers of his article should have at first a false impression that he was quoting some little-known Irish writer—the definite article before some family name being a courtesy title in Ireland—so that when they discovered their error, the name Giordano Bruno might perhaps awaken some interest in his life and work. Laymen, he repeated, should be encouraged to think.[10]

False leads of this type are common in Joyce's work from *Dubliners* on, as recent work of my colleague David Robinson, building on work by Hugh Kenner and others, has amply demonstrated.[11] Yet it is necessary to observe that *the* reader is a fiction projected by a text.[12] Either as critics or as individual readers we attempt to *become* that reader, ideally insomniac perhaps, by constituting the text in a certain way for a moment, staying the text even as a new constitution inevitably awaits. There is no guarantee of improvement in time, though there ought to be greater sophistication about what is and is not possible. If there is the undecidable, there is also the understandable. As the tradition of phenomenological hermeneutics has shown, every interpretation bears the mark of its temporal site or prejudice. But this means only that we must understand the text against the fact of the temporal.

Here I return to Yeats, who casts himself as the reader of the text of his instructors in *A Vision* and discovers himself in just such a regress, or rather ongress of reading—endless antinomiality that can only be momentarily but significantly arrested by some statement such as the following:

> Then I understand. I have already said all that can be said. The particulars are the work of the *thirteenth sphere* or cycle which is in every man and called by every man his freedom. Doubtless, for it can do all things and knows all things, it knows what it will do with its own freedom but it has kept the secret. (302)

As Yeats relaxes in this passage at the end of his book, we continue our work of reading sentences such as these, Our reading must remain tangled in the paradoxes these sentences tenaciously insist on, including the fact that Yeats knows that in one sense he has *not* said all that can be said—if he waits. He is expressing exhaustion and, in part, pleasure at having completed his book.

But he has not quite completed it, for there is a paragraph of important questioning yet to come and a poem as epilogue. Yeats, it seems to me, is a believer in fictions. This is the way I read Richard Ellmann's phrase describing his method as that of "affirmative capability."[13] I connect it with Blake's remark, "Every thing possible to be believed is an image of truth." From *A Vision* can be inferred a theory of fictions more sophisticated than Vaihinger's, which reduces literary fictions to "figments."[14] The theory puts emphasis on making books in language, not books of law or of explanation—closed, univocal, and requiring a priesthood of interpreters—but books antithetical to these, books of a different kind of truth, a truth always in the making or rather susceptible to being made and remade. We would perhaps have to call such books deconstructive antibooks if we remained in the language of deconstruction. But this would not be quite the right terminology, for Yeats insists everywhere on creation, even decoration, and the formulation of personal experience, the making of one's identity in words. Such a book would be antithetical to books of received doctrine and would attempt the construction of a "profane perfection," not a sacred one.[15]

It is perhaps in reading Yeats's poems that we are roused to act most completely, by which I mean to constitute critically the antithetical book of Yeats's poems. In asserting this, I suggest that Yeats invites us to move part way, but not all the way, toward recent deconstruction. He does not call for the abolition of the book, because he believes a book can contain an order of Heraclitean chaos. He does not call for a new kind of book, because he believes we have always had such antithetical Heraclitean books. He reminds us of this, and we are invited to query ourselves as readers in the best modern way. Yeats has constructed a book of poems with a mixed plot, that is, a mixture of narrative and mimesis. It has frequently been observed that one has to consider Yeats's poems in the light of each other, particularly in the light of those close by in the text.[16] As yet, criticism has not fully addressed what, to borrow a term from Wolfgang Iser, I call *blanks* in the text—the silent spaces between the poems.[17] We must constitute the text by inferring a content for these spaces. We find ourselves critically constituting a book rather than deconstructing one, the antithetical book being in many ways a deconstruction open to view. *A Vision*, with its treatment of a character named Yeats as a confused searcher for truth often looking in the wrong places or not quite getting things right, offers through its ironies about this matter the potentiality of constituting a way to search through the irony, to live with a new form of fictive belief or (un)belief, and to face the terror of history.[18] The book we constitute does not find its authority or center or presence behind itself or in the poet's life, even though Yeats was a quite personal poet. His work remains the construction of a fiction, a potentiality from which critical acts constitute the book. Many of the problems addressed by a host of theorists of narrative, of fictions, and of the reader are presented to us by Yeats's book. In spite of the great respect in which his work has been held, Yeats is a figure who has been for some time rather a puzzle to each fashionable critical speculation. The biographical critics did not really get outside Yeats's life, and the New Critics could not get into it or conceive successfully of Yeats's poems as more than discrete units. Present theory should at least have the benefit of greater wariness.

But what to do with a book whose play of language seems to disarm even the deconstructionist? *Finnegans Wake* seems to insist on a certain decentering, and already we have had work showing this.[19] Certainly the play of language is everywhere open to view. Certainly the text deflects us from trying to establish a single (or even multiple) fictive plot reference. Certainly repeated perusal of *Finnegans Wake* makes us doubt the usefulness of familiar modes of reading and traditional patterns. Let us take, for example, the venerable distinction between narrative and mimesis that goes all the way back to Plato. Recently Gerard Genette has declared all mimesis to be narrative, but it would be just as easy to declare all narrative to be mimesis.[20] Joyce confounds anyone taking a position on this by having it both ways in the form of what, for want of a better word, I call a struggle between the two. One shades into another for no apparent reason in *Finnegans Wake*. Dialogues and mock dramas come and go. Narration seems to have mimetic speakers, yet there is, as I have suggested, also a voice that seems to be merely "narration," not a characterized narrator, not a characterized voice, as in mimesis. Joyce's practice is what Blake would have called a "reprobate" and a "contrary" to the negation narrative/mimesis.

The same dilemma confronts us when we try to make a decision between two models for *Finnegans Wake*—the model of writing and the model of speech. Certainly the book is writing, and it seems, on the one hand, to be a radical insistence on writing as all there is of language, forcing of us to accept as fact *écriture* in the Derridean sense. No one can read it aloud—not even James Joyce—without substantial loss of potential significance in virtually any sentence, any phrase, or sometimes even any word. Joycean words are subject to multiple pronunciation;

phrases read in different tones yield radically different interpretations. On the other hand, the text invites reading aloud as a mimesis of speech, mumbling and garbled as that speech so frequently seems to be. The accents of the speakers, the presence of dialogue, the oratory, the interruptions of one voice by another—all these things require us to remember speech. Is the text phonocentric or not? The answer seems to be that it is both, as if speech and writing had become the same thing, with neither privileged. Rather than being based on a principle of dissemination or of the absolute play of difference—so inviting as an answer to the problem of Joyce's text—the book employs an antithetical logic similar to but more thoroughgoing than that of *A Vision*, which tends to dramatize the clash between antithetical and "primary" logic. This antithetical logic is the logic of tropes as conceived of by Vico and Blake, both of whom Joyce knew well. This logic includes the principle of both/and, as in the Freudian dream, and employs fundamentally the trope of synecdoche as a principle of serious thought in the antithetical mode. We discover that everyone in the text can be imagined as its author, that each part seems to imply the whole, and so on. The other fundamental principle is one which, as I have suggested, deflects our imposition of conventional critical paradigms. To show this I shall employ in a limited way an analogy to the work of one of the major predecessors of postmodern critical theory, Claude Lévi-Strauss. In his essay "The Structural Study of Myth," Lévi-Strauss argues that a myth is a chain of variants. For each variant Lévi-Strauss offers the image of a chart or card:

> We shall then have several two-dimensional charts, each dealing with a variant, to be organized in a three-dimensional order, so that three different readings become possible: left to right, top to bottom, front to back (or vice versa). All these charts cannot be expected to be identical; but experience shows that any differences to be observed may be correlated with other differences, so that a logical treatment of the whole will allow simplifications, the final outcome being the structural law of the myth.[21]

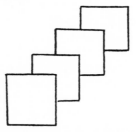

Joyce's notion is more complicated and sophisticated than this, which would have been for him too mechanical and reductive, implying unintentionally the idea of a sort of *ur* myth; for Lévi-Strauss's use of the term "variant" implies the existence of the *ur* myth, even as he denies it.

What Joyce does with a pattern such as this is suggest to us a way that *Finnegans Wake* might be "ordered," though he never allows us to privilege one possible way of ordering over another. There is, of course, the paradigm of the dream, including both/and logic, and displacement, temporal simultaneity and disorganization, and dream speech (or talking in one's sleep). There is the paradigm of Viconian *ricorso*, of which so much has been made. There is also the paradigm of linear development, though this seems to be displaced from plot to the activity of arranging the text. The paradigm that is similar in some ways to Lévi-Strauss's is the palimpsest or stack of cards. Indeed the other paradigms I have mentioned seem to be contained by this one. A reader cannot help noticing the very large number of repetitions (always with a difference) in *Finnegans Wake*. As long as we are using the linear or cyclical paradigms "repetition" is the right word. In the palimpsest paradigm it is inadequate. Imagine for a moment any chapter of *Finnegans Wake* as the card on the top of a pile of seventeen *Finnegans Wake* chapters, each a card. Imagine also that each card has a certain transparency. At every point of reading, previous chapters shine through to the surface card, but in bits and pieces and often in shaded and distorted form.

This is not the only such set of cards. Imagine *Finnegans Wake* itself as a card on top of a stack of cards each of which is another work of James Joyce. Elements of these works shine through occasionally to the surface. A third stack contains cards bearing the texts of Vico, Bruno, Swift, Carroll, Yeats, Mother Goose, and a good many others. There is also a stack of narrators, commentators, or voices; from submerged cards in this deck issue interruptions, parenthetical comments, and the like. Inside what passes as the linear plot there is still another stack. This one includes things apparently going on as the "story" proceeds: players in a game of darts, a chess game, a radio broadcast (a weather forecast, a report of a football game, race results), a trial, an inquisition, a play of children, a sightseeing tour, and so on.

The Four and Shaun would seek the *ur* myth (they don't have Yeats's instructors to dissuade them from this endeavor) in the form of a definitive understanding of ALP's letter, which is a synecdoche of the *Wake* itself. They don't know, of course, that they are part of what they seek to understand, and Joyce goes to some considerable trouble to prevent us or discourage us from discovering the letter as a text separate from, and understandable apart from, the text as a whole. Nor does he let us find out what "really" happened in Phoenix Park, if that is what it is called and if anything at all happened. For that matter, nowhere in the text is there actually mention of the names of the principal so-called characters, whom we infer are Humphrey Chimpden Earwicker and Anna Livia Plurabelle. We have only the initials HCE and ALP to hang on to. Otherwise, there are only what appear to be variants of the so-called names that we have constituted by inference. We have as much right to think the family name is Porter as to think it is Earwicker. Truth disappears as we abandon the surface of the text. Anthony Burgess has been entertaining and helpful but ultimately wrong to write about *Finnegans Wake* as if the first thing of importance were its conventional structure of plot and character.[22]

There is another paradigm, popular in some forms of contemporary exegesis, that the text actually seems to be inviting us to employ. It is a secularized version of typological interpretation. Joyce seems to have regarded *Ulysses* not as an ironic modern version of the *Odyssey* but its antitypical fulfillment. *Finnegans Wake* he seems to have regarded as the antitypical fulfillment of Western literature. Both would be secular new testaments to the preceding old testaments. (M. M. Bakhtin sees the novel as the inevitable replacement of the epic and defines it broadly in a way that would certainly make Joyce's work the successor to, perhaps the antitype of, the epic.)[23]

Yet, although *Finnegans Wake* is not describable as *about* something, in the usual sense of that word, it has ethical implications. Modernist and postmodernist criticism (a distinction that history is unlikely to sustain) have been anxious to avoid the accusation of moralism, for moralism has tended to be identified at least since the development of aesthetics in the eighteenth century as the search for didactic allegory based on a naively mimetic principle. Yet at heart modernist criticism wanted to recast the ground of morality from a single law or system based on what Vico called the "abstract universal" to one that accepts "poetic logic" as its base. The shift in recent centuries from an interest in science-inspired epistemology to language philosophy, in spite of the ensuing split between logical positivists and the rest, has been instrumental in making us consider yet again that literary fictions are not in their ends descriptive or explanatory of some pre-existing external being or existence. Nor do they constitute existence as if it were separate from the constitution itself, as it is fictively declared to be in science. Rather, their "as ifs" are directed toward constitution of an ethic. In this sense, *Finnegans Wake* is *about* something after all, but that is too loose a way of expressing the matter. It is *on the way* to aboutness, which is inferred by the constitutive critical act, which can only be part of a continuing conversation. Such conversations, though constitutive, do not pretend ever finally to close the book, or at least they invite a new opening. This in itself begins to constitute an ethic of interpretation, one of the principles of which would be that we are always a part of what we seek to understand and by synecdoche are constituted as our understanding.

Finnegans Wake is an antithetical book with ethical potentiality. It is a "dream" because it insists that it not be taken to be about an externality (apart from an internality) subject ot processes of verification. It is an antithetical book that celebrates common life in a secular way. There is nothing in life too mean, trivial, ridiculous, sentimental, or obscene not to be worth allusion in *Finnegans Wake*. Nor is there anything too great. Its concerns are universal and yet so particular that the question of origins—the question posed by the Four—is irrelevant. This is why it is not quite right—though it is a temptation—simply to say that *Finnegans Wake* turns on the question of original sin. The "sin" is so ubiquitous and the text's play on it is so vast that to query it in terms of historical causality seems pointless. The word *sin* in these senses is unlocable. If it is "original" it is so in the antithetical sense of being everywhere and nowhere. *Sin* is a word perhaps best treatable as attached to a set that has no common feature, like a Wittgensteinian word family; but the family includes everything. Everything conceivably related by trope to a physical, political, or mental act is implicated, including the rise and the fall of HCE's penis, Parnell's fall from power or his descent from Katherine O'Shea's bedroom, or Humpty Dumpty's fall from the wall. Ubiquitous is the primal act of procreation and the continuation of the species, expressed in the so-called Earwicker (or Porter) family romance. Thus sin is identified with secular resurrection or the simple cycle of nature.

In *Finnegans Wake* the sin is cut off from any theological or historical concept, though traces, of course, exist. In *Finnegans Wake* there is no incursion of divinity, no resurrection to a higher life, no transcendence of the human condition as we experience it. The sin that is ubiquitous in the *Wake* both is and is not sinful. Redemption is secular, of limited duration and efficacy, of only human ordinance, and cyclical. There is no recourse beyond human dispensation. The cycle involves the love and sexual relations of men and women, eventuating in the family with all of its conflicts. The cycle is endless, presided over by an endlessly reborn tempting and redeeming female figure, not a goddess but nevertheless the muse of the text. Like the seductress-redemptress of Blake's poem "The Mental Traveller," which lies prominently behind both *A Vision* and *Finnegans Wake*, the female cyclically tempts the male to fall and brings about his renewal in sex. She turns the wheel of his encouragement, his rise, his sin and fall, and his new encouragement and rising. She is also the secular priestess who presides over the eucharist-wake where the body of her man is fed to the community in the form of endless gossip about his sin. This sin is also the sin of the gossipers, who both expiate the sin and acknowledge it as their own in the same act. A scapegoat embodying communal guilt, HCE is also the community itself.

The family of *Finnegans Wake* is in turn synecdoche for the social world. Its existence is assured by the cycle of rise and fall, sin and redemption, which, as oppositions, end up as identical. *Finnegans Wake* is a book celebrating, that is, reminding us of, what is fundamental, simple, and profound in human life. It looks on the cyclicity of rise and fall, meeting and parting, as the perpetuation of life. It displaces ritual to the secular, where, as Blake observed, "Joy and woe are woven fine," and where neither can be expected without the other. *Finnegans Wake* judges this as the reality that must be acknowledged, and all action must be predicated on it with no recourse to divine interventions or to the assumption that even a totally communal human act can change these fundamental conditions.

The secular morality of common life in Joyce and the implication we draw from the search of the character Yeats through the mirror world of *A Vision* with its supposedly (at the outset) originating instructors, who seem to be seeking something from Yeats, are not examples of the negation of religious spirituality. Rather, they are Blakean contraries to it. For the most part, the great poets have known, in their writings at least, that the friendship of their poetry to religion was properly one of contrariety—the role of reprobate that Blake boldly assigned to Jesus himself. Poetry is secular, earthy, and physical. For Yeats, life had to be met with the "affirmative capability" of fictive (un)belief. For Joyce it was a matter of accepting both pleasure and woe, rise and fall. Everything contains both. Both writers offer an ethical challenge to formulate a secular criticism that constitutes the text, but a constitution acknowledging that it must always move on, and that we are always involved, a criticism suggested by Shem and by Yeats's instructors, who, he remarks, helped him to "hold in a single thought reality and justice" (25). This criticism is not suggested by the four old men, whose ass, like the ass of Balaam, knows better than they.

NOTES

1. James Joyce, *Finnegans Wake* (New York: Penguin, 1976), 296. Subsequent quotations are from this edition, cited parenthetically by page number in the text.

2. Richard Ellmann, *Yeats: The Man and the Masks* (New York: Macmillan, 1948) 229.

3. W. B. Yeats, *A Vision* (New York: Macmillan, 1938) 73, 193. Subsequent quotations are from this edition, cited parenthetically by page number in the text.

4. Margaret Solomon, *Eternal Geomater* (Carbondale: Southern Illinois University Press, 1969).

5. Joseph Campbell and Henry Morton Robinson, *A Skeleton Key to "Finnegans Wake"* (New York: Viking Press, 1961), 184–90.

6. *The Book of Kells, described by Sir Edward Sullivan*, 4th ed. (London: "The Studio," 1933).

7. Derek Attridge and Daniel Ferrer, eds., *Post-Structuralist Joyce: Essays from the French* (Cambridge: Cambridge University Press, 1985), 145–58.

8. Geoffrey Hartman, *Saving the Text: Literature, Derrida, Philosophy* (Baltimore and London: Johns Hopkins University Press, 1981) 2.

9. Recent criticism has been influenced mainly by French theorists responding principally to Continental writers, but, of course, Joyce has for some time charmed a variety of French critics.

10. Stanislaus Joyce, *My Brother's Keeper* (London: Faber and Faber, 1958), 146.

11. David Robinson, "Joyce's Nonce Symbols" (Ph.D. Diss., University of Washington, 1985).

12. See my *Joyce Cary's Trilogies: Pursuit of the Particular Real* (Gainesville: University Presses of Florida, 1983), 246–64.

13. Richard Ellmann, *The Identity of Yeats* (New York: Oxford University Press, 1954), 216ff.

14. See my *Philosophy of the Literary Symbolic* (Gainesville: University Presses of Florida, 1983), 187–200, 312–23.

15. The phrase is from Yeats's poem "Under Ben Bulben."

16. The most important essay here is Hugh Kenner's "The Sacred Book of the Arts," in *Yeats: A Collection of Critical Essays*, ed. John Unterecker (Englewood Cliffs, N. J.: Prentice-Hall, 1963), 10–22.

17. See Wolfgang Iser, *The Act of Reading* (Baltimore and London: Johns Hopkins University Press, 1978). My own current work studies Yeats's poems as a book with a narrative/mimetic plot. Its argument was made in a preliminary essay, "The 'Book' of Yeats's Poems," *Cornell Review* 1 (Spring 1977): 119–28. It is continued in my essay "Constituting Yeats's Poems as a Book," in *Yeats: An Annual of Critical and Textual Studies*, vol. 4, ed. Richard J. Finneran (Ann Arbor, Mich.: UMI Research Press, 1986).

18. *Philosophy of the Literary Symbolic*, 287–324.

19. For example, Margot Norris, *The Decentered Universe of "Finnegans Wake"* (Baltimore and London: Johns Hopkins University Press, 1976).

20. Gerard Genette, *Narrative Discourse* (Ithaca, N. Y.: Cornell University Press, 1980), 162ff.

21. Claude Lévi-Strauss, *Structural Anthropology*, trans. Claire Jacobson and Brooke Grundfest Schoepf (Garden City, N. Y.: Doubleday, 1967), 213–14.

22. Anthony Burgess, *Here Comes Everybody* (retitled *ReJoyce*) (London: Faber and Faber, 1968).

23. M. M. Bakhtin, "Epic and Novel," in *The Dialogic Imagination: Four Essays*, ed. Michael Holquist (Austin: University of Texas Press, 1981), 3–40.

6

Ghosts in the Churchyard: Ó Cadhain and Patterns

Robert Tracy

> But if present time were always to be present time, and never become past, then indeed it would not be time, but rather eternity.
>
> —St. Augustine, *Confessions*

> Eternity is in love with the productions of time.
>
> —Blake, *Proverbs of Hell*

"When you are writing about the world of the dead—and the damned—where none of the rules and laws (not even the law of gravity) holds good, there is any amount of scope for back-chat and funny cracks." The words are Flann O'Brien's, written to William Saroyan about *The Third Policeman* on St. Valentine's Day 1940,[1] but they offer a convenient summary of the contents and method of Máirtín Ó Cadhain's *Cré na Cille* (Churchyard Clay), which has been generally recognized, almost since its publication in 1949, as the most important novel ever written in Irish. But, though the importance of *Cré na Cille* has been generally recognized, like many masterpieces it has been generally unread. Even readers who read Irish easily and who are comfortable with innovative literary technique are often put off by the difficulties of Ó Cadhain's language. He chose not to write in the now standard Munster dialect as established by Father Peadar Ó Laoghaire and ratified by Father Dinneen, but instead in the dialect of Galway, more precisely in the dialect of Connemara, and even more precisely in the dialect of Cois Fhairrge, the south coast of Connemara. Indeed, he wrote in the particular dialect of his own sparsely inhabited parish. At the same time, he felt free to coin words or borrow them from other dialects, even from other Celtic languages—Ó Cadhain knew Scots Gaelic, and Old and

79

Middle Irish.[2] As for non-Irish readers, although *Cré na Cille* was chosen by UNESCO as long ago as 1953 as an important novel to be translated into the major European languages, no such translation has been available until the recent and as yet unpublished English translation by Joan Trodden Keefe.[3]

Ó Cadhain's use of a narrowly local dialect is central to any discussion of *Cré na Cille* because the novel is not a narrative in the ordinary sense, but rather a series of dialogues, presented without any sort of descriptive commentary and without any authorial identification of each speaker. It is a play without stage directions and without any allotment of speaking parts, though there are at least forty speaking characters, who continually struggle to be heard. Indeed, the dialogues or conversations are really attempts at monologues, since most of the characters are not much interested in what anyone else may have to say and would much prefer to talk themselves. They cannot, in fact, do anything else, because all the speakers are dead. *Cré na Cille* is a series of conversations, or attempted conversations, among those buried in the churchyard of a remote Connemara parish—conversations that lay bare the entire life of a *Gaeltacht* village. We learn all the scandals, the enmities, the spiteful curiosity, and the nasty secrets of a self-absorbed and at times self-loathing community. As in the Irish folk belief that the latest corpse buried in a graveyard must become the slave of all those buried earlier, until he or she is in turn relieved by the arrival of a fresher corpse—a belief that often caused unseemly struggles at churchyard gates as rival funerals battled to be first inside—here each new arrival must tell all the latest news of the village and its affairs,[4] a situation Leopold Bloom had anticipated during his visit to Glasnevin cemetery. "The dead themselves the men anyhow would like to hear an odd joke or the women to know what's in fashion," Bloom muses. I suspect that sentence, and the whole Glasnevin episode generally, may have partly suggested Ó Cadhain's subject matter and method, especially when Bloom's ever-active and inventive mind imagines a slightly different version of Ó Cadhain's garrulous dead: "Have a gramophone in every grave. . . . Put on poor old greatgrandfather Kraahraark! Hellohellohello amawfullyglad kraark awfullygladaseeragain hellohello amarawf kopthsth."[5]

"I wonder is it in the Pound Plot or the Fifteen-Shilling Plot I am buried?" *Cré na Cille* begins as *Ulysses* ends, with a soliloquy. The speaker is Caitriona Paudeen, lately arrived in the graveyard, anxious about the site her relatives have chosen for her burial and about the greenstone cross and the "railing round the grave like Shevaun the Shop has" that her son Patrick has promised her.[6] Her question has a double meaning. She soon discovers that she is in the fifteen-shilling plot and learns that the human voice, at least, survives death, but in the literary sense of the word she may well continue to wonder what plot she is in, what precisely Ó Cadhain is trying to do. "What sense is there in this clatter in the churchyard clay?" she wonders.[7] Neither the fictional plot nor the cemetery plot satisfies her.

When considering Ó Cadhain the word *patterns* too has a double meaning. In its ordinary sense *pattern* means a literary work that serves as a model for another literary work, but in the special sense it has acquired in rural Ireland, where *pattern* has coalesced with the word *patron*, it means both the festival of a parish's patron saint and the ritualistic observances carried out in a holy precinct during that festival. Most frequently this involves visiting several spots or objects situated close by one another in a carefully prescribed order, a ritual of repetition.[8]

To examine Ó Cadhain's literary patterns or models is to suggest, at least tentatively, some of the ways by which one may fit him into the general tradition of European literature, as well as into the tradition of Irish literature in Irish and in English. Along with Irish and Scots Gaelic, Ó Cadhain read French, German, Italian, and Russian, acquiring some of these languages in the Curragh Camp, or "University of the Curragh," where he was interned from 1939 until 1944 as a member of the Irish Republican Army (IRA). Apart from "practically everything worthwhile in Old, Middle, and Modern Irish," he had read widely in Aristotle, Dante, Shakespeare, Swift, Dickens, Yeats, and Joyce, and, among his contemporaries, Eliot, Auden, Spender, Dylan Thomas, and Edith Sitwell. He had read a number of French writers as well, including Rabelais, Villon, Racine, Corneille, Chateaubriand, Balzac, Vigny, Mérimée, Stendhal, Flaubert, Valery, and Mauriac. Among the Russians he had read Gogol, Turgenev, Dostoevsky, Tolstoy, Chekhov, and Gorky. He also read the Welsh novels and poems of Saunders Lewis and knew Croce's critical writings, the work of the great Slavic linguist Roman Jakobson, and the theological speculations of Teilhard de Chardin.[9]

This overwhelming list suggests a number of approaches to Ó Cadhain's novels and his other works, along the lines of "Máirtín Ó Cadhain and . . . whoever you like." No doubt such analyses will be written, and they may well illuminate certain darker corners of Ó Cadhain's creative processes. His interest in so many writers hints at the syncretic nature of his own work, despite his commitment to a local, almost parochial language and setting. In *The Waste Land*—another modern work set among the dead—T. S. Eliot invokes a multitude of earlier texts ("These fragments I have shored against my ruins" [l. 430]) to portray the collapse or eclipse of European culture. Ó Cadhain echoes this in a more localized way. *Cré na Cille* portrays the collapse of traditional Irish

culture; its fragments of monologue that never achieve dialogue demonstrate the splintering and disintegrating of that culture, its inability any
longer to cohere.

Ó Cadhain thus shares a theme that is also a technique with such
modernists as Eliot and Pound. But at the same time he depicts the
cultural fragmentation that is an almost invariable consequence of the
experience of being colonized, and so he anticipates such postcolonial
writers as Chinua Achebe, V. S. Naipaul, and Salman Rushdie. If modernism expresses the twentieth century's sense that a once unified Western culture has shattered into fragments, the postcolonial writers
describe the breakup of an indigenous culture under the impact of
colonialism, and the subsequent rootless and fragmented state imposed
upon the colonized people and their culture.

Perhaps this helps to explain why Ó Cadhain and other Irish writers
are so conspicuous among twentieth-century modernists. Ireland's
cultural dislocation and fragmentation predate Western Europe's larger
experience of the same phenomenon. Just as the Russian poet Osip
Mandelstam was able to proclaim Petersburg as the city of the future
because grass grew in its streets in the troubled times just after the
revolution, a portent of what all cities were to undergo, so Ireland
experienced the distinctively twentieth-century phenomenon of cultural
fragmentation sooner than the rest of Europe. Such cultural fragmentation is paradoxically at once a source and a subject for twentieth-century
art. In taking the title of his 1958 novel, *Things Fall Apart,* from Yeats,
Achebe neatly recognized the identity of modernist and colonialist perceptions of cultural collapse.

The echoes or analogues that recall the great writers of the European
tradition or more recent Irish writers hint at a further ramification of Ó
Cadhain's colonialist theme. As an Irish speaker from one of the poorest
parts of the *Gaeltacht,* and as a student of Old and Middle Irish literature,
he was well aware of how such writers of the revival as Yeats, Synge, and
Lady Gregory, and such earlier writers as Thomas Moore, had helped
themselves freely to themes and stories from the Irish past. Their ultimate purpose, to build an Irish cultural pride, was commendable, but
nevertheless their methods could be seen as exploitive. In the preface to
The Picture of Dorian Gray (1891), Oscar Wilde described modern aesthetic
attitudes towards realism and romanticism as the rage of Caliban seeing,
or not seeing, "his own face in a glass." Stephen Dedalus glossed this by
offering "the cracked lookingglass of a servant" as "a symbol of Irish
art."[10] Ó Cadhain seems to mock the revivalists' plunder of the Irish past
by echoing *them*—a defiant and self-conscious Caliban, flauntingly
decked out in his master's clothing.

To emphasize Ó Cadhain's echoing or paralleling of great European and Irish writers is not a matter of source-hunting but of establishing his affinities with those writers and his legitimate claim to share with them the larger Western literary tradition, not just the parochial tradition normally assumed when speaking of contemporary writing in Irish.

Ó Cadhain himself has recorded two events that combined to create the form and some of the content of *Cré na Cille*. Released from internment in 1944, he spent the winter "at home in Cois Fhairgge" and helped some neighbors locate and dig a grave for a local woman. She, of course, had to be buried in the right grave, with her own people. "We cleared two graves but the coffins there were the wrong ones," he later recalled. "We sent for the map of the graves but it resembled what a child would draw with the tongs, doing sums in the ashes of the hearth. . . . We said we would clear one more grave and that was it. Going home, one of my neighbors said 'Do you know where we finally slipped her in . . . on top of Michael Roe.' 'Oho!' said another, 'It's there will be the *grammar!*' "[11] This pun on the English *grammar,* suggesting an exploration of language in all its complexities, and the Irish *greamadach*—the grabbing, grasping, clutching hold of, and even biting—made the grave a much less private place than Andrew Marvell imagined, where the embraces are both intricate and long-lasting.

Ó Cadhain's internment in the Curragh Camp supplied an autobiographical element to his story of existence after death. Like the dead in the graveyard, the prisoners could not escape and could not mingle with or much affect the living world outside the prison. The Curragh prisoners could only talk, often in tedious monologues, or interrupt one another. They could not stand each other, yet could not get away from one another, and, like the dead, they were always eager for the latest news from the outside world. By setting *Cré na Cille* during the Second World War—"the Emergency," as it was called in Ireland—Ó Cadhain makes its action coincide with his own period of incarceration. He even includes a downed Free French aviator who is desperately trying to learn Irish; the Curragh was also used to intern various British, French, and German fliers who crashed or otherwise arrived in neutral Ireland, and during Ó Cadhain's time there the IRA prisoners organized courses in foreign languages and other subjects. Ó Cadhain himself taught Irish. That the founder of the churchyard, the first corpse buried there, was buried in 1916, suggests the political allegory that is implicit in *Cré na Cille*, especially when one remembers the resurrection associations, Christian and national, that inevitably cluster around the Easter Rising. Ó Cadhain's churchyard includes a republican and a Free Stater, who argue endlessly, but both are disturbed to hear that Eamon de Valera and Richard Mulcahy have appeared together on the same platform and pleaded for national unity. As Ó Cadhain well knew, the de Valera republicans had abandoned the pure republican cause and were responsible for his own imprisonment.

But apart from these personal or autobiographical elements, there are Ó Cadhain's literary models or patterns. Some of these are speculative, but probable. Visits to the place of the dead and conversations with them are features of the *Odyssey,* the *Aeneid,* and especially the *Divine Comedy.* In all three works, the dead are preoccupied with the world of the living—with the lives they lived there, the issues and enmities that engaged them there—and with the latest news from that world. But Ó Cadhain's underworld is a grimmer place than Homer's or Virgil's, and his account does not lead to a new and better order, as theirs do, nor to Dante's vision of salvation. Ó Cadhain is closer in spirit to Lucian's dark *Dialogues of the Dead* (Nekrikoi diálogi), a work W. H. Auden excluded from his *Greek Reader* (1948) as "too 'enlightened' for a generation as haunted by devils as our own." There too the dead are trapped in the underworld, without hope of change. "Not satisfied," as Menippus complains to Pluto, "with having lived bad lives, they remember the past even though they are dead, and hug it close."[12]

Homer, Virgil, Dante, Lucian—an honorable but perhaps rather obvious list of predecessors. One might well add Ezekiel and his famous question, "Can these bones live?" (Ezekiel 27:3), to which Ó Cadhain answers *No.* As we sift through the list of authors Ó Cadhain is known to have read, other possible patterns for his novel emerge. The most striking of these is Dostoevsky's short story "Bobok" (1873), in which a narrator overhears the conversations of the dead in their graves; they flirt, exchange gossip, and even play cards, all pastimes shared by Ó Cadhain's dead. Though Dostoevsky provides a kind of narrative frame, his story also consists almost entirely of dialogue/monologue:

> "Avdotya Ignatyevna, do you remember how, fifteen years ago, when I was a fourteen-year-old page, you seduced me?"
> "Ah, so it's you, you scoundrel. Well God has sent you at least, and to this place . . ."
> "You wrongly blamed your neighbor the merchant for the nasty smell. . . . I kept quiet, I just laughed. It came from me, you know; that's how they buried me, in a nailed up coffin."
> "Pah, how disgusting! I'm glad though, all the same. You wouldn't believe, Klinevich, you wouldn't believe what a lack of life and wit there is here."[13]

Dostoevsky's corpses know that they will decompose after about three months in the grave, and are determined to make the most of their brief but limited posthumous existence. They are haunted by the remembered dissolution of one of their number, who ends saying only "Bobok,

bobok"—either a diminutive form of *bob*, a bean, i.e. a beanlet—or the sort of liquid gurgle a dissolving corpse might make. To "grow beans" *(razyodeet' bobii)* is a Russian idiom for talking nonsense.

Ó Cadhain rather half-heartedly denied any debt to Dostoevsky's "Bobok," conceding only that he might have subconsciously remembered the story, but the resemblances are striking. He may also have been subtly influenced by the titles, though not the contents, of two works by Dostoevsky. In *Jottings* or *Notes from the House of the Dead* (1860–62), the Russian writer describes the death in life that was his own imprisonment for political reasons, and his *Notes* or *Jottings from Underground* (1864), convey the bleak self-portrait of a spiteful and self-lacerating personality. Ó Cadhain's often archaic or highly specialized vocabulary may also owe something to Dostoevsky's habit of endowing certain characters with special vocabularies. Marmeladov in *Crime and Punishment*, for example, speaks a kind of bureaucratic jargon—though here Dickens or even Rabelais may also have served as patterns.

Though Ó Cadhain also read Gogol, Turgenev, and Tolstoy, his own work does not show any debt to these writers, but he does seem to have learned from Gorky and Chekhov. He has recorded his own delighted discovery of Gorky in a French translation in 1939. The Russian writer's meticulous attention to the homely details of peasant life offered him a model for writing about his own people.[14] Chekhov, one or two of whose plays were performed at the Gate Theatre in the 1930s, was a more subtle but perhaps a more important influence. Like the speakers in a Chekhov play, the speakers in *Cré na Cille* rarely listen to one another. Each is concerned only to speak, to say what he or she wants to say. What appears to be dialogue is in fact a cluster of simultaneous interrupted monologues, a parody of communication.

Ó Cadhain may well have noted the trapped protagonists of Racine's tragedies, and at least the title of Chateaubriand's *Mémoires d'outre-tombe* (1849–50) (Memoirs from beyond the grave). But a more likely pattern for *Cré na Cille* is Jean-Paul Sartre's play *Huis clos* (1945), translated into English in 1946 as *No Exit* and, as Joan Keefe points out, broadcast that year by the BBC.[15] In *Huis clos* a trio—man, wife, mistress—are forced to spend eternity together in a tiny room, endlessly locked in resentful conversation, a situation later presented although much more austerely by Samuel Beckett in *Play* (1962).

Ó Cadhain could hardly have escaped knowing about two modern American works of literature that have some affinities with his novel as well. In Edgar Lee Masters's *Spoon River Anthology* (1915) the dead in the graveyard of a small midwestern town speak from beneath their gravestones, usually in bitter summaries of their lives. Masters's dead do not speak to one another, but rather to the reader/cemetery visitor, as Yeats does in "Under Ben Bulben." As one poem follows another one develops a sense of the village of Spoon River, its personalities and scandals. One also begins to realize the isolation and decay of small-town America, the disintegration of its way of life, a theme echoed by Ó Cadhain's apparent despair about the future of the Irish-speaking West. The other likely American pattern for *Cré na Cille* is Thornton Wilder's popular play *Our Town* (1938), which also depicts a small community and a way of life that is doomed; here too, in the cemetery scenes, the dead converse—less vindictively than the Ó Cadhain dead—and retain an interest both in the past and in the affairs of the living.

In Irish literature and folklore the dead often behave this way, and Ó Cadhain clearly owes much to the native tradition in both Irish and English. The *sí* (genitive *sidhe*) or mound people—that is, the dead—are always interested in the living, sometimes become involved with them. The dead live in their mounds as the living do in their houses and villages, and certainly they talk; we owe the *Táin* in its entirety to the garrulous corpse of Fergus mac Roich. Stories of the seductive and voracious dead exist in Old Irish—"The Adventures of Art, son of Conn," "The Death of Muircertach Mac Erca"—and in more recent works such as Sheridan Le Fanu's *Carmilla* (1872) and Bram Stoker's *Dracula* (1897). They are common among the vast store of supernatural tales in Irish folklore.

These themes of the persistently active dead have been frequently and brilliantly adapted by Yeats in poems and plays. Apart from the dead's eagerness to remain in some way among the living, and to continue to communicate—to speak—expressed in such poems as "Sailing to Byzantium" and "Under Ben Bulben," the theme is particularly noticeable in three plays: *The Dreaming of the Bones* (1919), *The Words upon the Window-Pane* (1934), and *Purgatory* (1939). In the first of these, two dead lovers are eternally together but can never touch, nor can they escape each other to find peace. They are "Diarmuid and Devorgilla/Who brought the Norman in" to Ireland, whose love provoked invasion from England and all Ireland's pain. Their half-existence cannot end until someone of Irish race forgives them for that deed; only then can they "snatch the sleep/ That lingers always in the abyss of the sky/Though they can never reach it." But the play's third character, a fugitive after the 1916 Rising, refuses to forgive them. Though his refusal is politically motivated, it is perhaps also part of his commitment to the living.[16] In *The Words upon the Window-Pane*, Yeats explores the terrifying possibility that the dead remain among the living and go on talking, talking, talking, endlessly returning to the issues that preoccupied them in life. A séance in an old Dublin house evokes the voice of Swift, who once spent time there. But perhaps Swift is always there, always talking, and only the accidental presence of a medium has made his voice audible. His hell may be an endless broken monologue, a little like *Krapp's Last Tape*. Swift himself, incidentally, had an intimation of Ó Cadhain's speaking but not communicating dead in Gulliver's encounter with the Struldbruggs, whose perpetual old age makes them "opinionative, peevish, covetous, morose, vain, talkative, but uncapable of Friendship, and dead to all natural Affection."[17]

Yeats again examines a bleakly repetitious afterlife in *Purgatory*, in which an old man and his son have returned to his ruined birthplace on the anniversary of his conception. The old man despises his parents—his mother for marrying beneath her station, his father for being a stableboy. He has murdered his father, and before the play ends he murders his son, the bearer of tainted genes. He knows that his dead parents must reenact their coming together to conceive him on the anniversary. He murders his son to put an end to the consequences of their coming together and so free them from their ceaseless reenactment and give his mother peace. But he is troubled metaphysically:

> she must live
> Through everything in exact detail,
> Driven to it by remorse, and yet
> Can she renew the sexual act
> And find no pleasure in it, and if not,
> If pleasure and remorse must both be there,
> Which is the greater?[18]

Though he kills his son and leaves the spot, the couple once again prepares to reenact their moment of sexual unity, and Yeats chillingly hints that their eternity may be this endless repetition, like the conversations of *Cré na Cille*.

Joyce's *Dubliners* begins with a dead priest who wants to talk, then proceeds through the " 'queer old josser' " of "An Encounter," whose monologue circles "round and round in the same orbit," repeating "phrases over and over again."[19] It then examines the city's inhabitants, who are sexually, politically, culturally, and spiritually dead, until the final story, "The Dead," features a Christmas party that is more like a wake, a Gabriel who calls no one to resurrection, and a visitation from the still restless and attached spirit of Michael Furey. There is a funeral in *Ulysses*, where Leopold Bloom speculates about the existence of the dead in their graves and moves, himself in black, among the spiritually dead inhabitants of Dublin. The ghost of Paddy Dignam walks in Capel Street after he has been buried; Stephen's mother and Bloom's son are unwilling to part from those they haunt. Finally, in *Finnegans Wake* Joyce anticipates Ó Cadhain's move into the realm of the dead by setting his novel in the realm of sleep and dream. For the dreamer to wake will be a kind of resurrection, as when Finnegan rose from the dead when touched by the revivifying water of life. But in fact Joyce's dreamer does not wake; the story does not end. It returns to its beginning, again and again. Joyce's dreamer is in eternity, where he can only repeat himself again and again, in words that continue to refuse to mean, in a language even more solipsistic than the dialect of Ó Cadhain's remote corner of Connemara. Joyce equates hell with the endlessly repeated act, a notion that reappears in *Waiting for Godot* and in many other works by Beckett, and in Flann O'Brien's *The Third Policeman*. But it also has a long history in older Irish literature, especially in the successive Etains in "The Wooing of Etain" and in the self-referential structure of the folk tale "The Man Who Had No Story."[20] Joyce perhaps called our attention to paralysis and repetition as literary subjects and literary methods, but they are not uncommon obsessions in ancient or modern Irish literature.

Ó Cadhain may also owe something to another graveyard story where the dead and the living in a sense intermingle, Seamus O'Kelly's "The Weaver's Grave" (1918). In that story two very old men are summoned to *Cloon na Morav* (the Meadow of the Dead) to point out the family burial place where another old man, Mortimer Hehir the Weaver, is to be buried. "Both old men had the air of those who had been unexpectedly let loose. For a long time they had lurked somewhere in the shadows of life, the world having no business for them, and now, suddenly, they had been remembered and called forth to perform an office which nobody else on earth could perform." The two old men are in no hurry to find the weaver's grave; they move slowly about the graveyard talking, "airing their knowledge, calling up names and complications of family relationships, telling stories, reviving all virtues, whispering at past vices . . . arguing in a powerful intimate obscurity that no outsider could hope to follow, blasting knowledge with knowledge, until the whole place seemed strewn with the corpses of their arguments."[21] When they seem unable to locate the grave, the weaver's widow consults an even older man who is bedridden. He must haul himself up with a rope to speak with her—a literal lifeline—but he does not give her the information she needs. Instead he shares a dreadful truth with her: the world is only a dream, and to wake from it is to wake to nothingness. When the grave is finally found one of the old men exults, but it is the exultation of one corpse over another. And the young widow is already aware that one of the gravediggers will come to her later. She has no knowledge of where her husband's grave should be, and no interest in the local lore that feeds the half-life of the old men. She hates genealogy and is resentful when she learns that different species of tree have different names.[22] To her a tree is a tree, and all the careful discrimination between them that language has achieved is as irrelevant as the spoken memories that preserve the community's past. In O'Kelly's story the living are indifferent to the dead—the old men are more among the dead than among the living—and to the nuances of relationship and language that they cherish. The dead themselves are bitterly resentful. "Several partially suppressed insurrections—a great thirsting, worming, pushing, and shouldering under the sod—had given [the graveyard] character." The dead do not haunt the living, but perhaps they haunt each other; when the gravediggers find the wrong coffin in the weaver's alleged grave, one of the old men remarks darkly that " 'many a queer thing happened in Cloon na Morav that had no right to happen in it. Julia Rafferty, maybe, isn't the only one that is where she had no right to be.' "[23]

To move from Yeats's one act plays, Joyce's short stories and the episodes of *Ulysses*, and O'Kelly's short story is to realize how deliberate was Ó Cadhain's choice of the inappropriate novel form. Sean O'Faolain and Frank O'Connor have taught us that the short story is the appropriate literary form for depicting a marginal or incomplete community, a "submerged population group. . . . Always in the short story there is this sense of outlawed figures wandering about the fringes of society" and "an intense awareness of human loneliness."[24] Ó Cadhain's *Gaeltacht* characters fulfill this description and invite treatment in short story form. Their fragmentary lives would be better presented in such fragments rather than as parts of a novel, which creates a complex and interrelated society such as the worlds of Balzac or Tolstoy. Joyce chose to present the marginal and incomplete life of Dublin first in a series of short stories, then in a novel that is not quite a novel (which began as one more short story for *Dubliners*), the episodic *Ulysses*. Ó Cadhain also chose the novel to undermine its form by using an episodic structure—*Cré na Cille* is divided into ten interludes, literally "interplayings"—and constantly interrupted and often incoherent monologues. He deliberately used these devices to emphasize the fragmentary and marginal nature of the society he was portraying, a society that was already dissolving socially, linguistically, and in this case literally. By choosing the novel form, with its traditional function of portraying a complex and active society, Ó Cadhain drew deliberate attention to the marginal and incomplete nature of the deaths these people live, the lives they die.

When Nora Shauneen begins to organize a cultural enrichment movement among the corpses, one corpse, The Writer (he publishes with *An Gúm*, the government publishing house for books in Irish) is excluded on the grounds that his work is "Joycean," a charge Ó Cadhain rightly foresaw would be leveled at his own work: "You have a low low mind to be writing a thing like that 'The Dinosaur's Dream.' A Joycean potboiler, in reality. . . ."[25] It is a graceful internalization of a literary pattern, but the title of that "Joycean" work emphasizes the obsolescence that is part of Ó Cadhain's theme. Like the dinosaurs his characters are nonsurvivors, and like the dinosaurs their kind can no longer survive in a world grown unsuitable for them. Not surprisingly, Ó Cadhain quotes a version of the elegiac sentence with which Tomás Ó Criomhthain (O Crohan) marks the end of the Blasket Island society he described in *An tOileánach* (1929): "Our likes will not be seen again."[26] Séan Ó Tuama has commented on the uniquely communal voice that speaks in *An tOileánach*, of Ó Criomhthain's interest in the collective life of his society rather than in details of his own autobiography.[27] That sense of communal life, essential to the novel, is missing in *Cré na Cille*. It has only individual protesting, complaining voices. The dead in *Cré na Cille* are as alive as they ever were, trapped then in a marginal and dying culture just as they are now trapped in the churchyard clay. They were always dead, or, to put it another way, this incoherent and rambling graveyard talk is their life.

Ó Cadhain's aim is to fix in words a way of life already fixed in time, as in a faded photograph—in Joyce's phrase, "a fadograph of a yestern scene."[28] These people cannot change or evolve; they can only go on repeating themselves over and over. There do seem to be lively, though petty, issues: will Caitriona Paudeen get her greenstone cross? will the Big Master's widow marry again? But as many of the interludes begin, the Trumpet of the Churchyard reminds us that the speakers are all dead. They are impotent to influence any actions among the living—Ó Cadhain's recognition of the impotence of his marginal community in the nation's affairs. And they speak in what Ó Cadhain had come to regard as a dead language. As he said later, "A dark cloud hangs over Irish again. A worse thing than lack of recognition at home and abroad weighs on the writer. It is hard for a man to give of his best in a language which seems likely to die before himself, if he lives a few years more."[29] Though he goes on to say that "this despair engenders a desire to fight fiercely for the language," and Ó Cadhain did fight fiercely, he betrays a bleak sense that the Irish language, along with the socio-linguistic attitudes it shapes and contains, and even the topographical history it contains, is doomed.

The decay of the Irish language and its probable disappearance have been frequent themes for Irish poets since the sixteenth century. "Gan gáire fá ghníomhradh leinbh,/cosc ar cheol, glas ar Ghaoidheilg," complains the seventeenth-century poet Aindrias Mac Marcais: "There is no laughter at children's doings,/Music is prohibited, the Irish language is in chains." Mathghamhain Ó hIfearnáin (d. 1640) advises his son to "Ná lean do dhíogha ceirde,/Ná cum do ghréas Gaoidheilge": "Follow not your useless trade, Fashion not your poem in Irish." The motif persists into the twentieth century, as in the Aran Island-born poet Máirtín Ó Direáin's poem of tribute to J. M. Synge:

My people's way of life is decaying,
The sea serves no longer as a wall,
But until Coill Chuain comes to Inismeáin
The words which you once collected
Will still live in a foreign tongue.

Pearse Hutchinson embeds the decay of Irish in an English poem called "Gaeltacht":

In the Liverpool Bar, at the North Wall,
on his way to join his children over there,
an old man looked at me, then down at his pint
of rich Dublin stout. He pointed at the black glass:
"Is lú í an Ghaeilge ná an t-uisce sa ngloine sin."[30]

The last line means, "There is less Gaelic than there is water in the glass." Finally, the plight of the Irish language has been movingly and effectively dramatized in Brian Friel's recent play, *Translations* (1980).

An all too familiar figure in the shrinking *Gaeltacht* is the old storyteller who has lapsed into silence because no one can or will listen anymore to what he has to tell. The inhabitants of Ó Cadhain's churchyard are more or less in the same position. They do not stop talking, but no one is listening. Their monologues have the meaningless repetitiousness of pilgrims at some remote holy site, who move from one spot to another in the order of a ritual pattern without knowing exactly why they follow that order. The Free French aviator buried in the churchyard is learning Irish, and is delighted to have discovered a truly dead language:

—. . . the Frenchman . . . is a devoted Gael. He is zealously learning the language . . .
—He is writing a treatise about the dental consonants in the Half-Guinea plot dialect. He says their palates are sufficiently flattened by now, so it is possible to do a learned study of their phonetics . . .
—The Institute considers that there is too much Irish—of the kind that isn't dead within the scheduled time—he has learned, and since there is doubt that an odd word of it is *Revival Irish*, he must unlearn every syllable before he is qualified to do the research properly.
—He is undertaking also to collect all the lost folklore and save it so that the generations of Irish corpses to come will know what kind of

life it was in the Republic of Irish corpses before them. . . . He thinks
it would be easy to make a Folklore Museum of the Churchyard and it
would be no trouble at all getting a grant for the purpose. . . .[31]

Later, when the Frenchman tries to give a colloquium, which turns out
to be his attempt at a monologue, he remarks that "learned research
cannot be carried out on a language which a great many people
speak. . . . Research cannot be done—nor is it worth doing—except on a
dialect known only to two or three at most. Three senile dribbles must
accompany every word. . . ." His discourse is of course interrupted by
Colley, the local *seanchaí*, who tries to tell a story:

> —Have patience now, decent man, and I will tell you how the cloak
> was torn off the knot of nonsense . . .
> —Colley, Shaun Kitty's version from our place is that he lost it . . .
> —Shaun Kitty from your place! It was often for a man from your
> place to be in the right . . .
> —. . . By the oak of this coffin, Kate Beg, I gave the pound to her, to
> Caitriona Paudeen . . .
> —A fur coat on her, Tom Roe, like the one Baba Paudeen used to
> wear, until she had to throw it to one side, because of the blobs of soot
> that fell on it in Caitriona's house . . .
> —You're lying, Brigid Thurley . . .[32]

With superb and suicidal appropriateness, Ó Cadhain makes his dead
characters speak a dying language. His penultimate sentence is scorn-
fully addressed to the oldest corpse in the churchyard, who has repeatedly begged permission to speak, but falls silent when that permission is
finally granted: "—. . . You have permission to speak now but it seems
the dead tongue sounds sweeter to you . . ."[33] The language they speak
will soon be quite dead; they too will perhaps eventually fall silent. By
writing in Irish, Ó Cadhain is not trying to reverse linguistic history; he
is grimly accepting it, and demonstrating its logical and inevitable end—
Irish as a dead language spoken only by the dead.

This anxiety about language is characteristic of modern Irish writers.
Joyce's Stephen Dedalus is uncertain about English in the presence of
the English Jesuit—"The language in which we are speaking is his
before it is mine. How different are the words *home, Christ, ale, master,* on
his lips and on mine! I cannot speak or write these words without unrest
of spirit. His language . . . will always be for me an acquired speech."[34]
Consider too the polemic writings of Daniel Corkery, Flann O'Brien's
column (written under the name of Myles na Gopaleen) for the *Irish
Times,* Beckett's decision to write in French, John Montague's "A Severed

Head" (1972), Michael Hartnett's *Farewell to English* (1975) and his decision to "come with meagre voice/to court the language of my people," and Seamus Heaney's *Station Island* (1985), where the shade of Joyce proclaims, "The English language/belongs to us."[35]

Ó Cadhain's response to this preoccupation most closely resembles those of Joyce and Beckett: Joyce ultimately writes in the private language of *Finnegans Wake*, Beckett writes in French to demonstrate language's inability to mean. But Joyce's private language explodes into a kind of universal language. "The more Joyce knew the more he could," Beckett told Israel Shenker in 1956. "He's tending toward omniscience and omnipotence as an artist. I'm working with impotence, ignorance. I don't think impotence has been exploited in the past."[36] Though most of Beckett's work appeared after the publication of *Cré na Cille*, he and Ó Cadhain seem to share the same bleak attitude toward the enterprise of writing.

Beckett's doubts about literary nationalism of the Yeats sort are clear in the mocking pages of *Murphy* (1938), where Neary tries to dash out his brains against the buttocks of Cuchulain's statue in the General Post Office—a monument both to the Easter Rising and to Yeats. And Murphy himself requests that his ashes be flushed down a toilet at the Abbey Theatre, "if possible during the performance of a piece."[37] Ó Cadhain's political and literary radicalism made him equally impatient with the pieties of Ireland in the 1940s. Beckett chose to write in French for a time, as a guard against easy eloquence and perhaps also as a wry comment on literary supernationalists who insisted that Irish was the only proper language to use. "Do you know, Maddy, sometimes one would think you were struggling with a dead language," exclaims Mr. Rooney in the radio play *All That Fall,* and she replies, "it will be dead in time, just like our own poor dear Gaelic"; later Mr. Rooney describes his visit to "the men's, or Fir as they call it now, from Vir Viris I suppose, the *V* becoming *F,* in accordance with Grimm's Law."[38] Ó Cadhain chooses his dying language in part as a guard against easy reading, in part to become the voice of a dead and incredibly remote past. To write in Irish, he declared, made him "as old as the Hag of Beara, as old as Brú na Bóinne, as old as the Great Elk. There are two thousand years of that stinking sow which is Ireland, revolving in my ears, my mouth, my eyes, my head, my dreams."[39] The reader of *Cré na Cille* in Irish must ponder each strange or obsolete word; even to read it in English is no easy task, for one must learn the style of each individual speaker, each one's verbal tricks and obsessions. As Billy the Post reminds us, there is no map of the churchyard to keep the graves, the corpses, the speakers apart.[40]

Beckett has spoken about the impossibility of writing, and also about the overwhelming compulsion to go on writing. "You must say words, as long as there are any," the narrator of *The Unnamable* insists,

> perhaps they have said me already, perhaps they have carried me to the threshold of my story, before the door that opens on my story, that would surprise me, if it opens, it will be I, it will be the silence, where I am, I don't know, I'll never know, in the silence you don't know, you must go on, I can't go on, I'll go on.[41]

Beckett's characters—Vladimir and Estragon, Hamm and Clov, Nagg and Nell—are locked together like Ó Cadhain's dead, unable to communicate, unable to mean, doomed to go on talking. Ó Cadhain has intensified his characters' plight by incorporating them in a novel that refuses to be a novel and making them speak a language almost no one can understand. He has deliberately embarked on a doomed enterprise— doomed formally, doomed linguistically—to demonstrate the end of a way of life, of a community, of the language that alone expressed that way of life and that community. "His writing is not *about* something," as Beckett wrote of *Finnegans Wake; "it is that something itself."*[42] Here it is a refusal to fall silent, a refusal to allow the inevitable and eternal silence to prevail until these speakers keen the death of their own speech and their unending talk becomes a howl, a scream of protest—until it becomes, in John Montague's words,

> a voice
> like an animal howling
> to itself on a hillside
> in the empty church of the world
>
> a lament so total
> it mourns no one
> but the globe itself
> turning in the endless halls
>
> of space, populated
> with passionless stars
>
> and that always raised voice.[43]

NOTES

1. Flann O'Brien (Brian O'Nolan) to William Saroyan, in Flann O'Brien, *The Third Policeman* (London: MacGibbon and Kee, 1967), 200.

2. Seán Ó Tuama, "The Other Tradition: Some Highlights of Modern Fiction in Irish," in *The Irish Novel in Our Time*, ed. Patrick Rafroidi and Maurice Harmon (Lille: Publications de l'Université de Lille, 1975–76), 3:43–44; Breandán Ó

hEithir, "*Cré na Cille:* Máirtín Ó Cadhain (1906–1970)," in *The Pleasures of Gaelic Literature,* ed. John Jordan (Dublin and Cork: Radio Telefís Eireann/Mercier Press, 1977), 73; Joan Trodden Keefe, "The Graves of Connemara: Ireland's Máirtín Ó Cadhain," *World Literature Today* 59 (Summer 1985): 368.

3. Brian Cleeve, *Dictionary of Irish Writers,* vol. 3, *Writers in the Irish Language* (Cork: Mercier Press, 1971), Cleeve adds Welsh and Breton to Ó Cadhain's Celtic languages; he translated from Welsh, English, and French, and read Russian, German, and Italian. Throughout, I have quoted from Joan Trodden Keefe's introduction to and translation of Máirtín Ó Cadhain, *Cré na Cille,* (Ph.D. diss., University of California, Berkeley, 1984).

4. E. Estyn Evans, *Irish Folk Ways* (London: Routledge and Kegan Paul, 1957), 293.

5. James Joyce, *Ulysses* (New York: Modern Library, 1961), 109, 114.

6. Ó Cadhain, *Cré na Cille,* 7.

7. Ó Cadhain, *Cré na Cille,* 5.

8. Evans, *Irish Folk Ways,* 262–64. Evans suggests that the word *pardon* also conflates with patron and pattern, 253.

9. Keefe, "Graves of Connemara," 365; Ó Tuama, "The Other Tradition," 43–44.

10. Joyce, *Ulysses,* 6.

11. Keefe, "Graves of Connemara," 373. The passage is from one of our chief sources of information about Ó Cadhain, his autobiographical essay *Páipéir Bhána agus Páipéir Bhreaca* (White papers and speckled [i.e. written on] papers) (Dublin: Baile Atha Cliath, 1969).

12. W. H. Auden, ed., *The Portable Greek Reader* (New York: Viking Press, 1948), 7.

13. Fyodor Dostoevsky, "Bobok," in *Polnoe sobranie sochinenii* (Complete collected works) (Leningrad: Izdatel'stvo "Nauka," 1980), 21:49–50. The translation is my own, as are the translations from St. Augustine and Lucian. There are English versions of "Bobok" in *The Short Stories of Dostoevsky,* ed. William Phillips, trans. Constance Garnett (New York: Dial Press, 1946), and in *The Diary of a Writer,* trans. Boris Brasol (New York: George Braziller, 1954).

14. Keefe, "Graves of Connemara," 364–65.

15. Ibid., 372. Dr. Keefe has suggested that the genre of radio drama itself—disembodied voices speaking from the void, a whole drama built only on voices—may have shaped Ó Cadhain's method and even his subject matter. Ó Cadhain may have known Fontenelle's *Dialogues des morts* (1683) and Fénelon's *Dialogues des morts* (1700–1718).

16. W. B. Yeats, *Collected Plays* (New York: Macmillan, 1953), 282, 284.

17. Jonathan Swift, *Gulliver's Travels,* in *The Writings of Jonathan Swift,* ed. Robert A. Greenberg and William Bowman Piper (New York: Norton, 1973), 181–82.

18. Yeats, *Collected Plays,* 434.

19. James Joyce, *Dubliners,* ed. Robert Scholes and A. Walton Litz (New York: Viking Press, 1969), 26.

20. In "The Man Who Had No Story" the protagonist cuts reeds in a place belonging to the *sí.* Benighted and lost, he is given shelter in a cottage, where the man of the house asks him to tell a story. When he admits that he has no story he can tell, he is sent out for water, but the bucket rolls away from him and he follows it. Eventually he enters another cottage, where a wake is in progress. Here he is successively called upon to act as fiddler, surgeon (he must cut the legs of the coffin-bearers to make them uniform in height), and priest; though he

protests his inexperience, he successfully performs each function. As priest he accompanies the corpse and its bearers to various graveyards where the corpse is denied entry. Finally the corpse is buried, the errant bucket is filled, and he returns to the first cottage. There he describes his adventures to the man of the house, who hears him out, then drily comments that henceforth he will always have a story to tell.

Sean O'Sullivan (Sean Ó Súilleabháin) told this version in a lecture at the University of California, Berkeley (April 1975); he includes a briefer version in his *Folktales of Ireland* (Chicago: University of Chicago Press, 1966), 182–84. The tale was widespread and popular in Ireland; 137 versions have been collected by the Irish Folklore Commission.

21. Seamus O'Kelly, "The Weaver's Grave," in *Modern Irish Short Stories*, ed. Ben Forkner (Harmondsworth, Eng.: 1980), 113, 118, 124.

22. Ibid., 140, 155.

23. Ibid., 114, 159.

24. Frank O'Connor, *The Lonely Voice: A Study of the Short Story* (Cleveland and New York: World, 1963), 18–19. Ó Cadhain declared that Dublin has not "been a community since Joyce's day. . . . It was Joyce who wrote the first of Dublin's novels, and perhaps the last." See his *Páipéir Bhána*, 22, quoted in Ó Tuama, "The Other Tradition," 44. Ó Tuama (45) remarks that "the characters in *Cré na Cille* . . . remain static, typed, underdeveloped, so that however valid a picture in *general* the novel is of a Connemara *Gaeltacht*, it is not in any way a deeply felt depiction of *personal* human life, in its complexity, as lived within that community." Ó Tuama is right about stasis and failure to depict a functioning community, but Ó Cadhain's point is that, living or dead, his people are not developing and no longer form a community. See Keefe, "Graves of Connemara," 367.

25. Ó Cadhain, *Cré na Cille*, 244–45. *An Gúm* rejected *Cré na Cille* as too "Joycean." See Keefe, "Graves of Connemara," 366.

26. Ó Cadhain, *Cré na Cille*, 245.

27. Ó Tuama, "The Other Tradition," 39–40.

28. James Joyce, *Finnegans Wake* (New York: Viking Press, 1958), 7.

29. Quoted in David Greene, *Writing in Irish Today* (Cork: Mercier Press, 1972), 60.

30. Mac Marcais and Ó hIfearnáin are quoted in Tomás Ó Fiaich, "The Language and Political History," in *A View of the Irish Language*, ed. Brian Ó Cuív (Dublin: Stationery Office, 1969), 105–7; Ó Direáin is quoted in Greene, *Writing in Irish Today*, 59–60. Pearse Hutchinson's "Gaeltacht" is in his *Watching the Morning Grow* (Dublin: Gallery Press, 1972), 10.

31. Ó Cadhain, *Cré na Cille*, 245.

32. Ibid., 274–76.

33. Ibid., 388.

34. James Joyce, *A Portrait of the Artist as a Young Man*, ed. Chester G. Anderson (New York: Viking Press, 1968), 189.

35. See John Montague, "A Severed Head," especially parts 1, 2, and 5, in *The Rough Field* (1972; Reprint, Dublin: Dolmen Press, 1979); Michael Hartnett, *A Farewell to English* (Dublin: Gallery Press, 1978), 67; Seamus Heaney, *Station Island* (New York: Farrar, Straus & Giroux, 1985), 93.

36. Israel Shenker, "Moody Man of Letters," *New York Times*, 6 May 1956, sec. 2, 3.

37. Samuel Beckett, *Murphy* (1938; Reprint, New York: Grove Press, 1957), 42, 269.

38. Samuel Beckett, *All That Fall*, in *Krapp's Last Tape and Other Dramatic Pieces* (New York: Grove Press, 1960), 80, 82.

39. Ó Tuama, "The Other Tradition," 44, quoting *Páipéir Bhána*, 42.

40. Ó Cadhain, *Cré na Cille*, 385.

41. Samuel Beckett, *Three Novels* (New York: Grove, 1965), 414; these are the last few words of *The Unnamable*.

42. Samuel Beckett, "Dante . . . Bruno. Vico . . . Joyce," in *Our Exagmination Round his Factification for Incamination of Work in Progress* (London: Faber and Faber, 1972), 14. The earlier portion of the passage is also relevant to Ó Cadhain's book: "Here form *is* content, content *is* form. You complain that this stuff is not written in English. It is not written at all. It is not to be read—or rather it is not only to be read. It is to be looked at and listened to. His writing is not *about* something; *it is that something itself.*"

43. John Montague, "Lament," part 8 of "Ó Riada's Farewell," in *A Slow Dance* (Dublin: Dolmen Press, 1975), 63.

7

James Clarence Mangan and the Paternal Debt

David Lloyd

The *Autobiography* of James Clarence Mangan opens with a quotation: ". . . A heavy shadow lay/On that boy's spirit: he was not of his fathers." This quotation, which Mangan attributes to Massinger,[1] opens the text with a threefold reflection. It predicates the text on a disjunction between the writer and the paternal line; it establishes the woe that may be either the condition or the sign of that disjunction; and its very status as a quotation radically separated contextually from an original that is not even named reflects upon the condition and effects of disjunction itself, which becomes both theme and procedure of the text it introduces.

The circumstances of the *Autobiography*'s origins virtually recapitulate the problem outlined above. Fishamble Street, the actual site of its writing according to Father C. P. Meehan, suggests immediately a topical repetition: in order to write the history of his life, Mangan returns to the place of his birth. Meehan's note also claims that it was "at [his] instance" that the autobiography was composed, which suggests that, if not specifically for therapeutic or ethical purposes, the *Autobiography* was written at the behest of a *father* confessor who was also a metafather.

The external injunction that determined the very composition of the *Autobiography* stems from a figure who repeats the "real" father, just as the site of its writing involves a return to Mangan's own place of origin. The ethical injunction itself is written large in the opening paragraph of the *Autobiography* in a figure that subsumes both fathers: Providence itself. What Providence demands of Mangan is, in fact, an autobiography that will serve as a "memorial" of his sin and suffering and be a warning to his fellow men. But if the "conviction" of this "imperative duty" impressed itself on Mangan "at a very early period" in his life, it is equally apparent that this conviction itself is at once the index of the sin and the nature of the suffering of which he must write:

> This conviction continually gained strength within me, until it as-
> sumed all the importance of a paramount idea in my mind. It was in its
> nature, alas, a sort of dark anticipation, a species of melancholy fore-
> boding of the task which Providence and my own disastrous destiny
> would one day call upon myself to undertake (*A*, 9).[2]

The origin of this text lies not in some specific event or set of events, but rather in the "anticipation" of the narrative itself. That "Providential" anticipation is the absolute ethical demand that produces both the "bodeful text" itself and its subject, a suffering that is constant anticipa-
tion. Mangan, however, is anxious not to "anticipate [his] mournful narrative," and anxious that these preliminary observations should not "appear as the commencement of a history" (*A*, 10). These remarks refer instead to the ends that precede the history, determining the shape of its reconstruction in keeping with the ethical injunction that elicits it. These ends turn out to be twofold. The first is a settling of accounts, a payment of *debts* that can, in effect, only be carried out by Mangan's delivering of himself, true and entire, to his readers:

> Meantime they [his enemies], as well as those excellent individuals
> whose kindness towards me throughout the period of my probation I
> have experienced to an extent scarcely credible, may in these pages
> read the simple and undecorated truth with regard to all that has so
> long appeared worst in my character and conduct. To all I owe a debt,
> and that debt I shall endeavour to repay to the uttermost (*A*, 11).

Yet far from being the case that, as he claims, his self is effaced in becoming a mere representation of "the hidden springs of human frailty" ("For myself, individually, I crave nothing" [*A*, 11]), the appeal to the reader's understanding involves a pursuit of the authentic Mangan, which both exceeds the apparent *ethical* intents of the *Autobiography* and fails to close the debt by *repaying* the reader's labors. We are faced with a text that in every sense seeks but never succeeds to make its ends meet.

Mangan recognizes a profound inadequacy in his rationalizations of his anxiety, and he is troubled as much by the gap between feeling and its conceptualization as by the threat itself: "I suffered as much from my inability to harmonize my thoughts and feelings as from the very evil that I dreaded" (*A*, 10). What blocks that "harmonization" of thought and feeling is perhaps the fact that his dread is based on the apprehension of a danger that is, in a quite literal sense, prefigurative: it has "neither

form nor outline," it is not to be figured or described. Had this confrontation clearly led in Mangan's case not to transcendence or increased
power, but rather to the "blasting" of "the Great Tree" of his existence,
one would have here a classic moment of the sublime, combining
obscurity with threat and "terror." It is, accordingly, no surprise that
when Mangan does find a figure of threat in which to locate the real
origin both of his misery and forebodings, that figure turns out to be his
father: "May GOD assoil his great and mistaken soul and grant him
eternal peace and forgiveness!—but I have an inward feeling that to him
I owe all my misfortunes" (A, 14). Throughout the first portion of the
autobiography, in the "impersonal autobiograpy," and in the letters to
James McGlashan, as well as throughout Mangan's life, his father appears constantly as a threatening figure, often as an unwelcome visitor
in his dreams, according to accounts probably based in part on the
impersonal autobiography (IA, 28; P, 16).

We begin, then, from the perspective of the father and with the
paternal figure's effect on the constitution of the "normal" subject. According to Freud, the "dissolution of the oedipus complex" occurs by
way of an introjection of the paternal figure and the moral sanction that it
represents "into the ego, [where] it forms the nucleus of the superego."[3]
At one level, the "castration anxiety" motivating this introjection is
merely a mechanism, so to speak, that enables what is of primary
importance—the formation of an ethical identity through identification
not with the real but with a subliminated father. But if the personal
identity of the subject emerges reflectively at the moment of the dissolution of the oedipus complex, it dissolves equally the narcissistic ego that
recognizes no difference between itself and the other. At this juncture,
the apparently merely mechanical function of "castration anxiety" returns and determines the more radically unsettling aspects of Freud's
elaboration of subjectivity. For castration anxiety is predicated, in the
first place, upon recognizing sexual difference, since the little boy is said
to perceive his sister's or mother's lack of a penis. An economy of
identity, the infant's relation to the mother, is fractured by the possibility
of difference. When, therefore, in the interests of anatomical identity,
the little boy reconstitutes his identity by identifying with his father, the
phallus continues to make a difference. In place of a narcissistic totality
in which the self-identity of the infant is assured, the child's identity is
constructed always through identification with an other. Far from guar-
anteeing the child's integrity, the accession to what is, in form as in
context, an ethical identity instead splits the child between a self-identity that is necessarily effaced, persisting always as only imaginary, and
an identification with the other that can never be complete, precisely
because of the trace of self-identity that it always leaves behind.[4]

Moreover, precisely because the moment of identification spells the end of the "pleasure ego" and of an economy in which the infant's needs are demands to be met by the mother, another economy is established, which may be conceived of as an economy based on *debt*. Given that the male child's identification with the father can never be total, he will perpetually be indebted to this figure to whom he owes his very identity. Structured from the start around an insufficiency in the self that stems from the recognition of difference, the subject's desire emerges as a perpetual striving for identification with the other that he is forever unable to achieve.

Within his *Autobiography* Mangan centers his relationship with his father around such a *debt*: "I have an inward feeling that to him I *owe* all my misfortunes." (The emphasis is mine.) The relationship to his father is like his relationships to others, as he indicates in the general observations in the opening chapter: "To all I owe a debt. . . ." Theoretically, then, it would be possible to pay off that debt in the very writing of an ethical autobiography that would provide an alternative paternity by developing "the hidden springs" of the subject's identity—on which, indeed, Mangan might seem here to have touched. The hindrance, however, is that the father here represents not the site of a transcendent fullness, in possession both of the phallus and of meaning, to which Mangan is indebted, but rather one who is in his own turn perpetually indebted. To identify with this father is not to enter into self-possession but to perpetuate that indebtedness into what becomes, in the father's own expression, "the desert of perdition" (*A*, 15). For Mangan's father succumbs early to bankruptcy, and in his losses the son's identity is lost.

The intricate connections between the debt of the father and the irredeemable indebtedness of the son is elaborated in an extraordinarily precise set of puns. The "fault" of the father, who should be both the provider for the family and its protector, is exactly *improvidence*. Failing to provide for the family, he spends his money and property on strangers. But if his material properties are the first to go, they are rapidly followed by those essential ethical properties, his "judgment and disposition," and he is led to exchange his grocery trade in "provisions" for that of vintner. What the father provides for the young James is in turn an atmosphere opposed to Providence: one "of curses and intemperance, of cruelty, infidelity and blasphemy—and of both secret and open hatred towards the moral government of God" (*A*, 14). In consequence, however, the father becomes himself the victim of "a retributive Providence" and, increasingly, a *debtor*:

Year by year his property melted away. Debts accumulated on him; and his creditors, knowing the sort of man they had to deal with, always proved merciless. Step by step he sank, until, as he himself expressed it, only "the desert of perdition" lay before him (*A*, 15).

Rather than becoming the symbolic figure of Providence—source both of law and plentitude, of *giving*—the father becomes a figure of privation, himself indebted and punished for improvidence.

In the larger study of which this essay is a part, I demonstrate that biography is intimately linked to the aesthetic politics of nationalism. The individual, consciously identifying with the nation, transcends the actual disintegration of the nation by prefiguring the nation's destiny. Here, as the political metaphors of Mangan's account suggest, his siblings adopt, in the face of their father's brutality, the line of action that repeats within the family the moral and political program of the nationalists. Identity is the necessary first stage in the nation's spiritual and economic "redemption." Mangan himself, on the other hand, adopts a strategy that might seem an intensification to the point of parody of their cultural and historical program:

> For me, I sought refuge in books and solitude; and days would pass during which my father seemed neither to know nor care whether I was living or dead. My brothers and sisters fared better: they indulged in the habits of active exercise, and strengthened their constitutions morally and physically to a degree that even enabled them to present a successful front of opposition to the tyranny exercised over them. But I shut myself up in a close room: I isolated myself in such a manner from my own nearest relatives that with one voice they all proclaimed me "mad" (*A*, 15).

Mangan almost literally brackets the spectacle of his siblings' opposition with that of his own withdrawal. The implied superiority of their strategy appears accordingly to be an "indulgence" that not only leads ambiguously to a "*front* of opposition," but more importantly aligns them with the father as the "one voice" of the family that declares him mad.

Mangan's withdrawal offers at first a double satisfaction. At the same time that it provides a negative refuge in solitude, it furnishes in the form of reading a more positive substitute for the investments that have been withdrawn from the family. It is possible to see this withdrawal as a regressive repetition and even an intensification of a more original moment of negation, in which the withdrawal of investments from unpleasurable objects founds at once the narcissistic ego and the beginning of the process of thought itself.[5] The direction of those thoughts in the first place toward the question of the child's own origin finds later form in the child's attempt to liberate himself from parental authority by establishing another parentage through his fantasies.[6] Mangan's withdrawal, which might initially involve regressive and defensive tendencies and suggest the basis for that "lack of a sense of reality" that is so frequently remarked on by his critics, passes over into an ambivalence that contains another, offensive thrust.[7] The pursuit of knowledge that his solitary reading involves would at once satisfy the desire to be wrapped up in another scene, and the more aggressive desire to construct another parentage, or, more radically, to deny the dependence that is itself structured around the threat posed by the father. The father as origin of self and of self-consciousness, is both displaced and, in a move that becomes increasingly significant at a later stage, decomposed by the multiplicity of texts to which the child has recourse in pursuit of independent origins.

The reasons for Mangan's inability to escape his psychic suffering seem to lie precisely in the reversible grammar of his relationship to his family. The respect and love that the child owes to his father and family are curbed by the threat that the father represents, transforming them through fear into hate. The subtle dissymmetry condensed in the difference between the phrase "to him I owe all my misfortunes" and its implicit opposite "to him I owe all my love," the difference between that *for* which one is indebted and the mode in which the debt is to be paid back, is in a way annulled: the misfortune of which the father is the source is turned back upon the father as hatred. But in Mangan's case, a further reversal ensued that prevents him from forming a "front of opposition," and which transforms his hatred of the father and of the family that shares his "one voice," into the sense of *being* hated. The onset of this paranoid representation of the world shores up Mangan's interior world, disconnected as it strives to be from "relations."[8] The "severe check" that Mangan, retrospectively, finds to have been in preparation for his faults (*A*, 17) manifests itself accordingly when both the material conditions that provided the possibility of his withdrawal and the adequacy of the paternal metaphor simultaneously disintegrate. The consequence is a series of breakdowns that appear to cross the "minimal split" between neurosis and psychosis.[9]

In the eyes of his son, James Mangan Sr.'s diminishment coincides with his final financial ruin and bankruptcy:

> My father's circumstances at length grew desperate: within the lapse of a very limited period he had failed in eight successive establishments in different parts of Dublin, until finally nothing remained for him to do but to sit down and fold his arms in despair. Ruin and beggary stared him in the face; his spirit was broken; and as a last resource he looked to the wretched members of his family for that help which he should have been able to extend to them (*A*, 17).

With the economic and psychic collapse of his father, Mangan loses the ambivalent figure that stands, at several levels, between him and an "outside world." On one hand, the diminished father is incapable of performing psychically the role of a figure of threat that both motivates and supports Mangan's interior world; on the other hand, his collapse removes both figuratively and literally the screen that protected that world from the intrusion of the other. The paranoic effects that colored the world are realized in Mangan's expulsion into a world in which contact with others can be experienced only in the form of physical and mental assault; he is forced in the scrivener's office "to herd with the coarsest of associates and suffer at their hands every sort of rudeness and indignity which their uncultivated and semi-savage natives prompted them to inflict" (A, 18).

These claims are almost certainly exaggerated if not entirely phan-tasmal.[10] What is more surely so is the depiction of the "house, or, if the reader please, hovel, in Chancery Lane" (A, 19) that, as he confessed to Meehan, "he dreamt" (PPM, xli n.). Given its hallucinatory status, it may also be considered the appropriate symbol of the collapsed defense, the loss of the "close room" (A, 15) that had been his refuge, and its transformation into a "den" through which the winds and rains "howled through the winter nights like the voices of unquiet spirits" (A, 19). The corresponding bodily image is the physical mutilation that Mangan attributes to his having shared when hospitalized a bed with a child "who was afflicted from head to foot with an actual leprosy" (A, 12), which he in turn contracts.[11]

Both the figure of the ruined dwelling and the phantom of a body ruined by the ravages of leprosy signify more, however, than the mutila-tions inflicted by Mangan's identifications. They also signify both the effective cause of Mangan's collapse and the identification that draws him into an alienation that can never be redeemed. His father's extrava-gance and ruin cast Mangan out from the shelter of introversion, leaving him "a *ruined* soul in a *wasted* frame" (A, 23), and he is obliged in turn to take on the father's role and with it his debts. James Mangan, Jr., substitutes for James Mangan, Sr., and, in identifying with the father, takes on also his economic and psychic ruin, while the parents become the younger Mangan's dependents. Identifying thus with the father as debtor rather than as Providence, the source of abundant production, the "succession" of his father's debts parallels the succession of diseases that culminate in his hospitalization with the leper and subsequent contraction of an "incurable hypochondriasis."[12]

Mangan's second breakdown resembles almost exactly his first: his displacement and replacement of his father give way again to the onset of illness, commencing more severely this time with hallucinations of being "shut up in a cavern with serpents and scorpions and all hideous and monstrous things, which writhed and hissed all around me, and discharged their slime and venom over my person" (*A*, 26).[13]

It is certainly possible to read the "serpents and scorpions" of his fantasy as a further fragmentation of the threatening father, who appeared initially as "a human boa constrictor" and is now multiplied in forms that are in turn the inverted image of the texts that were the boy's resources. For, at the same time, we can grasp how the ambivalent structure of Mangan's psyche remains in play in the midst of paranoid delusions. If the father persists here as a threat in the multiplied and fragmented form of a venomous other, it is equally the case that the father as such is no longer a threat, having become the younger Mangan's *dependent*. Having displaced and replaced his father, Mangan is in turn harassed by the "small creatures" that depend upon him economically, just as his father earlier regarded his children as mice to be chased into holes.

Mangan's phantasms thus figure quite precisely the decomposition of his identity back into a multiplicity of possible and contradictory identifications. There is, first, the persisting identity of the child, his "close room" transformed, perhaps by even a further regression, into the womblike form of a cavern itself not free from penetration by phallic beasts and their foul discharges. If this is the figure of the child elicited by the parent who destroys self-identity, a second identification may be that with the mother, seen in the figure of the younger Mangan submitting to the intrusive vermin that crawl all over him as multiple versions of the father. Such an identification may make some sense of the fact that throughout all his autobiographical writings, Mangan scarcely mentions his mother, and then only as the silent support of the father's will or desire.[14] Finally, there is an identification with the father, but one that is predicated precisely on a lack in the father and that, accordingly, cannot supercede and order the previous identifications. All remain in play at once, preventing Mangan from assuming a stable and "authentic" identity; in a more Freudian expression, he remains fixated at a stage anterior to the dissolution of the oedipal complex.[15]

As Mangan's psychic investments are transferred gradually from the family to the sublime domain of religion, the structure of his relations to the transcendental other, God, reproduces those already formed by the split between his real and figural father. Onto God the Father is transferred all the ambivalence that formerly attached to the father, accentuated and preserved, however, by the very transcendence of a God who can never be diminished. Throughout the *Autobiography*, Mangan refers to his father equally with admiration and dread. God the Father takes on the projection of precisely these qualities: on the one hand, he represents the refuge of innocents, the kindly father that Mangan lacks in his own parent; on the other, he is the unremitting chastiser from whom, as perhaps Mangan's breakdowns suggested to him, there is no escape, and to whom there is no appeal: "The gates of heaven seemed barred against me: its floor and walls of brass and triple adamant, repelled my cries; and I appeared to myself to be sending a voice of agony into an interminable chasm" (*A,* 28–29). This double aspect of God sustains as well as it reflects the interminable ambivalence that characterizes Mangan's career. At one extreme, God is represented as the refuge of the innocent dead where Mangan's desire remains suspended around an inviolate image of the self-sufficiency that might have been his as an infant; at the other extreme, God the Father, conceived as dwelling apart in a quite exclusive transcendence, takes on the affect of dread that is transferred from the real father only to be projected into an absence that, inviolable as it is, becomes the secure pivot of Mangan's own solitude. For if the projection of God into an "interminable chasm" guarantees the perpetuation of Mangan's suffering, it provides more importantly the promise of an inviolable space of singularity that can have, will have, nothing to do with "society." Having taken up the place of the father as provider for the family, Mangan becomes in turn the victim of Providence, a God who assumes on vast scale the *repulsion* that others characteristically felt toward the writer, and who accordingly becomes, far from the source of plentitude, the abyss into which the *irredeemable* subject pours his lost self.

Mangan's impasse is finally articulated, both in "form and content," in the last chapter by the introduction of a discussion with a young Catholic evangelist that centers on Pascal's *Pensées.* The allusion to Pascal opens a backdrop through which are recapitulated all the issues of the text, but on a critically reflective plane. Not only is Pascal familiar as the theologian of "le Dieu caché"[16] that Mangan has been seen to adopt as the transposed support of his psychic structures, but the unattainability of that God is reduplicated by what might seem the rather invidious act of concealing "le noeud de notre condition" beyond the attainability of knowledge through reason, in order to ensure the submission of that faculty to God himself.[17] In the distance that opens between a hidden God and the "hidden springs" of our condition, the nature of that condition constantly reveals itself to be a "misère" that is the only sign we have of our fall from some higher state.[18]

But from the suspension-in-suffering that for him characterizes our fallen condition, Pascal refuses to have recourse to nostalgia for a prelapsarian state, which is seen rather as a diversionary delusion than a true stimulus to faith: "What is it then that this desire and this inability proclaim to us, but that there was once in man a true happiness of which there now remain to him only the mark and empty trace, which he in vain tries to fill from all his surroundings, seeking from things absent the help he does not obtain in things present?"[19] Since the very structure of Mangan's psychic constitution prevents his being redeemed through accepting Pascal's ultimate injunction, namely, to fill the abyss with the presence of God, he remains in a state of perdition.[20] Crucially retained, however, is the radical doubt in relation to origins and to the recourse to a "trace vide" for the source of retrospective consolation. Closed out from either origin or end, the reprobate is suspended in an abyss in which he will persistently seek but never find the God to whom a sin that has preceded him has left him utterly indebted. He can see "nothing in creation but what is fallen and *ruined*" (*A, 33*).

DEPTHS OF CITATION

Mangan's invocation of Pascal at the close of a text that purports to be devoted to "developing the hidden springs" of his condition is peculiarly apposite not only to the theme of the illusory consolation to be derived from such pursuits, but also to the extensive use of such reflections in formal citation in Mangan's *Autobiography*. Drawn as one is to follow the network of quotations and allusions that permeates the text in pursuit of an anterior context that might permit a "translation" of the deeper truth of Mangan's writing, one is perpetually reminded by the insistence of the citations or allusions themselves that the writer remains irredeemably indebted even in the process of writing himself out: the supports of his texts constantly erode the authenticity of the self that is represented in them. In this "Iliad of [his] woes"—an expression he borrows from that other great text on "influence" and debt, De Quincey's *Confessions*[21]—the epic of the self falls back perpetually on a multiplicity of types whose formal analogue is the mannered effect produced in Mangan's prose by the recurrent intrusion of the quotations themselves.

But, as the metaphors at the opening of his fifth and last chapter remind us, to trace back through the type or fragment the archetype in which the complete identity of the self might be noted is a fruitless endeavor. In the years between any past moment and the present, "life upon life has followed and been multiplied on and within" the writer; any archeology of the self can in turn only disinter the ruins of a *present* self ("The Pompeii and Herculaneum of my soul") that are but an "imperfect picture" of their originals (*A, 31*). The history of the self is one of progressive ruin. In an allusion that once again encapsulates Mangan's ambivalent identification with and resentful debt to the father, his ever-increasing indebtedness is ultimately figured in the original father

of the race, Adam—at once the prototype and the source of Mangan's
sufferings as well as of rebellion that leads to his expulsion from the
enclosure of paradise into the suffering of labor; exchange of knowledge
for innocence initiates, like the parodic paradise of Mangan's reading in
a close room, a debt that multiplies indefinitely by endless self-reproduc-
tion.

Such reversability of intention appears constantly to define the function of quotation in Mangan's writings, and nowhere more than in the
Autobiography. Even the apparently innocent "Farewell the tranquil
mind! farewell content!" that prefixes both chapters 4 and 5, turns out to
be the cry of Othello believing himself betrayed by Desdemona, but
already betrayed by a "James" [Iago] who leaves him indeed with a
"mind full of scorpions." The sense of betrayal infects the entire text:
father betraying son, but also equally, in the motivation of the text itself,
son betraying father. So much is even compressed into the name Mangan inserts into the given name that would otherwise identify him with
his father. "Clarence" as a *borrowed* name inserts betrayal between James
and the "man" who "began" him, for "perfidious" is the epithet insep-
arable from the name "Clarence," false though his brother Richard's
accusation that he betrayed his father may have been. Already the
expression of an ambivalent relationship to the father, both resentful and
guilty, this name, like Mangan's other multiple pseudonyms, becomes
the license to a perfidious writing, consisting of treacherous translations
that "betray" their originals and their readers precisely by being, to use
Mangan's own apt expression, "fathered upon others." One need only
recall the sense of betrayal as *exposure* to have the entire mechanism of
Mangan's procedures crystallized in this word: Mangan's writing is
devoted to the exposition of its own dependence.

Not unlike translation or parody, citation becomes, as a formal device
as much as in the specific content of what is cited, the index of a deep
ambivalence with regard to the demand for authenticity that is contained
in the related demands for originality and sublimation of paternity. Far
from being the trace of successful appropriation of foreign matter into a
uniform text, Mangan's citations recur as an index of indebtedness, in
terms both of the stilted mannerisms of style and of the openings into
the treacherous "depths" of other writers who are the ambivalent fathers
of Mangan's own text. For citations at once efface and summon their
originals, being, like parody, both antagonistic and dependent. Like the
dead father who is said to have haunted Mangan, the body may be
buried but the spirit is invoked through citation itself, so that we are
drawn into a tracing of anteriority that may be endless. In the space of
irredeemable suffering that Mangan's indebted writing opens up
("deriving *calamity* from *calamus*, a quill") as a space equally defined by

the father who is its alternative source, a vertiginous sense of treacherous dependencies prevails. It is perfectly encapsulated in the phrase Mangan applies to the physical and mental disintegrations subsequent upon his contraction of leprosy: " 'within the lowest deep a lower deep' " (*A*, 21).

The phrase derives from Satan's bitter lamentation upon Mt. Niphates in Milton's *Paradise Lost*, where the rebel angel at once contemplates and mourns a paradise he can never share, but which is itself a mere parody of angelic joys, and laments the more critical fact that, since he is not his own original, having been created by God the Father, he is perpetually in a state of dependence:

> Which way I fly is hell; myself am hell;
> And in the lowest deep a lower deep
> Still threatening to devour me opens wide,
> To which the hell I suffer seems a heaven.[22]

If the sin of Pride of which he accuses himself so often identifies Mangan with Lucifer, it is a strangely passive pride that only opens up the ambivalence of a relationship to the father that alternates between identification, in which the identity of the son with the improvident provider is met by the identity of the father with the son as victim of the father, and withdrawal, in which the excluded father is substituted for by the chain of books/citations that provide alternate origins, and in which exclusion transforms into exile from any closed space. This reversibility is beautifully caught in the reversible phonetic patterns of the whole phrase: "It was *woe* on *woe*, and 'within the *lowest* deep a *lower* deep[']". Mangan's woe is characteristically in inverse relation to the debt he owes.

For Satan, the means to be quit of "the debt immense of gratitude of endless gratitude, So furthermore still paying still to owe" would be virtual identification with God the father, the taking of his place.[23] For Mangan, on the contrary, to take the place of the father is to assume the condition of debt all the more fully, a fact that is figured with deep irony in the disjunction between the tenor of the passage that he cites—refusal of debt to the author of one's being—and the indebtedness to another author that the vehicle of citation itself perpetuates. And where Satan may be seen to "strengthen his constitution" here with a view to presenting a "front of opposition to the tyranny exercised over him," Mangan's citation has as its referent rather the disintegrating influence of leprosy, whose "moral effects" are "incorporated with [his] mental constitution." Mangan's body, far from attaining the oppositional coherence of a rebel's, or the homogeneity of assimilation, is, as he puts it in the impersonal autobiography "all nerves"; it is a tissue of connections and cathexes just as the body of his texts is a tissue of connections with anterior texts. The paradox of Mangan's writing is crucially unresolved: initial foreclosure of the father, of an external origin, leads, with the discovery of the father's own debt, not to the enclosed space of an authentic identity, but to an abyss of indebtedness that is incarnated in the *multiple* readings that substitute for the father. The origin loses its singularity, becoming a place of disintegration and alienation rather than the figure of integration and autonomy. Where, in that tradition of psychoanalysis (and through nationalism), the internalization of the father confirms the subject's fiction of identity and originality, the *foreclosure* of the father prevents either the affirmation of identity or the assumption of originality. Equally, insofar as the end is predicated properly upon the rediscovered principle of the origin, upon the "developing of hidden springs," what is produced is a text that cannot develop or end: the remarks that open it, bearing upon the "prefigural" origin of his suffering, are not to be seen as the "commencement of a history," because they have to do with the abyss of an origin that never arrives and that can, therefore, never stand as the autonomous source of derivation.

In Mangan's dreams of ruin, which he confesses to have no relation to reality however they figure the real, the ethical cure that nationalist ideology offers to subjective and political disintegration founders. The history of "self-sustained energetic men" is parodied in a writing of the self that is the history of indebtedness and is incapable of concluding in decisive acts. The perpetuation of indebtedness assures the repeated production of an inauthentic subject who continually eludes identification in or with his writings; the transformation of the father from the site of plentitude into the abyss of ruin precludes the sublimation by which dependence can be converted into that autonomy on which the nationalist will to political self-determination is predicated. The contemporary call to identify, with all the ramifications that the term has been seen to produce, can only appear, given the logic of Mangan's writings, as an accentuation of alienation and as a delusion, merely displacing the locus of dependence. As Mangan is careful to maintain, it is at one and the same time to his writing and to his "life" that he is indebted for the suffering that is consequent on the unredeemed dependence whose multiple forms in life and writings he perpetually repeats. Writing, accordingly, can provide no aesthetic cure for the suffering, nor can a reformed life emancipate his writing from its own perpetually dependent modes. As the confirmed addict, or as the "reconstructed" psychotic, Mangan seems obliged to repeat compulsively around the empty trace of an original moment that, as his own narrative implies, is what was always in question.

NOTES

1. I have so far been unable to trace the source of these lines in Philip Massinger's *Dramatic Works*. The titles of some of his works, and the themes of others, suggest reasons for Mangan's attraction to him: *A New Way to Pay Old Debts*, or *The Unnatural Combat*, for example.

2. Quotations from James Clarence Mangan's works are cited parenthetically in the text using the following abbreviations:

A: *The Autobiography of James Clarence Mangan*, ed. James Kilroy (Dublin: Dolmen, 1968).

IA: The "impersonal autobiography": "Sketches of Modern Irish Writers. James Clarence Mangan," [signed "E. W."], *Irishman* 17 (August 1850).

PPM: *The Poets and Poetry of Munster: A Selection of Irish Songs by the Poets of the Last Century*, ed. C. P. Meehan, 3d ed. (Dublin and London: J. Duffy and Sons, 1883).

P: *Poems, by James Clarence Mangan, with Biographical Introduction by John Mitchell* (New York: P. M. Haverty, 1859).

3. Sigmund Freud, "On the Dissolution of the Oedipus Complex," in *The Standard Edition of the Complete Psychological Works* . . . , trans. and ed. James Strachey (London: Hogarth Press, 1953), 19:176.

4. This is further elaborated by Jacques Lacan in his "The Mirror Stage as Formative of the Function of the I," *Ecrits: A Selection*, trans. Alan Sheridan (New York: Norton, 1977), as "the transformation that takes place in the subject when he assumes an image" (2).

5. Freud, "Negation," in *Standard Edition*, 19:233–39.

6. Freud, "Family Romances," in *Standard Edition*, 9:235–41.

7. The strictures on Mangan's lack of a sense of reality stretch from Meehan's remarks on the *Autobiography* (*PPM*, xxiv–xxv) to Robert Welch's more recent ones, calling Mangan's failure one of "a temperament incapable of going out to encounter 'the reality of experience' . . ." in his *Irish Poetry from Moore to Yeats*, Irish Literary Studies, no. 5 (Gerrards Cross: Colin Smythe, 1980), 77.

8. Freud analyzes similar grammatic reversals characteristic of paranoia in "Psychoanalytical Notes," in *Standard Edition*, 12:63.

9. See Lacan, "Treatment of Psychosis," in *Ecrits*, 191–92, 215.

10. D. J. O'Donoghue, *The Life and Writings of James Clarence Mangan* (Edinburgh: Geddes, 1897), 12–16, questions the accuracy of Mangan's autobiographies on all these points.

11. Daniel Paul Schreber, *Memoirs of My Nervous Illness*, trans. and ed. Ida MacAlpine and Richard A. Hunter (London: William Dawson, 1955), also evokes the notion of leprosy as a figure for his sense of bodily disintegration. In this and in his account of his transformation into a body of nerves, he shows remarkable similarity to Mangan. Cf. *IA*, 18, where Mangan speaks of himself as being "all nerves."

12. Freud, "Psychoanalytical Notes," in *Standard Edition*, 12:56–57n, remarks on the intimate relation between paranoia and hypochondria; cf. MacAlpine in Schreber, *Memoirs*, 408–09.

13. Once again, an analogue of these scorpions and vermin can be found in Schreber, *Memoirs*, 99.

14. It is worth contrasting the effacement of the mother in Mangan's texts with the function of the mother as a kind of counterforce to the father in James Joyce's *A Portrait of the Artist as a Young Man* (New York: B. W. Huebsch, 1916), or in Edmund Gosse's *Father and Son* (London: Heinemann, 1925). Mangan's account bears remarkable similarities to Franz Kafka's "Letter to His Father" in *Wedding Preparations in the Country and Other Posthumous Prose Writings*, trans. Ernst Kaiser and Eithne Wilkins (London: Secker and Warburg, 1954), 183: "True, one could always get protection from her, but only in relation to you. She loved you too much and was much too devoted and loyal to you to have been able to constitute an independent spiritual force, in the long run, in the child's struggle." The similarity may be due to Kafka's and Mangan's both engaging in what Deleuze and Guattari describe as "grossir Oedipe" as a means to exceed paternal determination. See Gilles Deleuze and Felix Guattari, *Kafka: pour une litterature mineure* (Paris: Minuit, 1975), 19.

15. Hence, perhaps, the frequent references of Mangan's contemporaries to his boyish or feminine characteristics.

16. Blaise Pascal, *Pensées*, trans. W. F. Trotter (New York: Random House, 1941), 65–72.

17. Ibid., 141–45.

18. Ibid., 129–30.

19. Ibid., 134–35.

20. Ibid.

21. Thomas De Quincey, *The Works of Thomas De Quincey . . .* , 4th ed. (Edinburgh: A. and C. Black, 1878), 1:231.

22. John Milton, *Paradise Lost* in *Poetical Works*, ed. Douglas Bush (Oxford: Oxford University Press, 1969), 276.

23. Ibid., 275.

8

Factions in Prefamine Ireland

JAMES S. DONNELLY, JR.

Sir George Cornewall Lewis once said that the stage of civilization reached by different groups of human beings could be determined by the scope of their sympathies or allegiances. At the lowest level were those whose sympathies extended no further than their clans, tribes, or villages. Somewhat higher were those who identified with their social class or their party, political or religious. Loftier still were those public-spirited citizens who ardently desired the well-being of "the *whole civil community.*" And at the highest stage were those noble altruists who sought "to promote the interests of *mankind at large.*" Lewis insisted that the factions of prefamine Ireland "mark a state of feeling which has not yet made the first step, which has not risen from sympathy with one's clan to sympathy with one's order" or class.[1]

These supposedly primitive Irish peasants, chiefly those of the south and west, were remarkable for getting drunk, dividing into rival parties, and quarreling furiously over trivial matters at fairs, patterns, and race meetings. But their fights were not trivial affairs. Typically they involved from three hundred to six hundred combatants and occasionally even more. As a Tipperary writer observed in 1845, "Some farmers, according to their means and connections, could bring into the field from 200 to 1,000 men whenever their honour or that of their adherents was called into question."[2] Highly organized they may have been, but were factionists guided in their actions by a code of honor? Many persons above peasant rank doubted it. As a Limerick parish priest declared in 1824, "I can hardly define what a person in such a [low] situation of life as they were in would mean by honour; but I should think it would be better expressed by pride; they wished to be superior to the opposite party."[3] Partly because of their alleged primitivism, factions have been largely ignored by sober, cultured academics, regardless of the scope of their own sympathies. Nonetheless I intend to explore the vengeful, brutal, drunken, petty world that the factionists inhabited.

First, some important matters of chronology. Along with many other aspects of traditional popular culture, faction fighting had already declined precipitously before the great famine. We can be rather precise about dating this decline. The late 1830s constituted a watershed. On one side of this watershed, factionism was still a highly visible feature of social life in Munster and Connacht; on the other side it had dwindled to a feeble impulse. The experience of Tipperary was paradigmatic. Its fairs had been notorious for faction fights until the late 1830s, but by 1845 it could be said, "The Riot Act has not been read for the last six years in the county, nor the military called out to disperse a faction fight."[4] This striking alteration was largely attributable to major changes in the administration of the law and in the methods of preserving public order adopted under the Whig government of 1835–41.[5] To this subject I will return later.

Although the steep decline of faction fighting can be confidently dated in the late 1830s, its rise can be less easily characterized. According to one view, the scarcity of records of serious fights prior to 1800 "does not necessarily mean that many more did not occur. It simply means that they were not reported to Dublin and, consequently, were not recorded."[6] This view, however, is erroneous. Any dedicated reader of newspapers before 1800 will encounter fairly numerous reports of obviously traditional fights, such as the account of April 1775 noting that in Limerick city "the usual Easter battle was fought at Thomond-gate between the County Clare and County Limerick boys. . . ."[7] But the same reader, extending the inquiry into the years after 1800, will be struck by the much greater frequency with which fights are reported in the newspapers, not to mention in that great archive known as the State of the Country Papers. No faction feuds as persistent or as pervasive as those of the Caravats versus the Shanavests, the Three Year Olds against the Four Year Olds, the Coffeys versus the Reaskavallas, or the Cooleens against the Lawlors—all of early nineteenth-century vintage—emerge from the late eighteenth-century sources.[8] The only coherent scholarly attempt to explain this development has been that of Paul Roberts, who sees it as the outcome of increasingly sharp class conflict between the poor and the wealthier farmers.[9]

Faction fights were not only far more frequent after 1800 but were also accompanied by much greater violence. The weapons used by faction fighters became deadlier. Partly this resulted from rather nasty refinements that were made to the traditional sticks of blackthorn and ash. To the striking end of the *clogh alpine,* or knobby stick, were added iron ferrules, a piece of a musket or gun barrel, or a ring of nails; it also became common to pour lead into the hollowed-out ends of faction sticks by the early nineteenth century.[10] Presumably it was nasty refinements such as these that prompted Paud Brien, a "famous faction fighter from Askeaton, to name his two sticks *"Leagadh gan éirí"* ("Down and out") and *"Bás gan sagart"* ("Death without a priest").[11]

Supplementing the often deadlier sticks after 1800 were a variety of other lethal instruments. As a Tipperary writer pointed out in 1845, "The men of stones and skull crackers gave place to others, who might be seen half-naked, fighting with guns, pistols, scythes and pitch forks. . . ."[12] Two decades earlier, the police official Major Richard Willcocks called the attention of a parliamentary committee to the use of firearms as well as swords by faction fighters. He mentioned specifically "short guns of a blunderbuss description, cut-down muskets we call them, and pistols." The fighters, he remarked, concealed these weapons under their great-coats or slung them in their belts, again beneath their buttoned-up coats, and "unless you searched them, you would not be apprised of their being armed."[13] To resort to firearms in a faction fight was still widely considered an unwarranted breach of the popularly sanctioned convention that authorized only the use of sticks and stones. But in the extremely violent world of the early nineteenth century, the convention lost much of its force.

An almost inevitable consequence of these developments in weaponry was a much higher incidence after 1800 of death and serious wounding in fights. It would be easy to compile a very extensive list of faction fights between 1800 and 1835 in which the use of firearms led to deaths. The most appalling record of fatalities in a particular faction feud was achieved by the Caravats and Shanavests between 1806 and 1811. At the fair of Golden in May 1807 alone, no fewer than twenty people were killed. Though admittedly this was an extreme case, most fights between Caravat and Shanavest partisans in those years ended with several deaths. "Altogether," says Paul Roberts, the historian of this feud, "literally hundreds must have died."[14]

With the exception of Roberts, most modern writers on the subject of factions have glossed over the greatly increased violence and the endur-ing bitterness that it engendered. The eminent folklore scholar Caoimhín Ó Danachair (Kevin Danaher), for example, claims that "there was little real animosity between members of the different factions, who lived in neighbourly harmony when not actually engaged in com-bat. . . ."[15] And Patrick O'Donnell, whose short book *The Irish Faction Fighters of the 19th Century* records numerous savage encounters, asserts that "a legacy of continuing 'black hatred' was rarely to be found among the factions."[16] For these cheery views there is some support in the sources. Mostly, however, they are eighteenth-century sources, reliable enough for that period; the few early nineteenth-century writers who project the same attitude, such as Sir Henry Inglis, are generally not trustworthy guides to the subject.[17] The increasingly common deaths and serious injuries in faction fights after 1800 generated or intensified strong feelings of enmity and vengeance. Rather than waiting until the next scheduled encounter, bitter factionists were just as likely to waylay opponents far from any conventional faction field. The unpleasant reality was reflected in the recollections of a Cork countryman in the early 1850s: "But the faction fights war [sic] the bitterest of all—black hatred descending from father to son against the opposite faction, as if poor Ireland hadn't enough enemies without turning . . . to murder and destroy her own flesh and blood."[18]

What held factions together? What were their connecting tissues? Three main kinds of social links were involved: kinship ties, common residence or geographical loyalty, and class allegiance. Obviously these social relationships were not mutually exclusive. On the contrary, they often overlapped, and this was especially true of kinship and residence. The great importance of kinship in binding factions together is indicated by the phenomenon that so many factions took their titles from family names: the Powers versus the Mahonys in Waterford; the Hickeys against the Hogans in Tipperary; the Sheehans versus the Ambroses in Limerick.[19] The adoption of one family's surname to designate a particular faction did not necessarily mean that all or even most of its members belonged to that family or bore the same surname. Usually it reflected the fact that one family group was prominent in a collection of families, or that the leadership traditionally rested with a specific, and generally a powerful, family. Most factions comprised at least several different families related either by blood or by other social ties.[20]

Territorial allegiance was of course exceptionally strong in the pre-famine years, when xenophobia frequently characterized the relations of adjacent parishes, not to mention neighboring baronies or counties. This type of allegiance also gave structure to factions, either in conjunction with kinship ties or in independence of them. The customary fight at Easter in the late eighteenth century between "the County Clare and County Limerick boys" at Thomond gate in Limerick city was to all appearances a case of the latter type, as were numerous other faction fights in the early nineteenth century. But instances of the mixed type were probably even more common. Thus a fight at Dingle in 1824 pitted the Kennedy faction of Anascaul, located ten miles east of Dingle, against "the men from the west," with the westerners having been "picked from three parishes" on the far side of Dingle.[21] Fights between the adult male inhabitants of neighboring *clachans* in the western counties also illustrate the double bond of kinship and residence in the making of factions.[22]

Although kinship, common residence, and territorial loyalty have long been recognized as bonds for factions, Paul Roberts has recently suggested that class relationships also furnished the basic organizational structure of numerous faction feuds after 1800. Roberts propounded this thesis in studying the notorious rivalry between the Caravats and Shanavests in east Munster from 1806 to 1811. But he also suggested that other, later feuds in the same region and even elsewhere reflected class divisions. Roberts noted that, like the Caravats, their successors (the Three Year Olds, the Reaskavallas, and the Whitefeet) were composed overwhelmingly of the poor in countryside and town (that is, agricultural laborers, industrial workers, cottiers, and small farmers), and they often functioned as Whiteboys. On the other hand, like the Shanavests, their successors (the Four Year Olds, the Coffeys, and the Blackfeet) were made up mostly of wealthier farmers and other middle-class elements, although persons of lower social status were often found in the same ranks because of their economic dependence. Functioning partly as factions, the successors of the Shanavests were also, like them, middle-class nationalist and vigilante organizations "pitted against insurgent Whiteboy movements."[23]

Apart from the Caravat-Shanavest feud, however, the evidence for this interpretation has yet to be provided. This is not to say that Roberts's thesis is wrong. In fact, tantalizing evidence hints that some of the more notable faction feuds did have a class character. The longstanding rivalry in north Kerry between the Cooleens and the Lawlor–Black Mulvihills is a case in point. At the official inquiry that followed a murderous clash between these two factions in 1834, a magistrate testified that the Cooleens were "made up generally of a respectable class of farmer."[24] The limited information available on the Lawlor–Black Mulvihills suggests that they comprised mostly small farmers and laborers.[25]

Yet Roberts's picture of factions divided by sharp class antagonisms has a number of weaknesses. For example, he identifies the Reaskavallas of east Limerick and northwest Tipperary as successors to the Caravat Whiteboys. But in the early 1820s it was the Reaskavallas' opponents, the Coffeys, who were behaving like lower-class rebels, agrarian and otherwise. Leading them was James Coffey. "He is," said a magistrate early in 1823, "the head of a faction and walks about with arms, the terror of the whole district" around Newport.[26] Coffey was reputedly the main actor in three cases of abduction, all involving the same woman, whose hand in marriage (and no doubt familial wealth) he was resolutely determined to have.[27] (Abducting the heiresses of wealthy farmers had long been a common pursuit of poor young men belonging to both factions and Whiteboy bands.)[28] In addition to carrying out abductions, Coffey apparently assumed the role of Whiteboy captain. The Protestant curate of Newport put it this way in July 1822: "Connected with a very riotous faction, he has led many of them into breaches of the insurrection and other acts."[29] In the case of the Caravats and Shanavests as well, their class roles as portrayed by Roberts are sometimes reversed, with the Shanavests appearing as agrarian rebels and the Caravats as anti-White-boy vigilantes.[30]

Roberts seems more convincing when he considers the notorious though scarcely studied feud between the Whitefeet and Blackfeet in south Leinster during the late 1820s and early 1830s. Starting as a faction, the Whitefeet did indeed become a far-flung and (for a time) highly effective agrarian movement pursuing traditional economic goals.[31] Their greatest stronghold was the extensive south Leinster coal field, or the colliery district as it was generally known, a highly populous region where agricultural holdings were notoriously subdivided. But Roberts's thesis is at least partly invalidated when the social composition of Whitefeetism in the colliery district is scrutinized closely. Perhaps as many as nine or ten thousand people had taken oaths as Whitefeet in this district alone by 1832. The colliers themselves appear to have fur-nished the great bulk of the recruits.[32] But their leaders were of a higher class. A knowledgeable magistrate described them as "men rather above the lower order, who in the collieries are called contractors of pits, some of whom hold a good deal of ground and are in comfortable circum-stances." One leader was said to hold thirty or forty acres and another (his brother) considerably more. When queried about this curious junc-tion of the contractors with the colliers and smallholders, this magistrate remarked of the contractors, "They have been as great land-jobbers as others, and as oppressive perhaps; but being principals or heads of the Whitefeet party, they are exempted from attack."[33] As I have argued elsewhere, the great agrarian upheavals of the early nineteenth century, including that of 1830–34, featured a remarkable degree of cooperation cutting across the lines of social class below the landed elite.[34] In my view the interclass collaboration among the Whitefeet of the colliery district was at this juncture in no way peculiar.

But what of the Blackfeet? There is little evidence that they persisted beyond 1830, either as a faction or as any other kind of autonomous organization. On the contrary, by that point, under the impact of a sharp economic downturn and the rise of a great popular movement against tithes, many Blackfeet appear to have become Whitefeet or at least strongly sympathetic to their agrarian activities.[35] But in the late 1820s, a time of rising prices and generally good harvests (until 1829), the Black-feet do seem to have functioned both as a class-based faction of well-to-do farmers and as a vigilante organization. In these capacities they evidently enjoyed the encouragement or the tolerance of many magis-trates, and they were certainly regarded by Whitefeet partisans, then generally lower-class in social composition, as spies and informers.[36]

Indeed, before 1829 or 1830 the Blackfeet's collaboration with the authorities generated much of the Whitefeet's resentment and hardened the feud between the two parties.

What prompted factions to fight? We know little or nothing about how most feuds started. It was common for members of the landed elite to say that the reasons for the original outbreak of a particular feud were lost in antiquity.[37] Most factionists would have been unable to specify how their feuds had begun. This is thoroughly understandable. In the course of a feud that had lasted for years or perhaps decades, fresh resentments and grievances were continually manufactured, so many grievances that it was easy to forget, or hard to remember, the origins of a quarrel. Even when these origins could be recalled, they were often either too trivial or too particular to have much practical meaning for those who later carried on the feud.

Instead of asking how feuds began, it is better to ask how they were perpetuated. To this question there is a simple answer that, though far from complete, makes the phenomenon much more comprehensible. Faction fights were ways to gain physical revenge for injuries and insults. The ultimate injury, death, was the most prolific source of fresh fights. As a magistrate remarked after two men had been killed in a faction fight in Tipperary town in June 1829, "The feud for their deaths will be very extensive."[38] Beatings were also frequent grounds for perpetuating faction fights, especially beatings that were seen as the result of unfair tactics on the field of battle or that occurred beyond the faction field itself.

Besides seeking satisfaction for deaths and beatings, as well as simply for defeats in "fair fights," factions also sought revenge for insults and indignities inflicted on their members. To taunt and insult one's enemies was a standard ritual preliminary to a faction fight. "I have seen many a faction fight," declared W. R. LeFanu, "every one of which began in the same way, which was thus: one man 'wheeled,' as they called it, for his party; that is, he marched up and down flourishing his blackthorn and shouting the battle-cry of his faction: 'Here is Coffey aboo against Reaskawallaghs [sic]; here is Coffey aboo—who dar' strike a Coffey?' 'I dar',' shouted one of the other party; 'here's Reaskawallah aboo,' at the same instant making a whack with his shillelagh at his opponent's head."[39]

Within this ritual form there was wide scope for verbal ingenuity and maddening insult. For each wheel there was a so-called counter. In wheeling, a boastful faction leader might trumpet the names of redoubtable fighters on his side, producing a counter from the other camp, as in the following exchange:

WHEEL: "Hall, Wall, Lane, and Moss."
COUNTER: "I'll hang my hat on Hall,

> I'll piss against Wall,
> I'll shit on Lane, and
> I'll wipe my arse with Moss."[40]

Less inventive was the conduct of the provocateur at a fair in County Cork who was seen "running through the crowd and stopping before each man of the opposite party, whom he greeted with the foul phrase 'liar.' "[41] Insulting expressions of class prejudice and hostility could also be heard during the ritualistic beginnings of some encounters. In a fight at Shanagolden in June 1825 the leader of one of the factions, Kennedy O'Brien, shouted tauntingly at John Sheahan, the chieftain of the opposite party, "Come on, you coward, you spalpeen you!" This was probably not a loose use of the term *spalpeen* by O'Brien, for the police official who reported his death in this engagement remarked that O'Brien was "a wealthy farmer." (Sheahan was also killed in the conflict.)[42]

It is important to appreciate that the insults, taunts, and boasts that were so much a part of the ritual of faction fights were not confined to the traditional scenes of conflict. The trading of insults was, for example, a notable ingredient in the origin of the feud between the parties that became known as Caravats and Shanavests. Nicholas Hanley, hanged at Clonmel in 1805 for burning the house of a land grabber, had been prosecuted by factionists belonging to the party of "Paudeen Gar" (Sharp Paddy). At Hanley's trial Paudeen Gar declared that he would not leave the place of execution until he saw the cravat, a cant term for the hangman's rope and a bitter pun on Hanley's nickname, securely tied about Hanley's neck. Just before he was hanged, Hanley had to endure similar abuse about having finally gotten the right or the perfect cravat. Hanley's partisans in turn made sneering references to the old waistcoats worn by Paudeen Gar's faction, and from these exchanges about cravats and old waistcoats came the new names of the two factions.[43] The insults that pervaded feuds also frequently involved invading the opposite party's strongholds. This was usually done in some force, but a leader of the Four Year Olds, the formidable Billy O'Dwyer of Galbally, became notorious for the bravado of his single-handed incursions into the Three Year Olds' stronghold of Mitchelstown. O'Dwyer was accompanied only by two ferocious-looking bulldogs that, he boasted, "were a match for the devil," as they certainly were for any of the resident Three Year Olds.[44]

If the negative side of faction fighting, so to speak, was the avenging of injuries and insults, the positive side was the winning of contemporary fame and posthumous glory. Faction fights have often been characterized as a type of popular sport, and though Kevin Danaher is wide of the mark in describing them as "nothing more than a crude and dangerous form of sport,"[45] some of the leading purposes of athletic contests were undeniably fulfilled by participation in faction fights. Like athletic contests, faction fights were often conducted before a large audience of appreciative spectators. Of a lusty faction fight in Limerick city in about 1810, the Rev. James Hall, a visiting English clergyman, remarked censoriously: "To the disgrace of the inhabitants, many of them shouted and applauded those that were most active, calling them by name from their windows, 'Bravo! Well done!' while they hissed those disposed to be quiet."[46] By convention women were allowed a limited participation in fights: filling their aprons with the stones that men threw, wielding stone-filled socks, and hurling some missiles themselves.[47] Women were also among the most engaged spectators. The authorities often noted how they shouted encouragement and abuse from the sidelines. "The ladies," declared Rev. Horatio Townsend, the Cork parson and writer, in 1816, "enter into the spirit of the business very warmly, and instead of exerting their influence to moderate the rancour, do all that they can to exasperate [*sic*] and inflame it."[48]

Faction fights and fighters often became the subject of poetry, songs, and stories. These cultural forms celebrated the achievements of famous stick-wielders, eulogized fallen battlers, excoriated treacherous opponents, and in general transmitted the grand tradition. Though women were by no means alone here, they were certainly among the most notable contributors to these genres. As the folklorist Thomas Culhane pointed out, the Cooleens "had a *bainfhile* named Kate Flavin" to chant their praises, although she "was not nearly as poetic as Nancy Keane, who sang the glories of the 'Black Mulvihills,' or 'Bald Mulvihills' as their enemies derisively called them." Nancy Keane was especially adept at poetic insult of the Cooleens, as in the following verse:

Who is the wizened oul' skeleton
With his dim henchmen around him?
Isn't it dirty John from Killeely?
Grisly John of the snake's head.[49]

It was not unusual in faction fights for one or more of the leaders of each party to square off against one another in single combat. This practice showcased the physical dexterity and strength, or sheer endurance, of individual fighters and helped to fix them as heroes in the popular memory.[50] The wealth of stories and legends in Irish folklore demonstrates that many faction fighters achieved the status of local cult figures. Conor Cregan, for example, whose stick was broken at the fair of Newcastle West, was said to have "rearmed himself by pulling the shaft out of a sidecar and breaking it to a suitable length over his knee." And Sean Mor Hartnett was reputedly a man of such great strength that he was able to squeeze water "out of the head of a blackthorn that had been seasoning up the chimney for seven years."[51] Other faction fighters identified themselves rather completely with the weapons with which they had attained a lasting fame, like Paud Brien and his two named blackthorns. Shortly before his death Brien was asked by a priest for something by which to remember him, and he replied with a touch of pride, "I've nothing, Father, but my two sticks."[52] This kind of celebrity must be accounted a significant reason for the great vogue of faction fighting in early nineteenth-century Ireland. At a time when other routes to fame for men of humble rank were few and far between, the adulation bestowed on the more distinguished faction fighters was a powerful incentive to participate and excel.

The great prevalence of faction fighting in the early nineteenth century was largely the result of inadequate machinery to control it and official ambivalence about putting the machinery into operation. By 1800, admittedly, the days were gone when Irish landed gentlemen could often be seen actively assisting factions or even heading them in their encounters. But the complacent and corrupt ways of the past had certainly not been abandoned completely. Many landed gentlemen were content to let the common people fight among themselves in the belief that these conflicts would distract the factionists' energies from such targets as the land system, the established church, or the state.[53] A host of magistrates would have heartily concurred with the view expressed by a judge presiding over the trial of some factionists involved in an affray at Killenaule during which a policeman was killed. To the jurors this judge reportedly declared, "I protest to God, gentlemen, I would never interfere with them [faction fighters] one way or the other, if I had my wish, but that would not be a prudent thing to say publicly from the bench."[54]

Prompted by a variety of motives, many magistrates pursued precisely this course of inaction. They absented themselves from those large public gatherings where faction fights were expected to occur. Or if they did attend, they declined to read the Riot Act or to take the precaution of calling out the troops or police. Other magistrates known as "trading justices" were wide open to corruption. Often each faction in a given district had a protecting magistrate for whom they performed various gratuitous services, such as reaping his crops, digging out his potatoes, or drawing home his turf. In return for these services, they could expect that the magistrate would screen them if they got into trouble, arrange for them to be bailed if they were arrested, or seek to have indictments against them quashed.[55]

But corrupt or inactive magistrates were only part of the problem. The enormous difficulties facing justices of the peace in a sizeable market town like Killarney (with two zealous resident magistrates) were spelled out by magistrate James Lawlor in late July 1814. During a three-month period, said Lawlor, he had taken over fifty informations concerning affrays and his colleague Christopher Gallwey had probably taken an equal number, for an average of more than one a day for eighty-six days. Within four years, Lawlor pointed out, he had personally committed nearly five hundred persons to the bridewell of Killarney. Magistrates, he insisted, had an impossible job on fair days, "when at least 5,000 of the peasantry crowd in, without an atom of fair business & for no other purpose than fun as it is called, but more properly speaking, to partake of any mischief or riot that may go forward." Lawlor also explained that when a magistrate met resistance in quelling a riot and a bill of indictment was lodged, the grand jury often reduced the charge to common assault, and even then the petty jury might still acquit the rioters.[56]

In contrast to Killarney with its two active magistrates, there were numerous smaller towns or villages, even entire districts, where no justice of the peace resided, or where the magistrates, even if willing to do duty, were too old or too ill to serve.[57] In such places, of course, factions could and did battle without interference. In the Kilrush district of west Clare the absence of any zealous magistrate led to faction fights at every fair in the summer of 1813 (at least when troops were not summoned) and in 1814 to three murders in fights without a single arrest.[58]

Most localities were better placed than Kilrush in this respect. In such districts the authorities often sought and obtained the assistance of the army or the police (increasingly the latter after 1814 and especially after 1822). If the troops or the police arrived in time to take command of a town's streets before a clash had begun, they stood a good chance of preventing the planned encounter. Contemporary newspapers prior to the late 1830s contain many reports of the effective frustration of faction conflicts in this manner.[59] On the other hand, if the troops or police arrived after a fight had already started in earnest, if their numbers were too small to overawe the hundreds of factionists, or if they failed to position themselves properly between the warring parties, they risked a fatal collision with the populace. It was depressingly common under these circumstances for one faction and often for both to turn their stones (sometimes guns as well) on the soldiers or police, who, thus provoked, opened fire on the factionists. At a long string of fairs, patterns, and race meetings between 1800 and 1835 (but only a few after 1835), such official intervention resulted in death and serious wounding. The number of fatalities ranged from two or three in the typical case to as many as ten or more in occasional extreme instances.[60] The serious possibility of such murderous collisions between official forces and faction fighters persuaded many of the more tolerant or humane magistrates to abandon the resort to troops or police. Relatively few magistrates actively courted the dubious distinction and unwelcome notoriety that came from giving the fatal order to fire upon a crowd of factionists, even one engaged in stone throwing.

In pursuing their feuds, the factions regularly preferred private vengeance to public justice. To some extent this ingrained preference was part of their code of honor, though it also reflected the general hostility to the official system of justice. As landowner John Vandeleur observed of the feuding parties in west Clare in July 1814, the people held the law in such contempt that they would neither prosecute nor lodge informations in faction-fight cases, choosing instead to take revenge into their own hands.[61] That the code of honor was repeatedly broken by the Shanavests and later by the Blackfeet, some of whom stooped to becoming informers, helps to explain the intense resentment of their opponents. To check departures from the code, the factions adopted a relatively simple but highly effective strategy. When one party did lodge informations with the authorities in ordinary faction-fight cases, it became standard practice for the opposite party to do likewise. This custom, commonly known as "swearing cross informations," did not mean that the law was to be allowed to run its normal course. On the contrary, the practice encouraged a mutual agreement between the factions that their adherents would not prosecute each other.[62] In effect, it restored the broken code of honor and shifted the feud back to the sphere of private vengeance. Without willing private prosecutors, the Irish legal system before the late 1830s was badly handicapped, especially in matters affecting public order, and the factions greatly helped to make it so by their habitual cross informations.

Such avoidance of the official system of justice was least likely in cases of murder. Homicides were not supposed to occur in "fair fights" between contending factions; when they did, most believed that they had happened either by accident or because unfair tactics had been employed. Since the popular code of honor assumed that murder was out of bounds, prosecution for a homicide did not necessarily violate the code. An instructive illustration is the feud between the Powers and the Mahonys, who were described as the Capulets and the Montagues of the Lismore district in County Waterford. In the last week of 1813 and the first week of 1814 these factions engaged in two hurling matches, which were each followed by fights. On the second occasion of their sporting rivalry, the fight began when Bartholemew Power spit in the face of Michael Mahony. In the general melee that promptly ensued, John

Power was killed, apparently by the blow of a hurley stick. His brother James Power, seeking public justice instead of private vengeance, prosecuted Maurice Mahony for murder and six other members of the Mahony faction for aiding and abetting in the killing. But of the seven men who stood trial, only Maurice Mahony was convicted, and even he was found guilty not of murder, but only of manslaughter. Obviously the honor of the Power faction had not been satisfied by this disappointing outcome. But the Powers were not yet finished. As soon as the trial for the death of his brother ended, James Power prosecuted three of the Mahonys for Whiteboy crimes. One of the Mahonys, it seems, was a Whiteboy captain who commanded a band of sixty men. James Power had previously taken a solemn oath not to reveal the Mahonys' Whiteboy activities, but he considered himself released from this promise when the Mahonys killed his brother. In this second case the jury found the three Mahonys guilty of felony.[63]

As the legal proceedings between the Powers and the Mahonys suggest, in practice the law did not treat homicides in faction fights as murder but as manslaughter, with drastically less severe punishments. Rarely, in fact, did convictions for faction fighting result in serious penalties. Even when a fight led to one or more deaths, and those considered responsible were made answerable to the law, the most severe penalty was transportation to Botany Bay for seven years, and even that was only in exceptional cases. The transportation of eight members of the Hogan faction after a murderous clash with the Hickeys at Kilfeacle in 1826 so impressed contemporaries precisely because of the great rarity of such a punishment.[64] Indeed, the notorious leniency of judges and jurors in these cases and the difficulty of fixing personal responsibility for homicides in faction fights sometimes made these encounters a tempting cover for acts of premeditated murder.[65]

In less serious faction-fight cases, when indictments were pressed, the results were usually disappointing on at least two counts. First, a high proportion of those indicted were acquitted altogether.[66] Second, most of those found guilty escaped with a relatively light sentence—typically a short imprisonment not exceeding three months and perhaps a whipping. Moreover, in the great majority of cases those arrested for faction fighting were never even brought to trial. In Kerry, for instance, it was a constant practice, as the Killarney magistrate James Lawlor bitterly complained in 1814, for the county grand jury to receive releases in cases of riot and then, on the pretext of such releases, to ignore the bills of indictment entirely.[67] In short, as a deterrent to faction fighting the Irish judicial system before 1835 was ridiculously ineffective.

Yet within fewer than five years the authorities had not only gained the upper hand against faction fighting but could even claim that they had essentially stamped it out. The Whig government that presided over this dramatic change was headed by Lord Mulgrave (as viceroy) and Lord Morpeth (as chief secretary). But the driving force behind the reforms was Thomas Drummond, the under-secretary. The government's comprehensive campaign against faction fighting had two basic aims: prevention and punishment. With respect to both, the police force, restructured in 1836, played a crucial role. Under a detailed plan devised by the inspector-general's department and promulgated throughout the force, all constabulary posts in a district where a faction conflict was expected were to be placed on alert and to stand ready to reinforce the local detachment at the anticipated scene of disturbance. This policy of massing police (and sometimes soldiers) at fairs, patterns, and race meetings, previously effective but only inconsistently practiced, was now systematically enforced. The police were also placed under new orders to arrest all persons who came armed to the place of public assembly, an instruction that necessitated, among other things, the unbuttoning of greatcoats. If in spite of these elaborate precautions, a riot erupted, the police were commanded to arrest as many rioters as possible on the spot and to identify others for subsequent seizure.[68] To make the difficult task of the police more manageable, an extensive number of public gatherings notorious for faction fighting were simply banned altogether.[69]

Coinciding with these new preventive arrangements were substantial reforms in the judicial system. Most important was the extended prosecutorial authority given to both crown solicitors at the assizes and sessional solicitors at quarter-sessions. Their responsibilities were broadened to include categories of crime that had formerly been prosecuted only by private persons or else ignored entirely. Those offenses characteristically associated with faction fighting—common or aggravated assault, disorderly conduct, public drunkenness—became part of the crown business of the sessional solicitors and no longer depended exclusively on privately initiated criminal suits. These reforms struck heavy blows against the factions' strategy of cross informations to block prosecutions and against their widespread preference for private vengeance over public justice.[70]

Still, witnesses were essential for convictions, and while the testimony of police constables could be of signal importance, evidence from private persons was often required as well. The extreme reluctance of intimidated witnesses to appear openly in court had for generations been the great Achilles' heel of the Irish judicial system. The increased protection that the government now offered to faint-hearted witnesses was probably of much less significance in faction-fight cases than the new heavy fine for declining to appear in court to substantiate informations lodged earlier with a magistrate. Especially in Tipperary but in other counties as well, these fines, collectable on the basis of so-called green-wax warrants issued by the court of exchequer, were vigorously enforced.[71] Of course factions could still resort to bribing witnesses when intimidation failed, but the heavy fines made even bribery more costly and hence less likely. Already by 1839 these measures, taken in conjunction, were largely responsible for "a dramatic decline in the incidence of violence and faction fights at fairs."[72] In that year Drummond told a parliamentary committee that such fights "had virtually ceased" in Ireland.[73]

What made this achievement all the more remarkable was the absence in the late 1830s of any great agrarian upheaval. In earlier decades the passing of a wave of Whiteboyism had generally been followed by revived faction fighting on a large scale. By 1835 the Whitefeet and Terry Alt movements as well as the great tithe war itself had all petered out or been extinguished, and the stage was seemingly set for the reemergence of faction feuds, but the old cycle was then decisively broken. Some historians of factions might think that I have neglected the impact of the temperance crusade and the great Repeal agitation of the early 1840s on the demise of faction fighting. No doubt temperance and Repeal absorbed the energies of many former faction fighters after 1840, but what bears repeating is that the watershed came earlier, in the late 1830s. This is not to say that factions or factionism disappeared along with faction fighting. Long-tailed families would activate their tails for decades after 1840, but they would ever more rarely wield skull-cracking sticks.

NOTES

1. George Cornewall Lewis, *Local Disturbances in Ireland* (Cork: Tower Books, 1977; orig. publ. London: B. Fellowes, 1836), 227.
2. *Tipperary Vindicator* (hereafter cited as *T.V.*), 18 January 1845. See also Lewis, *Local Disturbances,* 228, 232.
3. *Report from the Select Committee on the State of Ireland; Ordered to Be Printed 30 June 1825; with the Four Reports of Minutes of Evidence,* p. 418, H.C. 1825 (129), viii, 293. William Carleton stressed the code of honor among factionists in "The Party Fight and Funeral," in his *Traits and Stories of the Irish Peasantry.*
4. *T.V.,* 18 January 1845.
5. M. A. G. Ó Tuathaigh, *Thomas Drummond and the Government of Ireland, 1835–41* (O'Donnell Lecture, National University of Ireland, 1977).
6. Quoted in Patrick O'Donnell, *The Irish Faction Fighters of the 19th Century* (Dublin: Anvil Books, 1975), 27–28.
7. *Finn's Leinster Journal,* 22–26 April 1775. See also 13–16 January and 3–7 April 1773.
8. For the Three Year Olds and Four Year Olds, see *Kerryman,* 5 February 1910. For the Coffeys and the Reaskavallas, se W. R. LeFanu, *Seventy Years of Irish Life, Being Anecdotes and Reminiscences* (New York and London: Macmillan, 1893),

33–37. For the Cooleens and the Lawlors, see Edward J. Herbert, "The Cooleens and the Lawlors: The Story of a Faction Feud," *Irishman's Annual* (Tralee, 1955), 27–33; Thomas F. Culhane, "Traditions of Glin and Its Neighbourhood," *Journal of the Kerry Archaeological and Historical Society* 2 (1969): 74–101; Caoimhín Ó Danachair, "Faction Fighting in County Limerick," *North Munster Antiquarian Journal* 10 (1966): 47–55. O'Donnell, *Faction Fighters*, 133–74.

9. P. E. W. Roberts, "Caravats and Shanavests: Whiteboyism and Faction Fighting in East Munster, 1802–11," in *Irish Peasants: Violence and Political Unrest, 1780–1914*, ed. Samuel Clark and James S. Donnelly, Jr. (Madison: University of Wisconsin Press, 1983), 64–101.

10. *Minutes of Evidence Taken before the Select Committee Appointed to Inquire into the Disturbances in Ireland, in the Last Session of Parliament (13 May–18 June 1824)*, p. 114, H.C. 1825 (20), vii, 1 (hereafter cited as *Select Committee on Disturbances*).

11. O'Donnell, *Faction Fighters*, 17.

12. *T.V.*, 18 January 1845.

13. *Select Committee on Disturbances*, 113–14.

14. Roberts, "Caravats and Shanavests," 88.

15. Ó Danachair, "Faction Fighting," 53.

16. O'Donnell, *Faction Fighters*, 98.

17. L. M. Cullen, "The Hidden Ireland: Re-assessment of a Concept," *Studia Hibernica* 9 (1969), 33; O'Donnell, *Faction Fighters*, 11, 29–30; Henry David Inglis, *Ireland in 1834: A Journey throughout Ireland, during the Spring, Summer, and Autumn of 1834*, 3d. ed. (London: Whittaker, 1835), 2:51–52.

18. S. C. and A. M. Hall, *Ireland: . . . Its Scenery, Character, Etc.*, new ed. (New York: James Sheehy, n.d.), 1:429.

19. *Limerick Evening Post*, 10 August 1814; *T.V.*, 18 January 1845; *Irish Independent*, 27 May 1964.

20. State Paper Office, Dublin, State of the Country Papers, 1st series (hereafter cited as SPO, SOCP1), 1823/2516/4; Lewis, *Local Disturbances*, 231, 233–34, 236–37; Samuel Clark, *Social Origins of the Irish Land War* (Princeton: Princeton University Press, 1979), 76–77.

21. O'Donnell, *Faction Fighters*, 175.

22. Clark, *Social Origins*, 76.

23. Roberts, "Caravats and Shanavests," 94–98.

24. O'Donnell, *Faction Fighters*, 158.

25. An informant of the Irish Folklore Commission remarked that "very often a [Lawlor–] Black Mulvihill servant boy would be working with a Cuílín farmer." This informant did not even hint that the reverse might frequently have been true (Ó Danachair, "Faction Fighting," 50).

26. Sir Benjamin Bloomfield to William Gregory, 18 March 1823 (SPO, SOCP1, 2518/11).

27. SPO, SOCP1, 1822/2354/42; 1822/2356/82; 1823/2518/11.

28. James S. Donnelly, Jr., "Irish Agrarian Rebellion: The Whiteboys of 1769–76," *Proceedings of the Royal Irish Academy* 83C (December 1983): 310; Lewis, *Local Disturbances*, 239–40.

29. Rev. William Lee to William Gregory, 15 July 1822 (SPO, SOCP1, 2356/39). Coffey, said Rev. Lee, "has some wealthy relatives, and they have been solicitting [*sic*] me to interfere for his pardon, promising very large bail for his future good conduct."

30. For a striking example, see SPO, SOCP1, 1814/1559/60.

31. For the Whitefeet movement, see *Report from the Select Committee on the*

State of Ireland, with the Minutes of Evidence, Appendix, and Index, H.C. 1831–32 (677), xvi, 1.

32. Asked to what class the Whitefeet of the colliery district belonged, the Queen's County magistrate Hovenden Stapleton replied, "Mostly of the younger class of persons; farmers' servants and sons, and working colliers, rather of the lower orders" (ibid., 95).

33. Ibid.

34. James S. Donnelly, Jr., "The Social Composition of Agrarian Rebellions in Early Nineteenth-Century Ireland: The Case of the Carders and Caravats, 1813–16," in *Radicals, Rebels, and Establishments,* ed. Patrick J. Corish (Belfast: Appletree Press, 1985), 151–69.

35. *Select Committee on the State of Ireland* (1832), 51, 144, 348, 352.

36. Ibid., 144, 176.

37. See Paul Roberts's comments on the ignorance of upper-class contemporaries about the origins and character of the Caravat-Shanavest feud ("Caravats and Shanavests," 67). Similar ignorance prevailed about the original causes of the feud between the Cooleens and the Lawlor–Black Mulvihills. The incidents mentioned as causes are known to have occurred long after the feud started. See O'Donnell, *Faction Fighters,* 134, 158.

38. O'Donnell, *Faction Fighters,* 58.

39. LeFanu, *Seventy Years,* 34.

40. O'Donnell, *Faction Fighters,* 51.

41. Hall and Hall, *Ireland,* 1:428.

42. O'Donnell, *Faction Fighters,* 67.

43. Randall Kernan, *A Report of the Trials of the Caravats and Shanavests, at the Special Commission for the Several Counties of Tipperary, Waterford, and Kilkenny, before the Right Hon. Lord Norbury and the Right Hon. S. O'Gready, Commencing at Clonmel on Monday, February 4th, 1811* . . . (Dublin: Hibernia Press, 1811), 29–31; *Kerryman,* 5 February 1910; Roberts, "Caravats and Shanavests," 68–73.

44. *Kerryman,* 5 February 1910.

45. Kevin Danaher, *In Ireland Long Ago* (Cork: Mercier Press, 1962), 148–49.

46. James Hall, *Tour through Ireland; Particularly the Interior and Least Known Parts: Containing an Accurate View of the Parties, Politics, and Improvements in the Different Provinces* . . . (London: R. P. Moore, 1813).

47. Hall and Hall, *Ireland,* 1:427; Danaher, *In Ireland,* 151.

48. Rev. Horatio Townsend to Robert Peel, 19 December 1816, in O'Donnell, *Faction Fighters,* 83–84.

49. Culhane, "Traditions of Glin," 90–91. See also O'Donnell, *Faction Fighters,* 137.

50. O'Donnell, *Faction Fighters,* 90, 115–16.

51. Danaher, *In Ireland,* 150.

52. O'Donnell, *Faction Fighters,* 64–65.

53. Lewis, *Local Disturbances,* 234–35.

54. *T.V.,* 18 January 1845.

55. Ibid. See also *Select Committee on Disturbances,* 157, 336, 373, 383–84; *Report from the Select Committee on the State of Ireland* (1825), 397–98, 418.

56. James Lawlor to William Gregory, 26 July 1814 (SPO, SOCP1, 1553/30).

57. Galen Broeker, *Rural Disorder and Police Reform in Ireland, 1812–36* (London: Routledge and Kegan Paul, 1970), 39–44, 149–52.

58. SPO, SOCP1, 1814/1553/4.

59. See, e.g., *Dublin Evening Post,* 10 January, 18 March, 27 April, 27 July 1824.

60. O'Donnell cites more than a half-dozen examples of intervention by troops or police that led to fatalities among faction fighters (*Faction Fighters*, 53, 54–58, 58–63, 89–97, 99–107, 113–33), and such instances could easily be multiplied.

61. SPO, SOCP1, 1814/1553/6.

62. *Report from the Select Committee on the State of Ireland* (1825), 327; *Select Committee on Disturbances*, 157–59.

63. *Limerick Evening Post*, 10 August 1814.

64. O'Donnell, *Faction Fighters*, 18.

65. See, e.g., SPO, SOCP1, 1815/1721/109.

66. For example, of nine men tried for involvement in a fight between the Magher and Hickey factions at the fair of Holycross in September 1822, only three were convicted (SPO, SOCP1, 1822/2356/55, 57).

67. SPO, SOCP1, 1814/1553/30.

68. Broeker, *Rural Disorder*, 226–27; Hall and Hall, *Ireland*, 1:426.

69. O'Donnell, *Faction Fighters*, 41.

70. Ó Tuathaigh, *Drummond*, 16–17.

71. *T.V.*, 18 January 1845.

72. Ó Tuathaigh, *Drummond*, 21.

73. In Broeker, *Rural Disorder*, 227.

9

After the Revolution: The Formative Years of Cumann na nGaedheal

MARYANN GIALANELLA VALIULIS

In 1924 the government of the newly established Irish Free State faced a revolt from within its own political party, Cumann na nGaedheal. This challenge to its authority stemmed from growing dissatisfaction and disillusionment with both the policies and the attitudes of the Cosgrave government in implementing the aims of the revolution. Not unrealistically, the dissidents had expected independence to bring about significant change in Irish society. In general, they wanted Ireland to reflect the political and cultural nationalist ideals that had molded their vision of a free, Gaelic, self-sufficient state. Specifically, they wanted a share in the power and a change in the ruling elite and in the prevailing ethos. They were certainly not radicals who sought to overthrow the system. However, having successfully fought a war of independence and a civil war, the dissident wing of the Cumann na nGaedhael party expected both symbolic and substantive change. Instead a conservative government seemed determined to continue policies that had more in common with middle-class Victorian England than with any definition of Gaelic Ireland. Hence, this dissident, populist element challenged the government.* It was the culmination of a power struggle between the conservative elements in the party, led by the government, and the populist elements to capture the soul of Cumann na nGaedheal. The dissidents lost. So did the party. After its initial ten-year reign, the Cosgrave government would never again hold power. And, tarnished

---

*I am using the term populist in the nonspecialized sense to mean a member of a political group claiming to represent the common people.

with the conservative image of the Cosgrave years, the Cumann na nGaedheal party would also never again hold power on its own and would rule as part of a coalition for only six of the first fifty years of independence.

This examination of the dissidents' criticisms of the Cosgrave government attempts to explain, at least in part, the rather spectacular failure of the government and the party to capture the mind, the heart, and the vote of the Irish people after 1932. Many of the complaints and much of the dissidents' dissatisfaction and frustration seem to have reflected popular feelings throughout the country about what independence should mean. The dissidents represented an alternative vision and voice to the conservative Cosgrave line, which—as it turned out—was destined to be a voice crying in the wilderness.

The struggle between the two wings of the party emanated from the contradictions and conflicts inherent in its founding. Because it was born of a revolutionary struggle, it adopted a party platform that reflected this idealism. Because it was founded amid the tragedy of civil war, membership in the party was based simply on acceptance of the Treaty of 1921 between Great Britain and Ireland. And, because it was formed after the establishment of the provisional government, it had an uneasy and subordinate relationship to the Executive Council.[1] It was in the working out of these conflicts that the major differences within Cumann na nGaedheal would surface and the ideological divisions become apparent.

The fundamental difference that separated the dissidents and the Executive Council centered on the nature of the society to be created. The council's main emphasis was on stability—economic, social, and political stability. Having achieved a degree of political independence, it was content to allow Irish society to develop along the lines laid out by the British. Change—if it did occur—would be slow, incremental, and, most important, in keeping with the dogmas of fiscal orthodoxy. The dissidents, on the other hand, distrusted the cautious attitude of the government. In the first place, they were concerned that the Executive Council would not use the treaty as a stepping stone to complete and total independence à la Collins, but rather as an end in itself. Second, the dissidents were less concerned with achieving stability than with implementing changes that would shift the focus of society. They wanted to alter the balance of power within the state so that power would be exercised in the interests of, and by, the Irish people, without any reference to the needs or desires of England. This segment of the party wanted changes to continue beyond political sovereignty. Or, to put it another way, they wanted to use independence to redirect Irish society.

These philosophical differences obviously led to conflict over policy and to mounting tension between the Executive Council and the dissidents. Dissatisfaction with the Executive Council was such that in the fall of 1924 the government faced a major challenge from within the party organization. The "October Manifesto" of the Standing Committee (Coiste Gnotha) was a searing and direct repudiation of the Cosgrave administration's policy. The manifesto articulated the disappointments, frustrations, and festering grievances that had been building for the past two years.

The Standing Committee began by declaring its disillusionment and disappointment with the lack of substantive change since independence.

> The establishment of the Free State has not put an end to the Wars of the Gael and the Gall. After the evacuation of the British military and police, foreign executive power had ceased in the 26 counties, but the imperial hold on the economic, social and administrative life of the country remained almost as before, by reason of the dominant position in public and social affairs which the possession of political mastery had, in the course of centuries, given to an alien ascendancy.[2]

Independence, in the committee's view, had changed the country's flags and symbols, but still had not given the Irish control over their own country.

Part of the difficulty, as the authors of the document pointed out, was that the locus of power had not shifted from the Ascendancy class to nationalist Ireland. The October Manifesto blamed the government for this lack of change and criticized the Executive Council for its overly solicitous attitude toward people who had been traditionally antinationalist. The dissident party members were not objecting to the official position that all who accepted the treaty and the party's program were welcome within Cumann na nGaedheal, nor to the ideal goal of the new state to synthesize divergent traditions into a common Irish identity.[3] Rather they were rebelling against the fact that former unionists seemed to be receiving preferential treatment from the government at the expense of its nationalist supporters. The Standing Committee clearly deemed this to be misguided government policy.

> If . . . there is a clash of interests between those who created the present regime and those who resisted it as long as they could, our interest as well as our raison d'etre compels us to side with the popular claims. The brief of Cumann na nGaedheal is for the common people of Ireland, and what the common people want under the Free State is to abolish ascendancy, to undo the Conquest and resume the course of their national life as masters in their own land.[4]

It was not an unreasonable demand. Nor did it represent an exclusivist, narrow, nationalist strain of thought. Party dissidents were, in fact, arguing against exclusivity and for a more equitable, open, democratic society. They were not criticizing the inclusion of unionists in the political life of the country, but rather the council's apparent attempt to ingratiate itself with this group at the expense of its followers. This pro-Ascendancy attitude seemed to weaken the party's nationalist commitment and reject its revolutionary origins.

Moreover, the alleged pro-Ascendancy bias of the council fueled the perception that the government refused to reward or even properly look after its supporters. The Standing Committee believed that the party was popularly perceived as "not giving reasonable satisfaction to the needs and hopes of its supporters."[5] Indeed, the committee itself felt that the party was basically powerless in dealing with the government. They argued that

the Organisation's influence on Government policy and its power to affect patronage has been negligible, if not nil. In parts of the country it is openly recognized that to be connected with Cumann na nGaedheal is in most cases a handicap and in many cases a complete bar to appointments, preferments or even a fair deal in Land or Compensation.[6]

Clearly, this state of affairs weakened the party's ability to attract members. Thus, the October Manifesto blamed the government for the fact that Cumann na nGaedheal was not numerically stronger or more popular throughout the country.

The Standing Committee singled out three specific areas to illustrate the Executive Council's failure to meet the needs and expectations of the people: economic policy, land reform, and civil service appointments. These were issues on which nationalists had traditionally criticized British administration, and hopes had run high that independence would bring significant change and improvement in those areas. The conservative policy of the Cosgrave government dashed those great expectations. For example, the Standing Committee accused the government of lacking an economic policy and blamed the council for not doing more to relieve widespread poverty and unemployment. Moreover, it charged that the resolve of the people to solve these problems was being undermined by the government's pessimistic pronouncements.[7] The Standing Committee rejected the gloomy estimates of Cosgrave and his ministers, arguing that the financial position of the country was sound and that the government could do more to alleviate distress.

The second item specifically mentioned by the October Manifesto was the land question, a subject that was charged with emotion and expectation. The hope had been that independence would quickly make more land available to the various classes of farmers. While there would obviously be conflicts, the point was that rural Ireland expected land, expected change. And, according to the Standing Committee, government policy had once again disappointed and dismayed its followers:

> The hopes raised by the Land Act of 1923 are not sustained by any evidence of early realisation. . . . The only tangible result of the Land Act in most places was that the legal, military and police organisation of the new regime was employed, in the collection of arrears of rents and rates, in a manner more abrupt and vigourous fashion than before experienced. The manner in which this was done was calculated to produce a lot of bad feelings because the stage of issuing processes was reached without delay.[8]

In addition, once again the Executive Council was perceived to be condoning discrimination against its own supporters. According to the October Manifesto, there was a "widespread lack of confidence in the Land Commission which a western member of ours described . . . as 'The Chamber of Horrors.' "[9]

Part of the problem, the Standing Committee believed, was that in the Land Commission as well as in other areas of administration, it seemed as if the same "old gang" were still running the country. The October Manifesto declared:

> In general, it is complained that those who won the fight have not done well out of the victory, whereas, the pro-British ascendancy who lost the fight have done disproportionately well and got a new lease on life from the Free State.[10]

In particular, the document criticized the civil servants as a class for thwarting change:

> *The civil servants* are the Government and there is a distinct uneasiness throughout the whole country because of the fear that vital Irish interests are in the hands of men whose allegiance does not lie in Ireland. This fear is increased by the belief that there is constant reference to London officials for decisions of all sorts of concrete administrative issues, particularly in the Revenue and Finance departments.[11]

In some ways, it seemed to the committee that the British had never left.

As they surveyed the political landscape of 1924, party members must have wondered about the fine sentiments and aspirations that had motivated their struggle for independence. Two years after the signing of the treaty, they believed they still had not realized the fruits of independence. Indeed, the Standing Committee believed that the great discrepancy between what its followers wanted and expected and the policy pursued by the government posed a threat to the national interest. The October Manifesto was a direct and forthright statement calculated to stir the Cosgrave government to action and to end "the insulation of the Executive Council from the currents of thought of its supporters."[12]

The government, however, responded to these criticisms by either denying their validity or claiming, for various reasons, that it could take no action nor offer any hope of redress. For example, on the question of civil servants, Kevin O'Higgins explained that, while "it would be pleasing to turn to unpopular officials and dismiss them because they had not an Irish outlook," they could not do this. Article 10 of the treaty obliged the Free State government to pension any dismissed civil servant.[13] This, he argued, the state simply could not afford. Neither O'Higgins nor the other ministers replied to the argument that the complaint concerned only those in a few key positions and not the entire civil service. The minister for finance, Ernest Blythe, whose civil servants in particular had come under attack,[14] dismissed the charges against the civil servants as arising from "disappointed job-hunters, or those who failed to get promotion."[15] Blythe believed that "the whole thing was only bunkum and the product of interested motives."[16] Other ministers complained that their achievements were being overlooked or were unknown to their supporters. But it was President Cosgrave's reply that more than any other revealed the wide gap between the Executive Council and its more populist nationalist supporters. Cosgrave claimed:

> The heads of department who were appointed as having an Irish outlook were in the majority. Those who denounced the policy of balancing the Budget did not know the first thing of what they were talking about. Income and Expenditure must balance and projects of works must be examined before being entered on. Praise, not criticism, was deserved by the Executive Council. . . . Merit, efficiency and suitability were the ideas that moved the Minister for Finance in appointments. We must have value for money. . . . This country was poor, and hard work, not the words of a written policy, was the only solution.[17]

It was hardly a reply calculated either to ease the fears or to stir the imagination of the dissidents. Victorian virtues, not the ideals of the Irish-Ireland movement, seemed to motivate the government.

The October Manifesto had identified those whom it held to be responsible for preventing the emergence of an Irish-Ireland—the civil servants, especially in the Department of Finance. At a meeting later that month between members of the policy committee of Cumann na nGaedheal and the ministers for finance, industry and commerce, and land and agriculture (Blythe, Patrice McGilligan, and P. J. Hogan, respectively), the committee recommended sweeping and revolutionary changes in the Finance Department. In effect, it recommended stripping this ministry of much of its power because it had interfered in the works of other departments. The committee suggested that each department of state take direct control of its own expenditure; that a new commission, independent of the Finance Department, be created to take charge of the civil service; and that the fiscal officer be "a responsible permanent Secretary . . . who will not be bound by British traditions, but an Irishman of loyal associations, in whom the country can have confidence."[18] Not surprisingly, Blythe strongly resisted the suggested changes for his department. According to the minutes of the meeting:

Mr. Blythe refused to discuss the personnel of the Finance Department. The memo was not correct as to the Organisation of the Department. The officials were Irishmen of loyal associations. As to the suggestion that officials controlled policy, Mr. Blythe's comment was: "The ministers are not bloody fools." No understanding was arrived at.[19]

Manifestos and meetings did not heal the rift between the dissidents and the Executive Council. Perhaps because of the growing divergence of views and the pointed criticisms, the government announced within the next month its intention to form its own committee to fight the nine upcoming by-elections. The new organizing committee was to be headed by J. J. Walsh, minister for posts and telegraphs, and included ministers, Dail deputies, senators, and representatives from the party. According to a council member (Finian Lynch), one reason for forming this new committee was to broaden the electoral appeal of the government. It seemed that the Executive Council wanted to send the message that "the general rank and file of the country (including old Parliamentary supporters, such as had come in in Mayo) that had been cold shouldered by the Cumann na nGaedheal organisation" would now be welcomed as supporters.[20] This news could only deepen the anxiety of dissidents who were already concerned about the commitment of the government to nationalist ideals. To consciously attempt to appeal to former supporters of the old Parliamentary party could be construed as simply further diluting the revolutionary aims and principles upon which the state had been founded.

Moreover, the council's decision to form its own electoral committee seemed to some party members suspiciously like an attempt to supplant the regular organization. It appeared to be a bid to exert direct control over the party throughout the country and thus weaken the power and authority of the upper eschelons of the party organization—for example, the Standing Committee and the Executive Committee. This would, of course, undermine the strongholds of dissent and sap the dissidents' influence. If this were the government's intention, it was successful.

In addition to being a power play within the party, the government's decision to set up a new organizing committee was a vote of no confidence in Cumann na nGaedheal's organization, structure, and personnel. This was indeed ironic because party members had complained that Cabinet members had conspicuously failed to provide the leadership necessary for building the party's organization. Instead the government seemed to disdain the ordinary workings of political organization and the need to build solid support among the people through a strong grass roots organization.[21] For example, at a party meeting discussing a planned appeal for funds, Richard Mulcahy, former minister for defense, suggested that President Cosgrave's name would be a more effective fundraiser than that of Eoin MacNeill, president of the party. With an indignant reply that testified to the disdain that a number of ministers in the government felt, O'Higgins rejected Mulcahy's suggestion and rather contemptuously added that he hoped that they had not yet reached the point where it was necessary for the president to appeal for funds.[22] Obviously, this attitude would not gain support for either the government or the party, nor would it help build local organizations so vital for electoral success.

The dilemma, therefore, that faced Cumann na nGaedheal was that in the popular mind it was the government's party, but it exercised little if any influence over that government. In addition, the government, which could have provided effective leadership in the party, chose instead to treat its members and their concerns with an attitude that bordered on arrogance. Thus, Cumann na nGaedheal floundered.

The unsettled state of the party created a climate in which rumors flourished. There was, for example, talk of Cosgrave's resigning.[23] In addition, there was speculation of a proposed "almagamation [of Cumann na nGaedheal] with the Unionist element."[24] The suggestion for such a union seems to have come from an editorial in the *Irish Times* that urged the government to seek a rapprochement with what they described as "the most prosperous, the most responsible, the most experienced, the most highly educated and the most constitutionally-minded citizens of Free State . . . the mass of the old 'Southern Unionists' and a high percentage of the 'old Nationalists' who supported Mr. Redmond."[25] To accomplish this, the *Irish Times* suggested that the government plant itself "definitely, frankly and whole-heartedly" in the British Commonwealth.

> If they take this course now, they will not send any considerable number of their present followers into the Republican ranks, and all the stable elements in the country will rally to their support whether that support be demanded on the Stock Exchange or at the polls.[26]

Such rumors spurred talk among party supporters that an almost inevitable delineation had to take place within Cumann na nGaedheal.[27] There seemed to be too many diverse elements within the party hindering its effectiveness. Sean O'Murthuile, former quartermaster-general and a leading figure in Cumann na nGaedheal, expressed this frustration:

> . . . no party who puts the Treaty first in its programme can become a really National Organisation. There will be too many conservative elements clinging to it—or rather, this, that if too many people who put the National Point of view first in their minds cling to an Organisation that puts the Treaty first on its mind, it will prevent the rise of a proper and politic National Movement in the country.[28]

O'Murthuile's position was typical in many respects of the dissident wing of the party. He wanted to move beyond the treaty to a postindependent national movement that would steer the country in the direction envisioned by the revolutionary leaders. Yet he realized that, at this point, splitting the party would have dire consequences. While O'Murthuile believed that "bolstering up the Cumann na nGaedheal party is simply bolstering up in power people who ought not to be kept in power," he also knew that the fall of the government would mean the fall of the treaty.[29] That he could not countenance. While O'Murthuile believed that the framework of the treaty provided the best opportunity for national development, he felt that the present government was using the treaty not to create an Irish-Ireland but rather to foster an Irish imitation of Britain.

Interestingly enough, Mulcahy and O'Murthuile, two of the generals most responsible for prosecuting and winning the civil war, looked to a future reconciliation with some segment of the republicans, albeit based on their acceptance of the constitution, as a way of correcting the drift away from the nationalist point of view. O'Murthuile felt that "some question must arise that will bring the whole Nationally minded people of the country together," but did not see this happening in the immediate future.[30] This rather forlorn hope for reestablishing unity among former comrades testified to the increasing isolation and powerlessness of the traditional nationalists within Cumann na nGaedheal. From their point of view, the gains of the revolution and the potential that the treaty had offered were being squandered by the government and its supporters. Yet, outside of day-dreaming about a reunited nationalist movement, they had very few options. To try to openly split the party would bring down the government, which would jeopardize the treaty. They could simply walk away from the party, as some did, but that would mean accepting defeat, discarding their dreams, and repudiating their sacrifices. De Valera, the man they held responsible for the civil war, remained an anathema to them. Their only alternative, therefore, seemed to be to remain within Cumann na nGaedheal and try to change its direction. It was a task worthy of Sisyphus.

The activities of the Boundary Commission further disheartened and disillusioned the dissidents. The failure of the commission to award the South predominantly nationalist areas of Northern Ireland, the rumor that the South itself would lose territory, and Eoin MacNeill's resignation from the commission led to a heated discussion at the December 1925 meeting. Three resolutions were discussed: 1) that the government not consent to "alienation of any scrap" of the Six Counties; 2) that under no circumstances could the Free State consent to the alienation of any part of the twenty-six counties; and 3) that all further negotiations about the Boundary question should be conducted directly with the British cabinet only.[31]

A passionate debate ensued. Members were outraged over the reports of the committee's findings and there was talk of military resistance.[32] Blythe spoke for the government. He vehemently rejected any talk of renewing the armed struggle with England. According to the minutes of the meeting, Blythe informed party members:

> That it is codology and codology and codology to think that we can fight the British Empire. Our Savings Certificates would fall. We would get foot and mouth disease and we would be on our knees in six months ('we did and we weren't'). That the Executive Council have nothing to accuse themselves of in connection with the Boundary— the only point is that MacNeill might have resigned earlier.[33]

Whatever its arguments to the British government, the Irish government was forced to make the best of the situation at home. Clearly, it was defensive about the commission and concerned with the repercussions of its findings. It was disturbed that the loose talk of resuming hostilities with the British or attacking Northern Ireland would undermine the financial stability of the state—one of its prime concerns. Government leaders were also worried that if the idea that the British had violated the treaty gained common acceptance, it would weaken their political position and strengthen the position of their republican opponents. This fact was not lost on some members of the party who viewed British actions as a transgression of the treaty that relieved the Irish of any further obligation to honor the document. To those who wished to see a reconciliation among former comrades of the revolutionary period, it seemed a perfect opportunity. As one party member noted:

> Many who accepted the Treaty, and with it partition, in every family, would have been on the other side if they had foreseen that Feetham [Chairman of the Boundary Commission] would be allowed to ignore the wishes of the inhabitants. As the Treaty was now violated, we should let it be known that if the abstaining T.D.'s entered the Dail the oath would not be tendered to them, and so we might end the more important partition in the South, and let England do her worst.[34]

While not everyone was prepared to view the situation in this way, even those party members who supported the Executive Council felt compelled to make some protest, "to make it clearly known to the British Empire that they have been false to us."[35]

Moreover, members of the party, ever sensitive to local opinion, predicted dire consequences would flow from the activities of the commission. Allegedly all of Cork was very indignant with the entire Executive Council.[36] And, from County Leitrim came the ominous warning that the Executive Council was "living in a fool's paradise. Forces [were] gathering that [would] completely wipe out the Party as well as the Executive Council."[37] Despite these warnings of doom, from the government's point of view, the meeting ended on a satisfactory note. Talk of rebellion or repudiation of the treaty was stifled as government supporters convinced those at the meeting "that any declaration from the meeting showing lack of faith in the Government would be disastrous."[38] The final settlement, however—status quo ante commission in return for a favorable financial agreement—left the government and the party open to the charges, in the words of one analyst, that they "betrayed their country, their cause and their companions-in-arms, for thirty pieces of silver and the tinsel of social prestige."[39]

After 1925 open dissension within the party seems to have abated. While issues such as land redistribution and tariffs remained areas of contention, the heart seems to have gone out of the dissident movement. Perhaps the Boundary settlement convinced them of the futility of opposition. Certainly the events of the next few years—the assassination of Kevin O'Higgins and the entry of de Valera and Fianna Fail into the Dail—had a chilling effect on dissent. Some left the party; others concentrated on institutional reforms in hopes of bringing the party back to its traditional nationalist roots. What seems clear, however, was that the Executive Council had managed to isolate and render ineffective those who disagreed with its policies.

It was a Pyrrhic victory. Having won the power struggle with the dissident wing, the Cosgrave government, in particular the Executive Council that was formed after March 1924, molded the party in its own image. Henceforth, Cumann na nGaedheal would enjoy the same reputation as the government and would, therefore, be castigated as the antinationalist, elitist, conservative faction in Irish politics. This reputation would help lead the party to defeat in 1932 and keep it in the political wilderness of opposition until 1944. Had it listened to its dissident wing, the party's electoral history might have been different. The traditional nationalist section of the party, schooled in the writing of Arthur Griffith and the ideas of Irish-Ireland and weaned on the lofty aspirations that the revolutionary struggle engendered, understood more clearly than the government the people's hopes for the first indigenous Irish government. The promise of independence was a concept that the Cosgrave government never seemed to understand.

In fact, more than simply not understanding, Cosgrave and his ministers seemed to forget that they came to power through a popular, nationalist revolution sustained by the support of the people. Now they seemed unwilling or unable to trust the people. They chastised them; they lectured to them; they did not, however, listen to them. While clearly the members of the Executive Council were dedicated democrats, determined to ensure that the foundation of the state was laid firmly and securely, their insensitivity to the concerns of the majority of the people, their arrogance toward both members of the Dail and their own political party, and their obsession with the treaty blinded them to political reality. Their failure to appreciate the strong emotional pull of the nationalist spirit, moreover, left them bereft of widespread and sustained popular support and unable to motivate or inspire the people. Perhaps their failure, their distance from their supporters is best typified by Cosgrave's statement in 1923: "If I have learned one lesson from the British, it is that they honour their bond. . . ."[40] Like John Redmond in 1916, Cosgrave seemed to have lost touch with the source of his power. It was no wonder then that he and his party would be easy prey for de Valera and Fianna Fail.

NOTES

1. On the party's relationship to the government, Ronan Fanning writes: "Cumann na nGaedheal were also disadvantaged electorally because its leaders were in government before they founded the party; *having* power they did not,

unlike de Valera, conceive of their party as an instrument for *winning* power."
Ronan Fanning, *Independent Ireland* (Dublin: Helicon Ltd., 1983), 101.

2. Statement of Views of Coiste Gnotha Relative to the Political Aspect of the
Present Situation, Richard Mulcahy Papers, P7/C/99, University College Dublin
Archives, hereafter UCDA.

3. See Cumann na nGaedheal Party Platform, Cumann na nGaedheal Papers, P/39, UCDA.

4. Statement of Views of Coiste Gnotha, Mulcahy Papers.

5. Ibid.

6. Ibid.

7. Ibid.

8. Ibid.

9. Ibid.

10. Ibid.

11. Ibid.

12. Ibid.

13. Minutes of meeting of Coiste Gnotha, 10 October 1924, Cumann na
nGaedheal Papers, P/39.

14. For a discussion of this point, see Leon O'Broin, *No Man's Man* (Dublin:
Gill and Macmillan, 1983).

15. Minutes of meeting of Coiste Gnotha, 10 October 1924.

16. Ibid.

17. Ibid.

18. Proposals on Policy for Organisation, Mulcahy Papers, P7/C/99.

19. Minutes of joint meeting of Policy Committee and Ministers, 20 October
1924, Mulcahy Papers, P7/C/99.

20. Mulcahy diary, 25 November 1924, Mulcahy Papers, P7/C/99.

21. This point was reaffirmed by Chief Justice Tom O'Higgins, who was one of
the leaders of the party in the post–World War II period. Interview with Chief
Justice Tom O'Higgins, Dublin, Spring 1985.

22. Mulcahy diary, 26 November 1924.

23. Mulcahy diary, 30 November 1924.

24. Mulcahy diary, 9 December 1924.

25. *Irish Times*, 29 November 1924.

26. Ibid.

27. Mulcahy diary, 30 November 1924.

28. Ibid.

29. Ibid.

30. Ibid.

31. Meeting of the Ard Chomhairle, 1 December 1925, Cumann na nGaedheal
Party Minute Books, P/39, UCDA; Mulcahy Papers, P7/C/99.

32. Ibid.

33. Mulcahy diary, 1 December 1925.

34. Meeting of the Ard Chomhairle, 1 December 1925.

35. Ibid.

36. Ibid.

37. Ibid.

38. Ibid.

39. Warner Moss, *Political Parties in the Irish Free State* (New York: Columbia
University Press, 1933), 131.

40. Unidentified newspaper clippings, 31 May 1925, McGilligan Papers,
P35c/162, UCDA.

10

Uneasy Alliance: The Gaelic League Looks at the "Irish" Renaissance

PHILIP O'LEARY

In May 1899 a rather self-righteous nineteen-year-old named Patrick Pearse declared war on the Irish Literary Theatre and its attempt to create a new national literature for Ireland in the English language. In a letter published in *An Claidheamh Soluis,* Pearse stated: "If we once admit the Irish literature in English idea, then the language movement is a mistake. Mr. Yeats's precious 'Irish' Literary Theatre may, if it develops, give the Gaelic League more trouble than the Atkinson-Mahaffy combination. Let us strangle it at its birth".[1] While Pearse here expressed himself in a particularly extreme fashion, his major premise was by no means an idiosyncratic one in Gaelic circles. Indeed the same idea had already been expressed by writers more influential than the then relatively unknown Pearse in forums that carried more weight than the correspondence columns. Thus in an editorial in the 22 January 1898 *Fáinne an Lae* one finds an attack on "sluagh mór daoine i nÉirinn, le céad bliadhan nó mar sin, dhá cheapadh gur féidir litridheacht náisiúnta do chruthughadh do'n tír seo as teangaidh Ghallda." (The great host of people in Ireland for the past hundred years or so who believe it is possible to create a national literature for this country in a foreign language.)[2] Again on 23 April 1898 *Fáinne an Lae* referred to "that strange sect who maintain that Irish may be written in English, and who, while ignorant of any 'Celtic' language, write and talk much of a 'Celtic' movement."[3] And a month before Pearse's letter was published, *An Claidheamh Soluis* editorialized with mock incredulity: "But there are to be found people who try to persuade themselves that Irish literature may mean literature in the English language. This heresy has done more to provincialise Ireland than has the Act of Union."[4] On 6 May 1899 Pearse's direct attack on Yeats and his colleagues was anticipated on the editorial page of *An Claidheamh Soluis*: "Such 'Irish' dramatists are far more the servants of English Imperialism than is their counterpart of the Munster Fusiliers, the Connacht Rangers, or the Enniskillings."[5]

This idea took form early in the history of the language revival and its press and persisted throughout the first decade of this century as both the Gaelic and Anglo-Irish movements gained strength and influence. A few quotations from *An Claidheamh Soluis* illustrate its tenacity. In a January 1903 editorial response to Séamas Mac Manus's contention that Anglo-Irish could contribute to Irish national literature, *An Claidheamh Soluis* categorically rejected the very term "Anglo-Irish": "It has really been invented as a sort of half-way-house, in which certain English writers may rest, flattering themselves with the thought that what they write is not English literature, and yet not Irish literature, to be sure; but something with the virtues of both—'Anglo-Irish' literature. 'Irish or Anglo-Irish?' Neither:—'English.' "[6] In April 1907, with the row over J. M. Synge's *Playboy of the Western World* still fresh in mind, Pearse, now editor of *An Claidheamh Soluis*, defended himself against Éamonn Ceannt's charge that he was tolerant of the Anglo-Irish movement with a ringing restatement of accepted League policy: "Literature which is in Irish is Irish literature; literature which is not in Irish is not Irish literature."[7]

Similarly, Eoin Mac Neill made clear in statements in both *An Claidheamh Soluis* and *Fáinne an Lae* under his editorship that, despite his cordial relations with the leading Anglo-Irish writers, he denied them a role in the building of a distinctively Irish cultural identity. He was utterly uncompromising on this point in a 1909 pamphlet: "In Ireland there is no possible foundation for a national culture except the national language. It can easily be shown that an attempt to base Irish culture on the English language can only result in provincialising Irish life."[8] While Gaelic aggressiveness abated as relations between the language and Anglo-Irish movements warmed somewhat after the death of Synge, *An Claidheamh Soluis* nonetheless felt obliged to affirm periodically its adamant position on this central question. In a September 1912 editorial on "Irish Literature," one reads: "To sustain our own claim to it we have of set purpose chosen the title adopted for this article. Though the term is still applied to Irishmen's efforts in the English language such an employment thereof remains just as false as when it first obtained currency. In other words, there can be no Irish literature except the Irish language be used as its medium."[9]

The melodramatic threats of Pearse's letter and the somewhat more considered judgments of other Gaels made clear that some in the language movement saw Anglo-Irish literature not as merely irrelevant to the creation of a distinct Irish culture, but as absolutely hostile to it. To these writers Anglo-Irish literature was, in the words of D. P. Moran,

"One of the most glaring frauds that the credulous Irish people ever swallowed."[10] Indeed Ernest Blythe remembered this as a fairly widespread view among Gaels in the early years of this century. In *Slán le hUltaibh* (Farewell to Ulster), he wrote of this period: "Cheapas, mar a cheap a lán Conrathóirí óga an t-am úd, nach bhféadfadh scríbhneoir Béarla gan a bheith ina namhaid d'Éirinn. . . ." (I thought, as did many young Leaguers at that time, that an English language writer couldn't help but be an enemy of Ireland. . . .)" Naturally this attitude was expressed in the Gaelic press. In June 1899 *An Claidheamh Soluis* stated flatly: "The so-called Irish Literary movement is a hindrance and not a help to a genuine revival."[12] A fortnight later another editorial expanded on this idea:

> Any movement whose end is the creation of works in English is in its essence English. With such a movement we have no quarrel till it calls itself Irish and national, thereby setting up a wrong ideal, and confusing and obscuring the minds of the people with regard to what constitutes nationality and a national literature. The leaders in such a movement, whether they be New Irelanders or Irish Literary Movement men, are some of the most seductive, and therefore most dangerous, emissaries of Anglicisation.[13]

Most interesting here is the hint that Anglo-Irish literature was most dangerous in its seductiveness, in its artistic success and beauty. This idea is found as early as 1897 in a favorable review of Sigerson's *Bards of the Gael and the Gall in Irisleabhar na Gaedhilge:* "Indeed to those ignorant of Irish literature I should hesitate to recommend the reading of Doctor Sigerson's translations, lest they should say, 'This is good enough for us. It cannot have been better in the Irish.' "[14] The Gaels' fear of their rivals' seductive powers was explicit in an *An Claidheamh Soluis* editorial on "The Irish (?) Literary Movement" in September 1899:

> Its effect upon the great mass of the people, however, will be to make them forget that it is only the second-best thing; the more excellent it is the more will they be inclined to give it an exaggerated value and to rest content with a maimed and defective product to the great detriment of the fairer, perfect and ideal embodiment of the national spirit—that in the national tongue.[15]

Eoin Mac Neill, who believed that creating true Irish literature in English was impossible, made the same point in his congratulatory letter to Lady Gregory on publication of her *Cuchulainn of Muirthemne.* His tone, while jocular, could not totally mask a legitimate and widely shared concern: "A few more books like it, and the Gaelic League will want to suppress you on a double indictment, to wit, depriving the Irish language of her sole right to express the innermost Irish mind, and secondly, investing the Anglo-Irish language with a literary dignity it has never hitherto possessed."[16] Again, this theme persisted. In a 1913 review of the work of the Gaelic theatre company Na hAisteoirí, one E. O'N. writes:

> We all may enjoy the Abbey Theatre and admire it, but unknown to us Gaelic Leaguers it is tyrannising over us, and silently trampling on our hopes of an Irish dramatic movement. Everything is so perfect in the Abbey that the Gaelic League feels ashamed of its occasional little dramatic attempts. Beautifully staged and splendidly performed plays in English are a danger to our hopes for self-expression in Irish—our language.[17]

This was a long way from bogtrotting philistinism. If anything, many Gaels had a peculiarly keen sense of the beauty of Anglo-Irish literature and were more often dazzled by the achievements of their contemporaries than blind to their artistic triumphs. In 1908 Pearse could go so far as to say

> Is leasg linn é rádh, acht 'sí an fhírinne lom í agus ní cabhair an fhírinne a cheilt, gurab i mBéarla nochtuightear bunáite dá bhfuil dá nochtughadh de smaointibh áilne doimhne i measg Gaedheal indiu. (We are loathe to say it, but it is the plain truth and it is no help to hide the truth. Most of the beautiful, profound thoughts being expressed among Gaels are being expressed in English.)[18]

In fact, Yeats and the other Anglo-Irish writers—with the glaring exception of Synge—usually received fair play or better from the Gaels as artists. The Gaels rejected not that the Anglo-Irish writers produced literature, but that they produced Irish literature.[19] One of the more plaintive notes in the pages of the Gaelic press is sounded repeatedly in the many favorable reviews of Anglo-Irish writers and their works. As the brief notice of William Boyle's *The Mineral Workers* lamented: "Truagh gan cluithchíbh mar so againn i nGaedhilg." (It's a pity we don't have plays like this in Irish.)[20]

Such appreciation of the artistic qualities of Anglo-Irish writing often led to a willingness to see its creators as allies rather than as foes in the struggle to forge a new national literature. In 1905 an older and wiser Pearse, then editor of *An Claidheamh Soluis*, most clearly expressed this more open attitude in a letter to Lady Gregory: "I have been trying in *An Claidheamh* to promote a closer comradeship between the Gaelic League and the Irish National Theatre and Anglo-Irish writers generally. After all we are all allies."[21] Again, this theme was not new. In July 1899 the future playwright T. C. Murray wrote to *An Claidheamh Soluis:* "To my mind, at least, the literary renaissance is a tributary, not a negative current, to the broad stream of the Gaelic revival. . . . The fact is, there is a great dividing gulf between Anglicisation pure and simple and the propaganda of the Gaelic League. The natural bridge between them is the literary movement."[22] The redoubtable An tAthair Peadar Ua Laoghaire employed the same image when he wrote of the work of Thomas Davis: "Thuig sé gur bh'fhearr usáid do dhéanamh de'n Bhéarla go dtí go bhféadfaí an Ghaeluinn do shaothrú; sórd drochaid a dhéanamh de'n Bhéarla i dtreó go bhféadfaí dul anonn mar a raibh an Ghaeluinn." (He understood that it was better to make use of English until Irish could be employed, to make a sort of bridge out of English so that one could go over to Irish.)[23]

Ua Laoghaire was not, however, impressed with the use Anglo-Irish poets after Davis had made of this bridge: "D'fhanadar 'n-a seasamh ar an ndrochad. Ní rabhadar thall ná abhus. Dheineadar abhráin. Níorbh' abhráin Bhéarla iad agus níorbh abhráin Ghaedheaacha iad. Ní raibh aon mhaith thall ná abhus ionta." (They stayed standing on the bridge. They were neither here nor there. They made songs. They weren't English songs and they weren't Irish songs. They were no use at all.)[24] The London correspondent to *An Claidheamh Soluis* was not pessimistic, writing of Anglo-Irish literature with a shift of metaphor in February 1903: "Some Gaelic Leaguers hurry a little haughtily past half-way houses, and shake their heads over those who bide therein. We, on the other hand, believe that Gaelic Leaguers ought to concern themselves in one way or another with nearly everything that happens in all the Irelands or the half-Irelands."[25]

While more Gaelic Leaguers seem to have viewed Anglo-Irish writers as allies than as enemies, none considered the alliance one of equals. In December 1899 *Fáinne an Lae* clearly defined the rather inglorious place of Anglo-Irish writers in the battle line: "We must regard our Anglo-Irish writers as skirmishers, as foreign agents, as sappers and miners, but not as our main force."[26] Six months later *Fáinne an Lae* reiterated this idea in a comment on the work of Fiona Macleod: "The English writings of three or four Neo-Celts do not make up a Celtic movement such as is stirring the Celtic nations to their very depths. They may be forerunners, scouts, or what you like. In future ages they may be looked upon as the apostles of the Transition. . . ."[27] In fact a *Fáinne an Lae* correspondent suggested the sort of practical work these Anglo-Irish scouts could do. After reporting on a speech by Yeats in Gort in which the poet had apologized for his inability to use Irish in his own work, the correspondent outlined how Yeats and his fellows could serve the cause:

Ca chuige ná déanfadh sé ádhbhar aistí i gcomhair a n-aistrighthe go Gaedhilg d'ullamhughadh. . .? Ní'l rud ar domhan is mó the-astuigheas ó'n nGaedhilg ná ádhbhar maith chum aistrighthe. . . . Dá gcuirfeadh ár mBéarlóirí Éireannacha agus ár nGaedhilgeoirí le céile, is breágh an litridheacht do chuirfidís ar bun. (Why wouldn't he prepare material for translation into Irish. . .? There's nothing in the world that Irish needs more than good material for translation. . . . If our English speakers in Ireland and our Irish speakers co-operated, we could establish a fine literature. . . .)[28]

The project never materialized.

Not only was Anglo-Irish to be the subordinate partner in this literary alliance, but it was also often seen as "a movement of defeat,"[29] doomed to irrelevance if not extinction by the coming victory over Anglicization. In June 1900 *Fáinne an Lae* prophesied confidently: "Anglo-Irish literature must and will suffer in this time of transition. Our poets and prose writers feel that they are something which is only half the real thing. They stand aside and await the coming of the Gaelic school." Once again, however, *Fáinne an Lae* suggested a way to employ future Anglo-Irish writers:

When our Gaelic literature has reached maturity . . . the question of a new Anglo-Irish school of writers may well come up for discussion. But its task will not be then to create an "Irish" literature in English, with a "Gaelic flavour", but to interpret the new thoughts and conceptions evolved from the heart of the Gaelic race to an outside world through the medium of a *lingua franca* inferior in power and subtlety, but more widely disseminated.[30]

Yeats and his contemporaries, however, asserted—through the creation of the Irish Literary Theatre and later the Abbey—that that *lingua franca* could create a self-consciously Irish literature. Although galvanized by that assertion, the Gaelic reaction to the theatrical movement and to individual Anglo-Irish figures, was by no means monochromatic. While some Gaels shared the young Pearse's vehement opposition to the Irish Literary Theatre, others were more open-minded and even warmly favorable. In January 1900 *Fáinne an Lae* editorialized: "Already the Irish National Theatre seems to be making the attempt to enter into Ireland— that unknown, mysterious country into which so many have in vain tried to penetrate. We heartily wish success to the Society, not so much for what they have done, or even for what they are doing, but for the manifest intention they have to struggle against being foreigners in their own country."[31] Two months later *Fáinne an Lae* pronounced the dramatic movement "bláth de'n chrann Náisiúnta" (a flower from the national branch.)[32] In 1901 *An Claidheamh Soluis* guardedly congratulated the Irish Literary Theatre on its production of Hyde's *Casadh an tSúgáin*: "We hope the Irish Literary Theatre is satisfied with the success of its experiment. Hitherto it was only a Literary Theatre, but only this year, for the first time, had the word 'Irish any right to be included in the title." But the editor was not fully satisfied by the production of a single Gaelic play, complaining that "the progress Irish-wards is, to our taste, oppressively slow."[33]

This ambivalance marked the Gaels' response to the Abbey as well. Among the more lucid attacks on the theatre following Synge's *Playboy* was Pearse's February 1907 *An Claidheamh Soluis* editorial "The Passing of Anglo-Irish Drama."[34] Indeed, some Gaels saw the Abbey as a traitorous foe to true Irish culture, as did the playwright Pádraig Mac Cárthaigh, who wrote in 1912:

> Bhí ionntaoibh againn as an ndream so an uair chuireadar chum na hoibre 'san chéad eascadh. Níorbh' fhada gur fhealladar orainn. . . . Bhí baint ag lucht stiúrighthe na hoibre seo leis na fealltóiribh atá dhár milleadh le faid de bhliadhantaibh. Measaid go bhfuil cos ar bolg aca orainn fós de dheallramh, acht tá dearmhad ortha. (We had faith in these people when they went to work at first. It wasn't long before they betrayed us. . . . The directors of this work were involved with the traitors who have been destroying us for years and years. They think they still have us down, but they're wrong.)[35]

Yet within two months of publishing his harsh editorial, Pearse could write: "Even the Abbey, be it good or evil, is at any rate an emanation from the soil of Ireland."[36] The following year he concluded a brief report on a Lady Gregory lecture to the League with warm praise of her theatre:

> Some writers and players of the Abbey may have sinned against our dearest sentiments, but the good they have done outweighs all their shortcomings, and while we deprecate indiscreet praise we must in justice admit that those who have succeeded in founding a home-made theatre, and who successfully run it independent of the worst influences of the modern decadent English stage deserve well of their nation.[37]

Still, many Gaels found the Abbey, however sincere and successful in its battle against vulgar Anglicization, as "oppressively slow" as the Literary Theatre in its march "Irish-wards." A January 1910 editorial in *An Claidheamh Soluis* expressed Gaelic impatience: "We have not classed the 'Abbey' with the other houses, because Mr. Yeats deserves well of Ireland for many reasons . . . but he is making no attempt at the

Gaelicising of the Irish stage, or at the creation of a purely Irish drama. . . . The production of plays in English is not to be condemned, but it is questionable if a theatre from which plays in Irish are excluded, can be called Irish."[38]

Here again appears the assumption that the Anglo-Irish movement is only really valid as the subordinate ally of the Gaelic movement. This assumption also colored the Gaels' response to individual Irish writers in English. The most significant of these was, of course, Yeats, whose activities and pronouncements were closely scrutinized in the Gaelic press. On the whole, positive judgments of Yeats far outweigh the negative, and the young Pearse's contemptuous dismissal of him as "a mere English poet of the third or fourth rank"[39] is utterly unrepresentative. For example, in *Fáinne an Lae* on 4 February 1899 one reads: "But no one will deny that Mr. Yeats strives most earnestly to follow the lead of the old Gaelic writers; whether he succeeds in giving expression to the true Gaelic spirit is a point to be decided by an admiring public."[40] In October 1905 Pearse called Yeats's *Cathleen Ni Houlihan* "the most beautiful piece of prose that has been produced by an Irishman in our day."[41] Three years later he wrote of the poet in *An Claidheamh Soluis*: "We may not all agree with his theories on art and literature, but we cannot forget that he has spent his life in an endeavour to free our ideas from the trammels of foreign thought, or that it was through his writings that many of us made our first acquaintance with our early traditions and literature. He has never ceased to work for Ireland. . . ."[42] A March 1910 *An Claidheamh Soluis* editorial stated in a favorable review of a lecture by the poet: "When Mr. Yeats speaks on the conditions under which literature is created, or the attitude that encourages its growth he has the wisdom of a sage, and Ireland owes him much for the example he has set in his devotion to literary ideals, even when she cannot agree with the ideals which Mr. Yeats sometimes holds before her."[43]

Yet it is hard to escape the conclusion that Yeats's stature in Gaelic eyes was often linked to the extent of his agreement with Gaelic ideals. Once again, the Anglo-Irish writer was to be a self-sacrificing foot soldier in the army of the revival. In *Fáinne an Lae* in August 1898 Yeats was enlisted in the cause: "Mr. Yeats, who might do for us what Kollar, with his patriotic poems full of sorrow and passion and hope, did for the Czech movement . . . has taken up Irish as a serious study and has already, we are informed, made considerable progress therein. . . . We look forward confidently to original work in his own language from Mr. Yeats."[44] In a March 1904 editorial Pearse commented on a Yeats speech in the United States in which the poet spoke highly of the Gaelic League and stressed the central position of the language in the creation of a new Irish literature:

It is a matter of congratulations that Mr. Yeats has come to see the inadequacy of the literary movement with which he has been mainly associated to touch the heart of Ireland or to utter Ireland's soul. He is now precisely at the same point as the Gaelic League, which holds that literary work in English, however largely it may draw its inspiration from Ireland, is at best only propagandist. We confess that we regard such an admission from Mr. Yeats as valuable, for it represents a conclusion arrived at by a long process of thought. In a sense, too, it is a courageous admission, for by a sort of self-denying ordinance it shuts out Mr. Yeats's own work from the Valhalla of Irish literature.[45]

Two years later Pearse granted Yeats a more actively creative role in the revival while still barring his work from the Gaelic Valhalla: "As for writers in English, they interest us only when they directly or indirectly help on our work, as, we think, Mr. Yeats himself has done in 'Cathleen Ni Houlihan,' in 'On the King's Threshold' and 'On Baile's Strand.' "[46] Nor was there ever much question in Pearse's mind about the ultimate significance of the literary contributions of even a Yeats:

Unlike most Gaelic Leaguers, we have a sincere admiration for much of the work of Mr. Yeats, Mr. Russell, and the other poets and drama- tists of what, without irreverence, we may call the Celtic Twilight School. We believe that their work is the finest that is being done in our time in English. But do Mr. Yeats and his fellows hold a place in the intellectual present of Ireland comparable to that held, say, by an An tAthair Peadar or Conán Maol? Mr. Yeats with a possible audience of four million is much less of a force in Ireland than An tAthair Peadar or Conán Maol with a possible audience of half a million. . . . The future is with the Gael.[47]

If the Gaels felt a healthy respect for Yeats even in disagreement and debate, they felt for Synge a bitter hostility throughout his lifetime. Declan Kiberd has amply documented Synge's stormy relations with the language movement,[48] but a few quotes from the Gaelic press illustrate the nature and extent of the revivalists' enmity. Even in his generous letter to Lady Gregory, Pearse could write: "Plays like Mr. Synge's, however, discourage me."[49] In a brief review of *The Well of the Saints* he explained this discouragement:

Leanann neamh-ghlaine éigin intinne do gach aon rud thigeas ó láimh an ughdair seo. Easbaidh eile atá air, agus ní beag an easbaidh í, ní thuigeann sé aigneadh an Ghaedhil, agus is baoghalach linn nach dtuigfidh go deo. (Some impurity of mind adheres to everything that comes from the hand of this author. He has another failing as well, and it's no small failing. He doesn't understand the mind of the Gael, and we fear he never will.)[50]

In a favorable review of Lady Gregory's *Kincora*, he offered the Abbey some advice: "Seachnaidís drabhfhuigheall de shaghas 'The Well of the Saints' agus 'In the Shadow of the Glen.' " (Let them stay clear of rubbish like "The Well of the Saints" and "In the Shadow of the Glen.")[51]

In these pronouncements Pearse fully represents mainstream Gaelic opinion. In Synge's lifetime all of his work, except *Riders to the Sea*, was condemned in the Gaelic press, and even that play was ridiculed in *An Claideamh Soluis* in February 1906: "Taobh amuigh de na brógaibh úr-leathair, ní raibh gaol ná cosmhalacht ag no daoinibh do bhí ar an árdán le muinntir Inis Meadhon thar mar bhí acu le muinntir Hong Cong." (Except for the pampooties, the people who were on the stage had no more connection with the people of Inis Mean than they did with the people of Hong Kong.)[52] While *An Claidheamh Soluis*[53] and particularly Pearse[54] were to take a more sympathetic and even appreciative view of Synge after his death, in his lifetime he was for Gaels the "evil spirit" of the Anglo-Irish movement.[55]

Among other Anglo-Irish writers, Lady Gregory, who always maintained close relations with the League and occasionally contributed to *An Claideamh Soluis*, was almost invariably treated with respect and affection, as was Edward Martyn, whose contributions to the League were financial as well as literary.[56] George Moore, on the other hand, was viewed with a healthy and well-deserved skepticism, although he was warmly welcomed when he publicly enlisted in the Gaelic cause. Nevertheless even then the *Fáinne an Lae* correspondent seemed unable to take Moore entirely seriously: "Suddenly we hear the sweet strains of a fairy tiompan, and the curtain flies up to discover Mr. Moore pushing aside the mummers (as is his wont) with one hand, while with the other he presents us with the acting copy of a play in Gaelic. . . ."[57] When Moore lost interest in the revival, the Gaels as quickly lost interest in him: "Mr. George Moore, too, has now gone back to his old love, and he is now trying to hold up Gaelic League leaders for the laughter of London drawingrooms in an English review."[58]

The tendency of revivalists to judge Anglo-Irish writers by their willingness to serve the cause is apparent when one considers the writers most consistently and highly praised in the Gaelic press. While denying that the English language could capture the Gaelic soul,[59] Leaguers nonetheless found an ineffably Gaelic flavor in the works of such writers as Séamas Mac Manus, a frequent contributor to League papers, his wife Eithne Carbery, Brian Higgins, and Mary Butler.[60] A review by Conán

Maol of Carbery's posthumous *The Four Winds of Eirinn* provides a rather florid example of this theme:

> Is mór an truagh gur i Sagsbhéarla atá "The Four Winds of Eirinn" sgríobhtha. Ní fhuil acht sgreamh Sagsbhéarla air ar a shon sain, mar is Gaedhealach é a chabhail agus a chorp. Tá intinn is croidhe na mná ba Gaedhealaighe lem' linn ó bhun bárr ins na hocht dánta is trí fichid atá 'san leabhar. (It is a great pity that "The Four Winds of Eirinn" is written in English. It is, however, only an English crust, for its whole substance is Gaelic. The mind and heart of the most Gaelic woman of my time is everywhere in the sixty-eight poems in the book.)[61]

Yet the League's imprimatur was not simply an attempt to boost the reputations of loyal, safely second-rate camp followers from the Anglo-Irish side. Two other writers also noted for this elusive Gaelic quality in their work were by no means either safe or second-rate. In a highly favorable review of Padraic Colum's *Land*, Seosamh Ó Néill wrote in *An Claideamh Soluis*:

> Is mór cás an leabhar so ar na scríobhadh i mBéarla, óir baint ná pairt ní'l aige le Béarla nó le Galldacht; Gaodhalach 'seadh é ó thús go deire . . . Gaodhalach ó'n gcnámh go dtí an smúsach. (It is a great pity that this book was written in English, for it has nothing to do with English or the Galltacht; it is Gaelic from start to finish . . . Gaelic from the bone to the marrow.)[62]

In March 1907 Pearse crowned Colum "the writer who, in intellectual stature, as in breadth and depth of vision, must henceforward be acknowledged the most considerable among the little band of Anglo-Irish dramatists . . . the most powerful and original mind in the present-day literary movement."[63] James Stephens received similarly warm praise when his *The Crock of Gold* appeared five years later: "Éireannach 'seadh Mac Stiopháin agus Gaedheal go smior é. Cé nach bhfuil sé acht ag tosnughadh ar an nGaedhilg d'fhoghluim tá sár-eolas aige ar an nós sgéalaidheachta bhí ag ár sean-sgéalaidhe." (Stephens is an Irishman and a Gael to the marrow. Although he is only beginning to learn Irish, he has a superb knowledge of the way our old storytellers told stories.)[64]

In a brief note on Stephens's winning the Polignac Prize for *The Crock of Gold*, Eoin Ó Searcaigh again praised the novel's Gaelicism while pointing out what he saw as the healthy influence of An tAthair Peadar on Stephens: "Leabhar an-Ghaedhealach is eadh 'An Corcán Óir'. Tá sliocht mór 'd'Eisirt' sníomhtha isteach ann." ("The Crock of Gold" is a very Gaelic book. There is a big passage from "Eisirt" woven into it.)[65]

Declan Kiberd has written perceptively and passionately of "the self-imposed quarantine" in which Gaelic writers placed themselves, particularly after the founding of the Free State, and of "an teorainn bhréige idir an dá litríocht" (the artificial border between the two literatures)[66] that intellectually partitions the country to this day. The roots of this stultifying misconception go well back into the early days of the language revival. Yet contemporary with Gaelic hostility toward and rejection of Anglo-Irish literature was a sincere and sensitive interest in and appreciation of the contribution of Irish writers of English. While most Gaels may not have been willing to accept their Anglo-Irish brethren as full partners in the war against Anglicization, they often welcomed and invited their support and praised them for it. One of the most tragic victims of the political and cultural struggles for independence was this promisingly constructive approach to creating an authentically bilingual Ireland. The adolescent Pearse's strident 1899 letter is too often quoted to represent Gaelic opinion toward the Anglo-Irish movement. Too little is heard of the more thoughtful views of a *Fáinne an Lae* columnist less than a year later:

Ní ceart dúinn a dhearmad go bhfuil an Béarla ann, agus go mbeidh sí i n-úsáid ag Gaedhealaibh de réir deallraimh an fhaid agus beidh sé i n-úsáid ag na Sasanachaibh féin. . . . 'San toisg is fearr, beidh dá theanga againn feasta, agus is fiú an bheirt acu do shaothrú go dicheallach. . . . (It is not right for us to forget that English is here, and that it will, it seems, be used by the Irish as long as it is used by the English themselves. . . . In the best sense we will have two languages from now on, and it is worthwhile to cultivate both of them to the best of our ability. . . .)[67]

NOTES

1. Patrick Pearse, *An Claidheamh Soluis,* 20 May 1899, 157.
2. "Litridheacht Náisiúnta" (National literature), editorial, *Fáinne an Lae,* 22 January 1898, 4. Brian Doyle was the English language editor of *Fáinne an Lae;* Eoin Mac Neill the Irish language editor.
3. "Notes," *Fáinne an Lae,* 23 April 1898, 7.
4. "Debasing Literature: Its Antidote," editorial, *An Claidheamh Soluis,* 29 April 1899, 104. Eoin Mac Neill edited *An Claidheamh Soluis* from its founding in 1899 to October 1901.
5. "Notes," *An Claidheamh Soluis,* 6 May 1899, 121. Even the dying exile Eoghan O'Growney entered the controversy, writing to the editor of the New York *Irish World* on 21 January 1899: "You may say that we could have a literature which while in the English language, would be truly Irish in sentiment and thought. This looks well in theory, but in practice it fails to work out." See "*The Irish World* Language Fund" in *Leabhar an Athar Eoghan / The O'Growney Memorial Volume,* ed. Agnes O'Farrelly (Dublin: M. H. Gill and Son, 1904), 257. Indeed, Alan Titley has written that in a sense founding the Gaelic League was an

attempt "séanadh a thabhairt don tuairim go bhféadfaí litríocht na tíre a thógáil ar Bhéarla faoi leith na hÉireann" (to refute the opinion that the country's literature could be based on the uniquely Irish form of the English language). See "Litríocht na Gaeilge, Litríocht an Bhéarla, agus Irish Literature" (Gaelic literature, English literature, and Irish literature), *Scríobh* 5 (1981): 127.

6. "Irish or Anglo-Irish," editorial, *An Claidheamh Soluis*, 10 January 1903, 740. Eoghan Ó Neachtain edited *An Claidheamh Soluis* from October 1901 to March 1903.

7. *An Claidheamh Soluis*, 13 April 1907, 9.

8. Eoin Mac Neill, quoted in Daniel Corkery *What's This About the Gaelic League* (Dublin: Conradh na Gaeilge, 1942), 25. Mac Neill's position here was not a new one. As early as May 1897 he had editorialized in *Irisleabhar na Gaedhilge:* "The Anglo-Irish or Hiberno-English idea of a National Irish literature is daily becoming a more evident delusion. That literature itself has failed to obtain any hold whatsoever on the Irish mind." See "Past, Present and Future," *Irisleabhar na Gaedhilge* 8 (May 1897), 3. Donal McCartney states that it was in deference to the wishes of Hyde that Mac Neill refrained from even stronger attacks on the Anglo-Irish movement. See "Mac Neill and Irish Ireland" in *The Scholar Revolutionary: Eoin Mac Neill, 1867–1945, and the Making of a New Ireland*, ed. F. X. Martin and F. J. Byrne (New York: Barnes and Noble, 1973), 93.

9. "Irish Literature", editorial, *An Claidheamh Soluis*, 14 September 1912, 7. Seán Mac Giollarnáth took over the editorship from Pearse in November 1909. Lest this view seem entirely fanatical wishful thinking, it should be remembered that it was shared by some prominent Anglo-Irish literary figures. Yeats himself, speaking in New York in 1904, recalled: "When this great movement [the Gaelic League] appeared in Ireland, it looked for a time as if there was nothing for men like myself to do. . . ." See W. B. Yeats, *Uncollected Prose*, ed. John P. Frayne and Colton Johnson (London: Macmillan, 1975), 2:323. See also Yeats's "The Literary Movement in Ireland" in *Ideals in Ireland* (London: The Unicorn, 1901), 90, and his comments on the future of Gaelic literature as reported in *An Claidheamh Soluis*, 5 March 1904, 5. In a similar vein, Frank Fay, as drama critic of *The United Irishman*, wrote in 1901: "An Irish theatre must, of course, express itself solely in the Irish language; otherwise it would have no *raison d'être*." See "Mr. Yeats and the Stage" in Fay's *Towards a National Theatre*, ed. Robert Hogan (Dublin: Dolmen Press, 1970), 50. Even Seán O'Casey could write as late as 1913: "We are out to overthrow England's language, her political government of our country, good and bad; her degrading social system. . . ." See "Euchan' and Ireland, a Challenge to Verbal Combat" in *Feathers from the Green Crow*, ed. Robert Hogan (London: Macmillan, 1963), 93.

10. D. P. Moran, "The Future of the Irish Nation," in *The Philosophy of Irish Ireland* (Dublin: James Duffy, 1905), 22.

11. Earnán de Blaghd, *Slán le hUltaibh* (Farewell to Ulster) (Baile Átha Cliath: Sáirséal agus Dill, 1971), 46.

12. "Notes," *An Claidheamh Soluis*, 10 June 1899, 200.

13. "Notes," *An Claidheamh Soluis*, 24 June 1899, 233.

14. Mac Léighinn, "A Vindication of Ancient Irish Culture", review of *Bards of the Gael and Gall*, by George Sigerson, *Irisleabhar na Gaedhilge*, September, 1897, 81.

15. "The Irish (?) Literary Movement," editorial, *An Claidheamh Soluis*, 26 September 1899, 423.

16. Quoted in Lady Gregory, *Seventy Years: Being an Autobiography of Lady Gregory*, ed. Colin Smythe (Gerrards Cross: Colin Smythe, 1974), 402.

17. E. O'N. review of performance by Na hAisteoirí, *An Claidheamh Soluis*, 19 April 1913, 9.

18. "Sgríbhneoirí" (Writers), *An Claidheamh Soluis*, 1 February 1908, 3. Two years previously, Mícheál Ó Brasaire had written in *Irisleabhar na Gaedhilge:*

> Is minic sinn ag trácht ar bhrigh intlidheachta an lae indiu ar fuaid na hÉireann; acht tuigidh uaim-se gur intlidheacht na nGall-Gaedheal í, agus go bhfuil an intlidheacht sin na bhfíor-Ghaedheal [sic] 'n-a spreas gan borradh gan bíodhgadh fós. (We often speak of the intellectual vigor found throughout Ireland today. But take my word for it that it is the intellect of the Anglo-Irish, and that the intellect of the true Gaels is as yet a dull and lifeless thing.)

See "Éirghidh, a Ghiollaí Leisceamhla!" (Arise, lazy lads!), *Irisleabhar na Gaedhilge* 16 (June 1906), 146.

19. See Pearse's comments in "About Literature," *An Claidheamh Soluis*, 29 April 1905, 7. He writes: "That Mr. Russell and his confreres ought to cease writing poetry because they do not know Irish we have, of course, never suggested. As literature we rate their work high. We regret that it has not been done in Irish, that it might be altogether ours. But we prefer that it should be done in English than that it should remain undone." While Douglas Hyde lived up to W. P. Ryan's characterization of him as "tolerance personified" by never actively entering this debate, it should be remembered that in his preface to the early collection of his poems in Irish, *Úbhla de'n Chraoibh* (Apples from the branch), he quietly took a firm stand much like that of Pearse above:

> B'fhearr liom aon rann binn amháin do thabhairt uaim ann san teangaidh atá mé d'á sgríobh anois, ná lán leabhair de bhéarsuigheacht do chumadh ann san mBéarla. Óir dá mbeidheadh aon mhaith ann mo bhéarsuigheacht Béarla, ní do mo mháthair Éire do rachadh sé i dtairbhe, ach do mo leas-mháthair Sacsana. (I would prefer to produce one sweet stanza in the language I am now writing than to compose a full book of verse in English. For if there were any value in my English verse, the profit of it wouldn't go to my mother, Ireland, but to my stepmother, England.)

See "Roimhrádh" (Preface), *Úbhla de'n Chraoibh* (Dublin: M. H. Gill and Son, 1900), v.

20. Review of *The Mineral Workers*, by William Boyle, *An Claidheamh Soluis*, 3 November 1906, 4.

21. Pearse to Lady Gregory, 29 April 1905, *The Letters of P. H. Pearse*, ed. Séamas Ó Buachalla (Gerrards Cross: Colin Smythe, 1980), 94. That Pearse was not merely flattering an influential friend is shown in a letter he wrote to J. J. Doyle when he was canvassing support for his candidacy for the editorship of *An Claidheamh Soluis*. Pearse included among his detailed suggestions for editorial changes: "Each issue would contain at least one literary article in English, dealing with some phase of Irish Ireland. These should be written by the best English writers at the disposal of the League. Such names as Lady Gregory, Stephen Gwynn, W. P. Ryan, Edward Martyn, W. B. Yeats, F. A. Fahy, Miss Hull and hosts of others occur to me. . . ." (Pearse to Doyle 27 February 1903, *Letters of Pearse*, 71–72.)

22. Thomas C. Murray, *An Claidheamh Soluis*, 15 July 1889, 278.

23. An tAthair Peadar Ua Laoghaire, "An Drochad" (The bridge),

Sgothbhualadh (Light threshing) 2 (Baile Atha Cliath: Muintir na Leabhar Gaedhilge, 1907), 146.

24. Ua Laoghaire, "Cé Áta Ciontach?" (Who is responsible?), *Sgothbhualadh* 2, 148.

25. "London Notes," *An Claidheamh Soluis*, 21 February 1903, 841. W. P. Ryan was probably the author of this column.

26. "Notes," *Fáinne an Lae*, 30 December 1899, 205.

27. "Notes," *Fáinne an Lae*, 16 June 1900, 188.

28. "Dubhghlas de híde san Iarthar" (Douglas Hyde in the West), *Fáinne an Lae*, 5 August 1899, 33.

29. "A Movement of Defeat," *An Claidheamh Soluis*, 6 February 1904, 5.

30. "Notes," *Fáinne an Lae*, 23 June 1900, 196.

31. "Notes," *Fáinne an Lae*, 27 January 1900, 28.

32. "An Theatre Éireannach" (The Irish theatre), *Fáinne an Lae*, 3 March 1900, 65.

33. "Notes," *An Claidheamh Soluis*, 2 November 1901, 537.

34. Declan Kiberd discusses in detail the harshly critical reaction of Gaelic nationalists to Synge in *Synge and the Irish Language* (London: Macmillan, 1979).

35. Pádraig na Léime, "Lucht Masladh" (Slanderers), *An Claidheamh Soluis*, 27 July 1912, 4. The occasion of this diatribe was the production of Lennox Robinson's *Patriots*. Mac Cárthaigh was answered two weeks later by one Fear na Feirsde, who defended both the play and the theatre. See "Searbhas na Fírinne" (The truth is bitter), *An Claidheamh Soluis*, 10 August 1912, 4.

36. "A Note on Acting," *An Claidheamh Soluis*, 6 April 1907, 8.

37. "Drama," *An Claidheamh Soluis*, 21 November 1908, 10.

38. "The Stage," editorial, *An Claidheamh Soluis*, 15 January 1910, 7.

39. Pearse, *An Claidheamh Soluis*, 20 May 1899, 157.

40. "A Gaelic Theatre," *Fáinne an Lae*, 4 February 1899, 36.

41. Review of *Caitlín Ní Uallacháin*, translation of Yeats's *Cathleen Ni Houlihan* by Tomás Ó Ceallaigh, *An Claidheamh Soluis*, 10 July 1905, 5. This review is unsigned, but Pearse stated that all unsigned material in *An Claidheamh Soluis* during his editorship was from his pen. (Pearse to Tomás Ó Flannghaile, 30 September 1905, *Letters of Pearse*, 98.)

42. "The Gael in Trinity," *An Claidheamh Soluis*, 28 November 1908, 9.

43. "Ireland and the Theatre," *An Claidheamh Soluis*, 19 March 1910, 7.

44. "Notes," *Fáinne an Lae*, 27 August 1898, 61.

45. "Mr. Yeats on his Failure," *An Claidheamh Soluis*, 5 March 1904, 5.

46. "Mr. Yeats on the Drama," *An Claidheamh Soluis*, 28 January 1905, 7.

47. "Some Thoughts," *An Claidheamh Soluis*, 10 February 1906, 7. In a similar vein, Pearse wrote in an editorial the following year: "When all is said and done, a Roibeard Weldon making homely rhymes by a fireside in the Déise is nearer the heart of Ireland, is accomplishing a nobler work for Ireland, is from every point of view, of greater moment to Ireland, than a W. B. Yeats trying over elaborate cadences to the accompaniment of a zither in a Dublin drawingroom." See "A Word to Our Readers," *An Claidheamh Soluis*, 21 December 1907, 9.

48. See Kiberd's *Synge and the Irish Language* and "John Millington Synge agus Athbheochan na Gaeilge" (Synge and the Irish language revival), *Scríobh* 4 (1979): 221–33.

49. Pearse, *Letters of Pearse*, 94.

50. "Mion-Sgéala" (Short notices), *An Claidheamh Soluis*, 11 February 1905, 3.

51. "Mion-Sgéala" (Short notices), *An Claidheamh Soluis*, 15 April 1905, 3.

52. "Ráflaí" (Rumors), *An Claidheamh Soluis*, 2 March 1906, 3. What was perceived as Synge's exoticism was also attacked by a critic who wrote of one of Synge's Aran articles in the American paper *The Gael*: "Mr. J. M. Synge, whoever he be, appears to be inclined to look down at the natives of Arann from a very high eminence indeed. He discourses of them in a quasi-learned style, as if they were some tribe of Central Africa, instead of Irish islanders of simple and unaffected manners." (*Irisleabhar na Gaedhilge*, 11 [May 1901], 95.) *Riders to the Sea* was, however, translated into Irish by Tomás Mac Domhnaill, a teacher at St. Enda's, Pearse's school. The play was tentatively scheduled for production by the Theatre of Ireland at the 1910 Oireachtas, but was eventually cancelled due to "some difficulty . . . as to the acting rights." See *An Claidheamh Soluis*, 21 May 1910, 8; and 4 June 1910, 10. According to Mac Domhnaill, Pearse had expressed an interest in publishing this translation in *An Claidheamh Soluis*, though he never did so. See Kiberd, *Synge and the Irish Language*, 244–45.

53. "John M. Synge," *An Claidheamh Soluis*, 30 April 1910, 5. The anonymous author of this piece wrote: "Gaedheal ar fearaibh iseadh Synge. Is Gaedhealaighe go mór é ná Eoghan Ruadh Ó Súilleabháin. . . . Aon-fhuil do Cholum Cille agus do Synge. . . ." (Synge was a Gael among men. He was far more Gaelic than Eoghan Rua Ó Súilleabháin. . . . Colm Cille and Synge were of the same blood. . . .)

54. See "From a Hermitage" in *Collected Works of Padraic H. Pearse: Political Writings and Speeches* (Dublin: Phoenix, n.d.), 145. In June 1913 Pearse stated: "When a man like Synge, a man in whose sad heart there glowed a true love of Ireland, one of the two or three men who have in our time made Ireland considerable in the eyes of the world, uses strange symbols which we do not understand, we cry out that he has blasphemed and we proceed to crucify him."

55. "The Passing of Anglo-Irish Drama," *An Claidheamh Soluis*, 9 February 1907, 7. Some Gaels remained unforgiving. For example, Cáit Ní Dhonnchadha, who actively urged Gaels to support the Abbey, always found Synge's work distasteful:

Tá sé amuigh air go raibh féith áluinn cluichtheachta ann, acht pé donas a bhí ag gabháil dó is beag má éirigh riamh leis taithneamh a thabhairt do phobal a thíre féin. Ba dheacair labhairt le foidhne nó leis an urraim is dual do'n mharbh ag cur síos le hoireamhaint ar chuid dá cheapadóireacht. (It is said that he had a beautiful dramatic talent, but whatever misfortune afflicted him, he never really succeeded in feeling affection for the people of his country. It is difficult to speak with patience or with the respect due the dead if one is to discuss properly some of his work.)

See "Amharclann na Mainistreach" (The Abbey Theatre), *An Claidheamh Soluis*, 11 February 1911, 4.

56. In 1915, *An Claidheamh Soluis* went so far as to call Martyn "the strongest mind of the earliest Irish Literary Theatre," and a man who "remained dominantly Gaelic and sensible." See *An Claidheamh Soluis*, 9 January 1915, 4.

57. "Notes," *Fáinne an Lae*, 3 March 1900, 68. This somewhat skeptical attitude was shared by the actors Moore directed in Hyde's *Casadh an tSúgáin*, a play whose language was unknown to him. See "Duine Acu" (One of them) in *Casadh an tSúgáin*" *Banba* 1 (December 1901), 7–8.

58. "The Abbey Theatre and 'The Playboy,' " *An Claidheamh Soluis*, 6 January 1912, 8. In the 1915 article in which Martyn was so highly praised, Moore was dismissed as "the godless hedonist."

59. Actually, in 1904 the young Tomás Ó Ceallaigh, who in the following year

translated Yeats's *Cathleen Ni Houlihan*, seems to have crossed the thin line and conceded the existence of the much-derided Celtic note in English literature. With the work of Yeats firmly in mind, he wrote: "It seems not unnatural to expect that the peculiar qualities of the Celtic nature should shine through the work of an Irishman even when he writes in English, giving it a lustre which is recognizably Irish." See "The Future of Literature in Ireland" in *An tAthair Tomás Ó Ceallaigh agus A Shaothar* (Father Tomás Ó Ceallaigh and his work), ed. Tomás S. Ó Láimhín (Gaillimh: Complacht Foillsighthe an Iarthair, 1943), 283.

60. On Mac Manus see, for example, "Mion-Sgéala" (Short notices), *An Claidheamh Soluis*, 7 October 1905, 3; or "Séamus Mac Mághnuis," *An Claidheamh Soluis*, 1 August 1908, 6.

On Ó Higgins see, for example, Séamus Ó Searcaigh, "Ó Chúige Uladh" (From the province of Ulster), *An Claidheamh Soluis*, 8 February 1908, 5; or "File Gaedhealach" (A Gaelic poet), *An Claidheamh Soluis*, 30 July 1910, 3–4.

On Butler see, for example, "A Soul and the Movement," Pearse's review of Butler's *The Ring of Day* in *An Claidheamh Soluis*, 29 September 1906, 5. In 1902 the League published translations by Tomás Ó Concheanainn of three of Butler's stories under the title *Blátha Bealtaine* (The flowers of May).

61. Conán Maol, review of *The Four Winds of Eirinn* by Ethne Carbery, *An Claidheamh Soluis*, 21 June 1902, 254.

62. Seosamh Ó Néill, review of *The Land* by Pádraic Colum, *An Claidheamh Soluis*, 7 January 1905, 6.

63. "Plays and Players," *An Claidheamh Soluis*, 30 March 1907, 8. Predictably, as Colum continued to write in English and drifted from the Gaelic movement, criticism of him sharpened. See "A Word of Encouragement," *An Claidheamh Soluis*, 29 April 1911, 7.

64. Buailtéan, "An Sgéalaidhe Gaedhealach" (The Gaelic storyteller), *An Claidheamh Soluis*, 26 October 1912, 5.

65. Eoin Ó Searcaigh, "Craobh na nUghdar" (The authors' branch), *An Claidheamh Soluis*, 6 December 1913, 5.

66. Kiberd, *Synge and the Irish Language*, 6. Kiberd, "Seán Ó Ríordáin: File Angla-Éireannach" (Seán Ó Ríordáin: An Anglo-Irish poet), in *An Duine is Dual: Aistí ar Sheán Ó Ríordáin* (The native person: Essays on Seán Ó Ríordáin) (Baile Átha Cliath: An Clóchomhar, 1980), 93.

67. "Nuaidheacht" (News), *Fáinne an Lae*, 24 February 1900, 57.

11

The SDLP and Sinn Fein: Whither the Nationalist Vote?

Padraig O'Malley

During the last couple of years the words Catholic alienation have become one of the "in" phrases in the political lexicon of Northern Ireland. This phenomenon, it is argued, accounts for the rise of Sinn Fein. The corollary warns that unless steps are taken to alleviate this alienation, Sinn Fein will emerge as the majority voice of nationalism in Northern Ireland with all kinds of dire consequences to follow.

When local elections are held in Northern Ireland on 15 May [1985] *it will be more accurate to say that two sets of local elections are being held: On the one hand unionist voters will choose between the Democratic Unionist Party (DUP) and the Official Unionist Party (OUP); on the other hand, nationalist voters will choose between the Social Democratic and Labour Party (SDLP) and Sinn Fein. The Alliance Party probably will do no worse in these local elections than in the Assembly, European, or general elections, and it therefore will remain peripheral, although its impact on the SDLP vote, which coopted the Alliance vote in the 1984 European elections, should not be discounted.

I would like to address the nationalist side of the equation and to suggest that the factors that will affect the distribution of the nationalist vote are both more numerous and more complex than can be subsumed under the simple but nevertheless appealing nomenclature of alienation.

These factors can be broken down into the following categories: (1) those that undermine the SDLP; (2) those that limit the degree to which the SDLP vote can be undermined; (3) those that boost Sinn Fein; and

---

*This essay predates the 1985 election. For a more recent perspective on present issues and strategies, see the Afterword at the conclusion of this essay.— Eds.

(4) those that limit the degree to which the Sinn Fein vote can, in fact, be boosted.

Factors in all four categories are interrelated, and to a large degree mutually inclusive. They are not fixed, immutable quantities. They can be manipulated, and the relative importance of the variables within each group finally depends on the SDLP's and Sinn Fein's overall political strategies. For example, if Sinn Fein believes that its electoral strength might pressure the British to concede what in Sinn Fein's view would be cosmetic changes, but which could be hailed by both the SDLP and Dublin as some kind of breakthrough, then Sinn Fein may decide not to attempt to maximize its potential vote. On the other hand, Sinn Fein cannot afford to appear to be "beaten" by the SDLP since this might undermine its concept of the armalite and the ballot box as complementary components of a long-term strategy. Thus Sinn Fein must do well enough to vindicate its essential political strategy, but not well enough to set in motion a political dialogue that might result in a set of political arrangements acceptable to all except Sinn Fein. Such a situation would, of course, undermine support for the armed struggle. Both the SDLP and Sinn Fein are therefore prisoners of particular sets of circumstances; how they both do at the ballot box may have more to do with their respective abilities to deal with these circumstances than with any grand strategy carefully designed and masterfully executed.

In one sense the SDLP's problems can be directly related not only to the political forces that brought the party into existence but, in a broader sense, to the historical continuum that is an essential part of the nationalist tradition in Northern Ireland. After the settlement of 1921 the pervasive belief among nationalists "that the border was a temporary expedient led to intermittent abstentionism from the Stormont Parliament."[1] Nationalists did not recognize the legitimacy of the new state. They did not bother to organize themselves either as a political opposition or, worse still, as a political party. Nor did they bother to contest constituencies that did not have a secure Catholic majority. As a result, they had no formal membership, which in turn led to informal conventions—more often than not dominated by the local Catholic priests—for selecting candidates for office.[2] Thus the tradition: the Nationalist Party might or might not contest an election; it might or it might not abstain. The principles that were the mainstay of Northern nationalism precluded the need for political organization—the vote, after all, was simple to identify. And for the nationalist voters the choice, too, was simple: they either voted for the Nationalist candidates, whoever they were and however they were selected, or they didn't vote at all.

The SDLP, which had its roots in the civil rights movement of the late 1960s, was an umbrella party bringing together the remnants of the old

Nationalist Party, which stood for unity with the rest of Ireland and little else, the National Democratic Party, and the Republican Labour Party. From the beginning the SDLP saw itself as a *cause* rather than a political party as such, and so put no large scale premium on political organization, especially since the party faced no electoral challenge in the nationalist community. This problem—now acute because of opposition within the nationalist community—has several aspects: the party has little understanding of how important it is to organize at the grass roots level; little familiarity with the nuts and bolts of politics, the delivery of basic constituent services; and no reservoir of skills necessary to develop a grass roots organization.

The SDLP's organizational problems are compounded by a number of others. First, there is the problem of political identity. That it stands against the use of violence is clear. That it opposes the Irish Republican Army (IRA) is clear. Both of these, however, are aspects of a negative identity. What it stands *for* is less clear. In the early stages of the party's development it emphasized an internal settlement within the United Kingdom with an Irish Dimension. This position was formally endorsed in November 1973, when the SDLP joined with the Unionist and Alliance parties to form a power-sharing executive in Northern Ireland, while the Sunningdale Agreement—which the executive, the Irish Republic, and Great Britain were parties to in December 1973—provided for an institutional link with the South. After the collapse of the Sunningdale Agreement in May 1974, the failure of the 1975 convention, and subsequent initiatives, two policy-orientations emerged within the party. One advocated more attention to an internal power-sharing executive with less emphasis on the Irish Dimension, while the other believed that a solution could be found only within the broader Anglo-Irish framework. Gerry Fitt, leader of the party, espoused the former view; John Hume, the deputy leader, advocated the latter. Matters resolved themselves in Hume's favor with Fitt's resignation as leader and from the party itself in 1979.

But there remains within the party a broader, perhaps even more significant divergence of opinion regarding policy that has yet to be resolved. Seamus Mallon, the party's deputy leader, represents the more "green" or traditional nationalist wing of the party, which aspires resolutely toward national unity; those who are less "green" would settle for an accommodation that would not necessarily involve a united Ireland. These differences, which are also reflected in the respective positions of Fianna Fail and the coalition parties (Fine Gael and Labour) in the Republic, give the *New Ireland Forum Report* its peculiarly schizophrenic qualities, since it attempts to reconcile two irreconcilable views of Irish nationalism and its future course.[3]

Ultimately the report is a negotiating document, but to this day [April 1985] the SDLP remains studiously unclear on several points. No one knows if it accepts that there will be a united Ireland in the foreseeable future, or if it would accept a settlement that would fall short of a united Ireland but that would nevertheless provide structures for the full expression of the Irish identity in Northern Ireland, or if it would accept that the constitutional status of Northern Ireland should not be changed without the consent of a majority of the people of Northern Ireland. Indeed, on the question of consent the SDLP remains unsparingly unclear, leaving unresolved the question of whether it believes consent should be induced or freely given, whether the right to give consent is counterbalanced by the right to withhold it, and whether its frame of reference is Northern Ireland, the island of Ireland, or the UK itself. The SDLP is unclear about these issues partly because it is a coalition, and a fragile one. The common bond among its members, an adherence to nonviolence and constitutional politics, might not be sufficient to hold the coalition together. Furthermore, the fudging needed to hold together competing elements within the SDLP coalition prevents it from clearly defining its political identity. Voters do not know precisely what the SDLP stands for. For example, a Marketing Opinion Research Institute (MORI) poll taken at the time of the 1984 European elections indicates that while an overwhelming number of nationalist voters disapprove of British government policies in Northern Ireland, only one-third of the SDLP's voters believe that the SDLP does.[4] On the other hand, Sinn Fein has a simple, clear-cut political identity, an easily understood statement of what it stands for, and voters who don't need to be reminded that it disapproves of British government policy.

A second problem reinforcing the SDLP's identity dilemma is its need to accommodate both of the Republic's major political parties—the Fianna Fail and the Fine Gael/Labour coalition. Despite the profound differences in tactical and strategic positions of both parties toward the North, and the absence of bipartisanship that has marked the Haughey/FitzGerald era, the SDLP must dance with both simultaneously. This calls for adroit footwork and the ability to switch partners, often at short notice, without losing the favor of either. It cannot offend either suitor, but neither can it succumb to the advances of either. The more clearly defined divisions between Fianna Fail and the coalition parties now make it increasingly difficult for the SDLP to maintain its delicate balancing act without revealing the cracks in its own facade. Nor is the SDLP sure of its own political orientation. It sees itself in the context of Northern Ireland; however, its frame of reference is the island of Ireland.

A third problem facing the SDLP is that it does not appear to have "delivered." British initiatives since Sunningdale have foundered. The reception given to the *New Ireland Forum Report*, culminating in Mrs. Thatcher's now notorious dismissal of the report's three options as "Out! Out! and Out!" following the November 1984 Anglo-Irish summit, added to the perception that the SDLP has little to show for its efforts. Its decision to abstain from the 1982 Assembly elections to appease the more "green" wing of the party may also have aggravated the perception that its policies have not borne fruit. This has blurred the distinction between the SDLP and Sinn Fein. Voters do not recognize the principles behind decisions to abstain. Abstentionism is simply abstentionism. Once the electoral yardstick is conceded, even in principle, it is difficult to redeem in the brutality of practice.

On the contrary, the SDLP's policies suggest that it is now dependent on the British government, the Irish government, or both to rescue it with some new initiative. Such a process is underway at the moment. Discussions between the two governments have been going on for some time; many hope that within months a package of arrangements designed to give full expression to the Irish identity of Northern nationalists will be formally agreed to by both governments. However, those talks are taking place in the context of the communiqué that followed the November 1984 summit in which both governments agreed that the constitutional status of Northern Ireland would not change without the consent of the majority of the people of Northern Ireland. For the Irish government this means getting something in return for its implicit acknowledgement that unionist consent for some form of association with the rest of Ireland is not forthcoming. The quid pro quo the Irish government wants is Britain's acknowledgment that the unionist right to oppose an all-Ireland state does *not* extend to a right to say no to every form of government Britain proposes for Northern Ireland, nor to a right to sabotage closer institutional relations between Britain and Ireland that would express the Republic's legitimate interests in Northern Ireland.

Whether the package is sufficient to be both fully acceptable to the SDLP and enforceable remains to be seen. Not the least of the difficulties it will face will be Mr. Haughey's vociferous opposition, to say nothing of the unionists' "not an inch" retrenchment. Needless to say, if it is sold as an interim step on the way to a united Ireland it will, more likely than not, go the way of Sunningdale. In short, for such a set of arrangements to work it must be seen as a *final* solution rather than as an interim one. Moreover, if the proposed arrangements were to fail, even with the SDLP's endorsement, the SDLP would find itself critically, if not permanently, undermined in the nationalist community. In this sense the SDLP has one roll of the dice left, one chance to dispose convincingly of Sinn Fein's contention that constitutional politics will never force the

British to address the legitimate grievances of the minority community in Northern Ireland. A Haughey veto of a FitzGerald/Thatcher agreement on the grounds that only a unitary state is acceptable would divide the country,[5] split the SDLP, and almost certainly kill the initiative, making Sinn Fein by default the clear beneficiary.

Meanwhile the SDLP can only argue that the bilateral talks between the two governments are the product of the forum process. However, matters are largely out of the hands of the SDLP. In a sense it is a bystander, its behavior at best passive-aggressive in its continued insistence that the British government must support the forum report or see the eclipse of the SDLP and the triumph of Sinn Fein. At worst it can be only passive, hoping that the two governments will find not only common ground but also the wherewithal and commitment to deliver, even if it means the British government must be willing to coerce the unionists, or at least to brandish the big stick. To the extent, therefore, that the SDLP is dependent on extraneous forces it is not in control of its own fate.

The results of these influences are threefold. First, they account for the centrifugal influence of party leader John Hume, who has so far managed to bridge the internal divisions, defuse the often conflicting implications of the SDLP's external associations, and substitute his own identity for the identity of the party. Second, there is little decentralization of the decision-making process, little serious attempt to establish a grass roots political structure, and little understanding that politics largely depends on the delivery of local constituent services. The SDLP's sense of itself as cause and its preoccupation with the larger national issues have clouded its understanding of the importance of the mundane local ones. Not having delivered on the larger issue, and not having concerned itself in a structured way with the local ones, it may fall between them both. Third, the feeling in the party itself that its efforts have not produced political progress has resulted in a pervasive, vague demoralization and a lack of motivation and sense of direction among its former activists. Half the party's supporters were opposed to the policy of abstentionism in the Assembly elections. The failure to contest Fermanagh–South Tyrone in 1981 undermined not only the SDLP's credibility among moderate Catholic voters but also its *raison d'être:* the settlement of differences in a parliamentary procedure.

The rise of Sinn Fein can be directly associated with the 1981 hunger strikes at the Maze Prison that resulted in ten deaths. For the first time the IRA had human symbols to mitigate the hard edge of its violence; the strikes allowed the IRA to reestablish itself in the heroic mold and to reaffirm its legitimacy in a historical context, making it more difficult to dismiss the IRA as mere terrorists with no political constituency representing nothing more than demented, fragmented dreams. Indeed, the MORI survey in 1984 found that 40 percent of SDLP voters saw the IRA as patriots or idealists while fewer than 33 percent of SDLP voters did not.

But the hunger strikes had a far more significant impact on Sinn Fein. They taught the movement invaluable lessons. It learned that mobilizing public opinion around a particular issue, especially an emotional one where support for the principles involved could be exploited as support for the movement, was a powerful propaganda tool; that contesting elections provided a base on which to build an enduring political organization; and that a political organization was a necessary prerequisite for taking power. Thus Sinn Fein set out to mobilize the nascent hard-core republican vote that had abstained in the past—the vote of the alienated and disaffected who remembered internment, rubber and plastic bullets, house searches, indiscriminate screenings, petty harassments, the prisons, and repressive, often zealously enforced security laws. Because Sinn Fein had not contested elections before 1982 it was assumed that such republican voters did not exist. But they did, as did other groups who had abstained in the past, especially the young and the ghetto-wise for whom the IRA was a symbol not only of resistance but of hope.

Support for Sinn Fein is also a product of what I call the "prison culture." In the North the prison population rose from 686 in 1967 to 2500 in 1983 and now represents the highest number of prisoners per capita in Western Europe. For every prisoner there are networks of family, friends, and relatives affected by the prison culture; they adopt its values, share its ethos, and cultivate its deprivations and resentments. Paradoxically the more the security forces apprehend and prosecute members of the IRA and the prison population swells, the more dominant the ethos of the prison culture grows, and the more successful Sinn Fein becomes. The free bus shuttles it runs everyday from the Falls Road to the Maze Prison are just one indication of its understanding of the situation. The 1984 MORI poll found that 70 percent of Sinn Fein voters believed that violence is justified while only 22 percent did not. Sinn Fein has no problem articulating its political identity; it is pristine and sharp—"Brits Out!"

The MORI survey, however, reveals the paradoxical attitude of nationalists. Although 63 percent of Catholics reject violence, only 46 percent of SDLP voters would reject Sinn Fein, if the SDLP were not on the ballot. Thus support for Sinn Fein cannot simply be construed as support for the IRA or for violence.

One of the more conspicuous factors accounting for support of Sinn Fein is its record of constituency services. In eighteen months it opened thirty-one advice centers, eleven in Belfast alone, compared to the

SDLP's two. The Falls Road center handled fifteen hundred cases in 1983. Attendance at community action political education courses is compulsory for Sinn Fein staffers. Voters who support Sinn Fein invariably make the point that Sinn Fein provides practical help, that it gets things done, and that it has empathy with the working classes.

From the beginning the electoral strategy of Sinn Fein vis-à-vis the SDLP has been simple: it contests elections only in constituencies where Sinn Fein believes it can defeat the SDLP, to whittle away the SDLP's claim of spokesparty for the nationalist community.

To date, Sinn Fein has participated in three elections: the October 1982 Northern Ireland Assembly elections, in which it received 30 percent of the nationalist vote; the June 1983 British general elections, in which it received 43 percent of the nationalist vote; and the May 1984 European elections, in which it received 38 percent of the nationalist vote. Both the October 1982 and June 1983 votes were interpreted as "victories" for Sinn Fein since in each case the margin of its "loss" to the SDLP was less than generally expected. By doing better than expected, Sinn Fein made the SDLP appear to do worse. In the European elections in 1984, which pitted John Hume, leader of the SDLP and the sitting member of the European Parliament, against Danny Morrison, the director of publicity for Sinn Fein, Sinn Fein made a tactical error. It predicted rather confidently that Morrison would defeat Hume, and led leading media analysts to suggest seriously that he just might. The subsequent margin of Morrison's loss was, therefore, greater than had been expected—creating the perception of a setback for Sinn Fein and raising the specter that its vote had in fact "peaked" and that since apparently it could not become, as it had boasted, the majority voice of nationalism, support for its dual strategy would evaporate, leaving the physical force advocates once again firmly in control. As a result, Sinn Fein has modified its strategy for the May 1985 local elections. There is no talk of "defeating" the SDLP and expectations are being kept low, often on the good grounds that legislation prohibiting some of its better-known members who were prisoners from running for office will weaken its capacity to pull its vote. Instead, Sinn Fein will challenge the SDLP in local council areas in which nationalists are in a majority and in which, therefore, the SDLP already holds power. It will attempt to split the nationalist vote, presenting the SDLP with two options: either form a coalition with Sinn Fein to preserve nationalist control of the council, or not join a coalition and give control of the council to the unionists. The latter would pose severe problems for the SDLP in the nationalist community, since politics in Northern Ireland are above all else tribal. Sinn Fein hopes to co-opt the SDLP by forcing it into coalitions, thus further undermining the SDLP's political identity and strategic independence.

Sinn Fein's potential for eating into the SDLP's vote is apparent from the 1984 MORI poll that indicates that the SDLP can rely on only half of its own voters to reject Sinn Fein completely, that one in seven SDLP voters would consider voting for Sinn Fein, and that 54 percent of the SDLP's voters believe that any attempt to solve Northern Ireland's problems must have the cooperation of Sinn Fein. On the other hand, one-third of Sinn Fein's voters would consider switching to the SDLP, which indicates that the Sinn Fein vote is not in itself monolithic. In fact, a significant proportion of Sinn Fein voters would vote for the SDLP if they believed that its policies were going to bring about meaningful political change.

This elasticity in the nationalist vote accounts for both Hume's recent willingness to meet with the IRA[6] and Sinn Fein's unwillingness to appear overtly threatening to the SDLP. In the absence of an Anglo-Irish summit before the local elections, Hume was more concerned with shoring up the SDLP's support within the nationalist community than with reaching out to unionists. Unionists may have howled their disapproval, but since they were not going to vote for the SDLP in the local elections their disapproval, at least in the immediate term, was irrelevant. Those who mattered—voters in both parts of the nationalist communities—approved, and to this extent Hume's moves must be seen as an attempt to woo the "soft" Sinn Fein vote. Meanwhile, Sinn Fein fears that if it appears to be on the verge of "defeating" the SDLP, the British government will respond with a package of "cosmetic" arrangements that would uphold the constitutional status of Northern Ireland as part of the United Kingdom, but would also be acceptable to the SDLP, the Irish government, and a clear majority of nationalist voters in Northern Ireland, including a substantial part of the "soft" Sinn Fein vote. In that case the SDLP would not only regain but enlarge its electoral constituency. However, even if Sinn Fein did "defeat" the SDLP it would still face formidable obstacles in holding onto nationalist sentiment in the event of a political initiative, cosmetic or not, since part of the Sinn Fein vote would represent a protest against the absence of such an initiative. Thus the political equation: at one end, the potential one in seven SDLP voters who could switch to Sinn Fein if they give up on the SDLP's ability to deliver a political initiative or local constituent services; on the other end, as many as one in three Sinn Fein voters who would desert Sinn Fein if the SDLP's efforts were to produce political movement.

Factors checking the growth of Sinn Fein are interconnected with the factors that limit the degree to which the SDLP vote can be undermined. First, 81 percent of the SDLP voters reject the use of violence, and for one-half of the SDLP vote that principle rules out altogether any consideration of support for Sinn Fein. Second, for Sinn Fein's electoral strategy to continue to be successful there must be a "ratchet" effect—each successive election must further undermine the SDLP. However, as this perception gains currency it adds to the pressure on both governments to intensify their efforts to come up with political arrangements that would vindicate the SDLP's constitutional emphasis and lead many voters who support Sinn Fein out of disillusionment with the SDLP's apparent lack of success to abandon Sinn Fein for the SDLP. To this extent, Sinn Fein too is not in control of its fate; its very success provides the ingredients for its undoing. On the other hand, Sinn Fein's failure to maintain a certain momentum will strengthen the hand of the IRA's hard-liners who find tailoring a military campaign to political expediency a repugnant reversal of the revolutionary natural order of things since military operations are held in check when political campaigns are in full swing. Many security officials in Northern Ireland attributed the reemergence of the Irish National Liberation Army (INLA), which had been thought to be defunct after the arrest of thirty-nine of its members in 1982, to the defection of a sizeable number of IRA volunteers who were impatient with Sinn Fein's preoccupation with the Assembly elections and the consequent curb on IRA activities. Moreover, certain kinds of violence, such as the Christmas 1983 bombing of Harrods in London, are not acceptable to many Sinn Fein supporters. In fact, in retrospect Sinn Fein attributes part of its relatively poor showing in the European elections of 1984 to the Harrods bombing. Third, in the long run it is difficult to build a successful political operation on a policy of abstentionism. Yet to abandon abstentionism, even if only in the South, would bring to the surface the division that exists within Sinn Fein itself and almost certainly split the movement.

At its basic level, the story of Northern nationalism is a story of endemic division. Divisions appear within the SDLP over a course of action to follow; between the SDLP and Sinn Fein for the leadership of the nationalist community; and within Sinn Fein both between the traditional nationalists and the radical socialists and between the IRA and INLA for military leadership. These divisions are a microcosm of the deeper divisions that permeate Ireland, North and South. These divisions exist not only between nationalist and nationalist, but also between nationalist and unionist, and unionist and unionist—making Ireland today, in the haunting words of Seamus Heaney, "an island of comfortless noises."

AFTERWORD

In the May 1985 local elections the SDLP won 101 seats (out of 566) and Sinn Fein won 59 seats. The SDLP won only 3 seats fewer than it did in

1981 but with a slightly increased share of the vote (17.8 percent of the first preference vote in 1985, compared with 17.5 percent in 1981).

Sinn Fein's seats were gained largely at the expense of the ultranationalist Irish Independence Party and independent republicans who were elected in 1981 during the hunger strikes. However, Sinn Fein secured 11.8 percent of the first preference vote and 40 percent of the nationalist vote—an outcome that buttressed the Dublin government's contention that alienation among the minority in Northern Ireland was widespread, that it required some dramatic political initiative to alleviate it. That initiative came in November 1985 when the Dublin and London governments entered into an agreement giving the Dublin government a role in Northern Ireland that is something more than consultative but less than fully executive.

The Anglo-Irish Agreement also stipulates that no change in the constitutional status of Northern Ireland can take place without the consent of the majority of the people there. The agreement was hailed by the SDLP as a vindication of its emphasis on the process of the New Ireland Forum as the way forward, condemned out of hand by both unionist parties as a breach of British sovereignty and the first step toward an all-Ireland state, rejected by Fianna Fail as being contrary to the forum's stated preference for a unitary Irish state, and rejected by Sinn Fein as a joint security arrangement on the part of two governments to smash the IRA.

The unionists resigned the fifteen seats held in Westminster Parliament to protest the agreement. However, in the special elections held in January 1986, which the unionists insisted on calling a referendum on the agreement, the SDLP's Seamus Mallon, benefiting in part from a streamlined, grass roots party organization, won a seat formerly held by the Official Unionist Party, and there was a 30 percent swing in the nationalist vote away from Sinn Fein to the SDLP. On the agreement's first anniversary, support for it in the nationalist community remained significantly strong, in part because the continuing opposition of unionists to the agreement reinforced the attitude among nationalists that there had to be something of benefit in the agreement for them. Meanwhile, at its annual conference in November 1986, Sinn Fein voted to end its abstentionist policies toward seeking seats in Dail Eireann, and the party split when many of the old guard and some of the young walked out and formed Republican Sinn Fein.

December 1986

NOTES

1. Ian McAllister, *Political Opposition in Northern Ireland* (London: Macmillan, 1977), 355.

2. Ibid., 356.

3. The political parties that participated in the New Ireland Forum—from the South, Fianna Fail, Fine Gael, and Labour parties, and from the North, the SDLP—set out their proposals for a "New Ireland" in the *New Ireland Forum Report* (Dublin: Stationery Office, 1984). While a unitary Irish state was the preferred option, the Report also examined proposals regarding federation, confederation, and joint authority, and remained "open to discuss other views which . . . [might] contribute to political development."

4. The survey data in this article come from the poll taken by the Marketing Opinion Research Institute on behalf of Brass Tacks, a British Broadcasting Corporation public affairs program.

5. Although Mr. Charles Haughey, leader of the then-opposition party Fianna Fail, was at first quite scathing in his denunciation of the Anglo-Irish Agreement when it was entered into by the Dublin and London governments in 1985, his opposition became more tempered when it became apparent that the agreement enjoyed overwhelming support in the Republic and in the nationalist community of Northern Ireland. Mr. Haughey has not said that he would abandon the agreement if elected taoiseach, although he is on record as saying that nationalists in Northern Ireland are worse off under the agreement.

6. In January 1975 during a radio program with Gerry Adams, president of Sinn Fein, Hume indicated that he would be willing to talk with members of the IRA Council to set out his views of the Northern Ireland problem. The council agreed. The meeting took place on 23 February 1985 at an undisclosed venue, but it broke up after a few minutes when Hume refused an IRA demand that part of the meeting should be video-recorded. Unionists protested the planned meeting, accusing the SDLP of being willing to meet with members of what was, in their eyes, a terrorist organization but not with unionists. Hume denied that he was unwilling to meet with unionists.

12

Living Together: Conflict, Community, and Expressive Culture in Newtownbutler

MARGARET STEINER

The complexities of Catholic-Protestant relations in rural Ulster are not well understood. The emphasis has been on polarization in Belfast and Derry, and the picture that emerges is one of barricades and "peace lines." The 1962 study by Barritt and Carter, for example, continues to stress polarization even when it deals with rural communities.[1] However, as was demonstrated in a later seminal study by Rosemary Harris, Catholics and Protestants in rural Ulster interact on a day-to-day basis, and must therefore juggle conflicting impulses toward neighborliness on the one hand and prejudice and conflict on the other.[2] Harris's study is the first, and perhaps the best, work that specifically deals with the ambivalence characteristic of some rural communities in Ulster. Though she does a marvelous job in covering matters of kinship, neighborly relations, swapping arrangements and the like, she ignores expressive culture. By contrast, Henry Glassie's works are interlarded with allusions to conflict and expressive culture although this is not his primary focus.[3] Having looked at statements elicited during interviews as well as at anecdotes and songs, and having observed interaction in "mixed" situations, I have identified a range of responses to conflict that are, as we shall see, situationally determined.

Before proceeding, however, some general statements about Newtownbutler are in order. The area is in East Fermanagh. To the north and east it borders County Monaghan, and to the south and west County Cavan. The "town" itself is roughly half Catholic and half Protestant, while the surrounding area is two-thirds Catholic to one-third Protestant, the reverse of the figures for Northern Ireland as a whole. Schools today are segregated, although in the past some country schools, such as

173

Drumlone, Gubb, and Feugh, were mixed. Each "side" has its own parochial hall, which is the focus of social activities. Catholics indulge in Gaelic sport and have a pipe band, while Protestants participate in the Orange Order. However, there are no distinctly "Catholic" or "Protestant" residential areas. As resident Frank McGahern put it regarding one particular road, "They're all mixed up. Every other house is Catholic-Protestant."[4] All three pubs in town are owned by Catholics, and all three have a religiously "mixed" clientele. Nonetheless, even with close day-to-day interaction between Catholics and Protestants, the "troubles" are an ever-present and terrible reality in the community.

Just how terrible has the conflict been in Newtownbutler in recent times? In the early 1950s, when an annual feis was held in the community, serious rioting often erupted, especially in 1955.[5] In 1972 a man was pitchforked to death on his farm by a number of British soldiers because, as the Catholic community maintained, of his membership in the Northern Ireland Civil Rights Association. In 1973 Main Street was all but destroyed by a bomb, and in 1979, during my second field trip, a clothing shop was also bombed. In 1981 a Protestant shopowner was shot while waiting on a customer.

Needless to say, the conflict also takes its toll in the degree of fear, suspicion, and despondency that is frequently manifest. The brother of the man who was killed by the British army would afterward sit for hours in the pub, his mood shifting from morose to bellicose depending on the amount of alcohol he had consumed. A woman whose son was in prison for paramilitary activities could not speak of him without crying. Sometimes tensions could result in avoiding people of the "other side." After the bombing in 1979 a Catholic woman reported that the Protestant shopkeepers, with whom she had good casual relations, were not speaking to her. "They don't speak to us. They think we're all in the IRA. You can see it in their eyes." The same woman, after the murder of the Protestant shopkeeper in 1981, wrote that it was a great tragedy. She asserted that everybody in the community liked him, but that he must have done something very treasonable to have been shot. In 1983 a man, who is the virtual epitome of sociability in his conscious role as singer and sportsman and who is always to be seen in the pub or at weddings, confided to me that he rarely went out anymore for fear that he would be shot on his way home on a Saturday night. "And they might not find me till first mass in the morning." When asked why anyone might want to shoot him—he was not an IRA man—he replied, "because I'm a Papish."

People in Newtownbutler fully realize the magnitude of the conflict. It is also true that in this rural, agrarian community people must depend on their neighbors just to ensure survival. Dwelling on the conflict and avoiding people of the "other side" would be a grave threat to the community. Therefore, residents have found a number of ways of living together and keeping tensions in check.

During normal times, good neighborly relations seem to prevail, and there is even a tendency to minimize the existence of bigotry or prejudice. Sean McMahon, when asked if the Orange Order was active in his youth, replied,

> Well, just at the Twelfth of July and Twelfth of August,[6] but apart from that they were all right, sociable, neighborly. Like, there was no great bitterness. . . . At that time everybody associated together. They weren't separated or segregated. They went to dances together, and I seen often when we were going maybe to church, maybe meetin' up with a couple of Protestant neighbors. And then, as they say, they went to their church, I went to mine, and we'd see one another on the way home. It often did happen, you know. . . . So there was no such thing as anything like bigotry as there is now.

Neighborly cooperation was the rule, whether one were Orange or Green.

> We helped other farmers, and it could have been Protestant or Catholic, it made no difference. . . . Everybody was obliging. It did not matter whether they were Catholic or Protestant because we found out that Protestants were even more obliging than Catholics if it came to a loan of something.

This latter sentiment I heard expressed repeatedly by Catholics and Protestants alike. Sunny Kearns was equally vocal in his stress on good neighborly relations.

> Your neighbor that would be Protestant, Muhammadan, or Catholic, whatever it is, it doesn't matter a damn what he is if you get along. . . . There's no remarks passed with the neighbors in country places, and when the Twelfth of July comes or anything else, well if a man comes out to the Twelfth of July for his day, a Protestant man, [he'll ask his neighbor] maybe . . . to do turns, and he'll go and do them for him and pass no remarks. Maybe when he comes home you tell him, you'd say, you's do with a bit of the touch today.

Two Catholic men told me that Protestants had every right, and even duty, to stand up and fight for what they believed.

With regard to kinship, Frank McGahern asserted with reference to a particular area,

Ah, but they're all mixed marriages. Every damn one of them. The
one is as black as the Devil, and the other is as Fenian as the Devil.
————,his wife was a Protestant. She was————up here and she
turned. His grandfather he was a Protestant and he converted to the
Catholic. . . . Well, down the next house is————and there's two of
them married to Protestants. They turned altogether Protestant,
beatin' drums on the Twelfth of July. Aye, real Orangeman. The next is
————and two of his girls are after marrying two Protestants. . . . Every
other house around this country, they're all mongrels.

What he does *not* say, of course, is that often when mixed marriages
occur the one who marries out often loses contact or, at the very least,
has tension-laden relations with his or her kin and is forced also to sever
other ties with church or lodge or the like.[7]

There are those who regularly socialize with people from the other
side and are praised for doing so. A Protestant woman informed me that
she regularly attended events in the Catholic hall because, as she
averred, "Nothing much ever happens in our hall." I was constantly
hearing good words from Catholics about a Protestant man who responded goodnaturedly to taunting by Catholic friends, and who would
be known to kick a Gaelic football. The only Protestant singing family of
my acquaintance was described to me as "good mixers," and they themselves had spent many a night at ceilis with their Catholic associates.
"We're Irish, like it or not," affirmed Mrs. Lattimore. This family is also
very active in Orange activities.

In addition, Catholics and Protestants often seek to minimize the
conflict and cooperate toward ensuring a time of "good crack." Solidarity, and even what Victor Turner calls "communitas," are sometimes
achieved.[8] Communitas is what Martin Buber would call an "I-thou
relationship," which "arises in instant mutuality [with] each person
[experiencing] the being of the other" and in which the needs of the
individual are subsumed by the needs of the group. During one "sing-
song," for example, Protestant Joey Wilson asks the Catholic singer,
Jimmy Halpin, to sing "The Bold Fifteen," a song about Newtownbutler's winning the county Gaelic football championship in 1953. It
must be remembered that Gaelic football is generally associated with
Irish nationalism and that Protestants rarely play or even attend games.
On this occasion, however, Joey persists in coaxing Jimmy and asks him
to sing "for the value" and "for the crack." When Jimmy exhibits somewhat unsportsmanlike behavior by claiming that he will be receiving five
hundred pounds "for a fucking record" [braggadocio is strongly dis-
couraged], Joey and another patron appeal to Jimmy as a sportsman.
Says the patron, "You're the only sportsman in Newtown." And Joey
adds, "You're the only sportsman I know of, anyway." Joey even sings a

bit of the song, and eventually he succeeds in getting Jimmy to sing it. This incident reflects the achievement of communitas, because it demonstrates how men of both "sides" cooperate to ensure "good crack." As we shall see, shared values such as sportsmanship are invoked, and the focus is on Newtownbutler itself.

Another attempt toward communitas can be seen in the act of praising singers during performance. Comments such as "good man" and "up Halpin" [or the name of the particular singer] are regularly heard during performances, and wishes of "good luck" abound. The good feeling that is often a feature of "singsongs" exists across the political-religious divide, and is the ultimate goal of such events.

In general, residents neither minimize the conflict nor seek to be destructive of community. In ordinary social interaction, as well as in expressive culture, "the motifs of every day are brought into some new perspective."[9] At least four types of responses seem to be evident:

1. Intra- and interparty joking.
2. A strict code of etiquette in "mixed" company.
3. A redirection of focus from the dangerous conflict to smaller conflicts or rivalries in sport, and
4. Emphasis on Newtownbutler itself.

Intra- and interparty joking is a regular feature of social interaction. All humans tend to joke about that which makes them uncomfortable, about those situations and persons they would rather avoid, as, for example, in mother-in-law, racial, or ethnic jokes. Certainly Catholic-Protestant avoidance in Northern Ireland is, to varying degrees, a fact of life. This story was told to me by Protestant George Lattimore, in which a fellow Protestant is the butt of the joke.

> There was a, maybe I told you before, but Paddy Sherry's father was in Lisnaskea Fair, and seemingly if you give these ballad singers a few pence they'd play any song you fancied, any tune you fancied. So this was a Protestant man who gave the ballad singer a couple of pence to sing a Protestant song. But Paddy Sherry's father was a bit of a divil anyway, and he went on the quiet and he gave the ballad singer a couple of pence to play a Fenian song or a rebel song. And the man that had got him to play a Protestant song didn't know the difference one tune from another. So whatever he had've played he patted him on the back he says, "That's the best wee tune I heard in a long time."

Interparty joking regularly took place between Charlie Mulligan, the Protestant man described above, and his Catholic drinking buddies, including two singers, Jimmy Halpin and Francie Conlan. During my first afternoon in McQuillan's Pub, after Francie had sung "The Manchester Martyrs," Charlie threatened to "sing The Sash." (Orange sashes are worn by members of the Loyalist Orange Order on 12 of July parades.)

CHARLIE. I [unintelligible] I wouldn't sing The Sash.
FRANCIE. I dar' ye.
CHARLIE. [unintelligible]
FRANCIE. Go on boy.
JIMMY. I'll sing it for him. I'll sing it for you.
CHARLIE. What?
FRANCIE. The Sash.
JIMMY. I'll sing a song for you . . . I'll sing it for you. I'll cover for Mulligan.
CHARLIE. Go on ahead. Go ahead. Sing for me.
JIMMY. I'll cover for Charlie.
CHARLIE. Yeah, cover for me.
JIMMY. No difference . . .
CHARLIE. You are one of the best [unintelligible] in the whole county in Cornavray [where Jimmy lives] . . . You cover for me, yeah.
JIMMY. [to me] Good girl.
CHARLIE. Good luck.

Jimmy sang The Sash, assisted by Francie Conlan, while Charlie laughed. At the conclusion, Jimmy sang,

Lie down and [unintelligible] you Orange cunt surrender or you'll
    die
We'll make 'em say "God bless the Pope" on the Twelfth Day of July
[spoken] Where?
On the green grassy slopes of the Boyne.

Jimmy followed the sash by singing "Thomas Williams," which contains the lines:

May their empire crumble like lumps o' clay
And the Belfast junta likewise decay.
May the yes men in Ireland be not there to tell
When her king and empire is blown to Hell . . .

In other circumstances, to sing a song with these sentiments would be a breach of etiquette. However, here was a group of associates who knew each other well, and the situation had been defined as one of good-natured taunting. Later in that same session, Charlie found himself the subject of more taunting. While singing "Biddy Mulligan," Francie made the following adaptation to the chorus:

And where would you see a fine a widow like me,
Biddy Mulligan from sweet Sandy Row?
[Sandy Row is an ardently Protestant area of Belfast.]

We can see that in this session Charlie and his friends agreed to acknowledge the tension and hostility that divide the two groups in Northern Ireland and then to diffuse and redefine it through shared laughter. The wish of "good luck" both before the song began and at its conclusion affirmed their neighborliness and camaraderie, ensuring that whatever tension and hostility might exist in this group would be, at least temporarily, defused.

Such interparty joking can only occur in a group of friends who know each other well, although taunting and other provocative behavior could always have negative consequences. Therefore, a strict code of etiquette is normally invoked. This is especially true when a large crowd is present, and when patrons who are not necessarily friends are uncertain about the sensibilities of others present. As might be expected, overtly political or religious discussions are taboo in "mixed company." Certainly those who are neighbors have some idea of each other's positions in these matters, but one can never be very sure of those he or she does not know. When one man from outside the area tried unsuccessfully to determine which political party I belonged to and, having failed to do so, called me a British spy, he was immediately pounced on verbally by the others in the pub and told by the barman that if he didn't keep quiet he would have to leave.

This code of etiquette is also applied in the realm of song. John Maguire is well aware of this. When singing in public he always likes to remain neutral in his song choices. For this reason he does not like to sing "Matt Fitzpatrick," although, as we shall see, he did so on one occasion under duress. It is deemed permissible for him to sing Gaelic football songs and the two that he invariably chooses are "The Bold Fifteen" and "The Hearty Sons of Dan." However, only on one occasion, when in a group of about ten Catholics, did I hear him sing the first verse:

Come all ye gaels from Erin's Isle
And listen unto me awhile
While I relate the praises of a club so near as them
It was called after that grand old man his name it was immortal Dan
Who struggled hard to try and get our little country free.

He usually omits this overt reference to Irish nationalism. The rest of the song, which depicts the exploits of the team, is a rallying cry reinforcing civic pride, and the chorus is usually sung lustily by those present in the pub.

Also, as Glassie found in Ballymenone, when party songs were sung, the songs that were selected tended to celebrate heroes and martyrs rather than to denigrate the "other side."[10] In both "The Manchester Martyrs" and "The Wild Rapparee" the narrator expresses the hope that the martyrs have taken their places in heaven along with Saint Patrick.

> Their beds are made in the highest Heaven
> Three holy angels around them stand
> Saint Patrick meets them with a crown of glory
> Saying "You're welcome soldiers from Ireland."
> > "The Manchester Martyrs," verse 4

> Now the Lord will have mercy on the soul that has fled
> He's now gone to rest with the glorious dead
> And when up in Heaven the angels will sing
> They'll welcome the outlaw, the Wild Rapparee.
> > "The Wild Rapparee," verse 6

"Matt Fitzpatrick" fits into this general mold too. The difference is that Matt had been reared in Wattle Bridge and his memory, not to mention the Troubles of 1921, was still fresh in the minds of a good many of the older people in the area. During one session [Easter Monday, 1979] John Maguire was asked to sing "Matt Fitzpatrick." He protested that he would rather not sing it, but gave in and sang the song, assisted by Francie Conlan. Francie, who has a habit of personalizing his songs and improvising on the spot, did so on this occasion, perhaps sensing the tension that had been created by singing that song.

> It was to the funeral in Drumully and to the church they went
> With the remains of Matt Fitzpatrick [unintelligible]they went
> They went unto Drumully, that place of peace and rest
> Where Matt Fitzpatrick was laid in a grave, of a[unintelligible] man of
>   the best.

> So here's to you young fellows, and the truth to yous I'll tell
> The night that Matt was shot at Clones I remember quiet and well
> I was sittin' in Lambrock House with neighbors of my own
> When the news come round that Matt was shot
> Every man [unintelligible] on his loan.

> Oh I remember quiet and well I was lyin' in me bed in a place they
>   call it Lambrock where me and us do dwell

The knock come to me father's window, I hope in heaven does rest
He talked to the boys through the window and the backdoor they
    come in.

Well I can name every man; quite well I remember it now
There was men from Derrykerrib and Wattle Bridge just as well
But me father didn't turn them out; he brought them in and give
    them tay
He went down the bog lane and come up with a big pint of poteen.

[Roars of approval from patrons]

. . . Boys to perfection, which I never will forget
There was one man stopped at home that day in a house they called
    Lambrock
His name was Johnny Tummon from Derrykerrib shore
And me father always said to them, "Good luck, good luck galore."

What Francie does, then, is redirect the tension created by singing a
song about an IRA commandant; he shifts the focus to neighborliness
and camaraderie by specifically mentioning a man who is locally well
known as well as the drinkable symbols of hospitality, tea and poteen.

Other songs, such as "Patrick Sheehan" and "Skibereen," catalogue
injustices. It is true, for example, that "Skibereen" concludes with the
lines, "Revenge for Skibereen," and "Patrick Sheehan" warns young
men,

If you join the English ranks you're sure to rue the day
And if you are inclined a'soldiering to go
Think of poor blind Sheehan on the Glens of Aherlow.

The songs, however, are primarily narrative rather than simple rallying
cries. Notably absent from the repertoire are songs like "A Nation Once
Again" or songs that openly taunt the other side. Ever present, even in
party songs, is the stress on solidarity.

Now boys get together in all kinds of weather
Don't show the white feather wherever you go
Just be like a brother and love one another
Like true hearted boys from the County Mayo.

Since I only knew of one family of Protestants who sang, and since they
did not usually go to the pubs, I have no data to indicate what would
happen should a Protestant sing a party song in "mixed" company, nor
have I heard stories of circumstances that might have led to fisticuffs or
worse among neighbors. My data indicate that the type of songs that

were sung very much depended on the singers' perceptions of their audience. In general, people are careful to keep latent hostility latent and to avoid any behavior likely to cause hostility.

They tend to redirect focus from the explosive conflict in a variety of ways. One way is by shifting emphasis from the "great conflict" to smaller conflicts and rivalries in sport, for example. Newtownbutler has two darts teams, a Gaelic football team, and a hunting club. These are formal organizations, where meetings are held and membership dues are charged. Both hunting and Gaelic football are the subjects of numerous songs that are favorites in the pub, such as "The Huntsman's Horn in the Early Morn," "Hark All Jolly Huntsmen," "The Fair at Roslea," "The Bold Fifteen," and "The Hearty Sons of Dan." It is no accident that most of the singers are sportsmen and that their audiences show a keen interest as well. Pictures of Newtown's past football teams adorn the walls of the pub, and people are constantly replaying past games in conversation. Even when Newtownbutler's sport is not being talked about, attention will likely be fixed on a horserace on television, and bets will be placed. For example of how emphasis on conflict can be redirected, consider the incident in which the Protestant man asked the Catholic singer, Jimmy, for "The Bold Fifteen." The transcript of this segment reveals that the conflict enacted is not the Ulster conflict, but rather a rivalry between the Newtownbutler team and St. Pat's, the team from Donagh two miles away, to which Jimmy owes his allegiance.

PATRON. This is between two teams in Newtownbutler. The team in Newtownbutler won the championship.
JIMMY. It's not my team now.
MARGE. Not your team?
JOEY. Not his team.
PATRON. Newtownbutler—
JOEY. He knows the song.
JIMMY. My team is goin' now on Sunday . . . the fuckin' championship.
JOEY. St. Pat's—
JOEY. And I hope they're beat . . .

Jimmy repeatedly protests, stating that Newtown is not his team, but finally, under duress, he sings the song.

On another occasion, most of the patrons in the pub were singing

Newtown, that's the place for us,
Whether we're on the cycle or we take the Ulsterbus.
Newtown, in sunshine or in rain.
No matter when we leave it, sure we'll always come back again.

Several of the St. Pat's supporters tried to drown out the singing with cries of "Up St. Pat's!"

Sometimes other types of tension in the community can be the source of song and conversation, like one youthful collaboration in 1953 between Catholics and Protestants making Halloween mischief. It resulted in a song, jointly made by a Catholic and a Protestant. The local breadman, a Protestant, had a gate taken off during the merrymaking, did not think it funny, and informed the police. The mischief-makers had to appear in court and were fined a pound apiece for their participation. Because the breadman failed to take in stride the fact that the youths were striving to "Uphold that ancient custom that can not be put down/ To take off all gates along the road and throw rockets in the town," he was subjected to ridicule by both Catholics and Protestants. As resident Ina Lattimore recalled, "He lost a lot of trade and he wouldn't speak to them for a long time, for years after." Thus Catholics and Protestants together reinforced the shared value of good sportsmanship and exercised social sanction on the breadman through song, not to mention ostracism.

Other shared values are emphasized as well. Among these, of course, is the pride of place, the solidarity that stems from "belonging to" Newtownbutler, Fermanagh, and Ireland as a whole. Thus Newtownbutler, as well as other villages in the area, has its own sporting songs that celebrate the superiority of the Newtownbutler hounds or football players. Songs that celebrate the beauty of particular localities are also popular, especially "The Lovely River Finn," "Lovely Fermanagh," and "Lovely Lougherne and Her Islands so Green." Here are the first and last verses of "The Lovely River Finn" as sung by Sunny Kearns:

> Well I was born in the year of eight in a place called Ballyhoe,
> Where underneath the old stone bridge the River Finn does flow.
> It winds its way through meadows gay through Newton and
>   Lisnakea,
> Where it joins the Erne, the winding Erne, and it flows down to the
>   sea.
> Now I'm old, I'm gray, I must away, for all things must die.
> In the green graveyard by Connan's church let my old bones gently
>   lie;
> In the heavens above, with the God of love, a new life will begin.
> And nevermore will I walk the shore of the lovely River Finn.

Ties with family are also important in this community of traditional values. It is not surprising, therefore, that "mother songs" are favorites in the pub, including "Good-bye Johnny Dear," "Shall I E'er See You More, Gentle Mother," and "A Mother's Love's a Blessing."

> A mother's love's a blessing no matter where you roam.
> Love her when she's living, for you'll miss her when she's gone;
> Love her as in childhood, when she's feeble, old and grey;
> For you'll never miss your mother's love till she's buried beneath the
>   clay.

Some of these parlor songs, as well as some of the current broadside stories, reinforce traditional values by contrasting them with their opposites. For example, the two ballads that I collected about the murder of John Flanagan by Joseph Fee "for a fifty pound check," though rarely sung in the pub, are sung to inveigh against disruption in the community; murder (as opposed to killing for one's country) is a heinous crime that traditionally has been rare indeed. And in the four versions of "Carey and O'Donnell" that I collected, the issue in the song texts as well as in the singers' comments is not that Carey and O'Donnell helped commit the Phoenix Park murders (indeed, this fact is never mentioned) but rather that Carey was an informer.[11] In fact, in much of the behavior described in this essay a fear of treachery implicitly underlies the shows of friendliness and neighborliness.[12]

Here is an anecdote told by Frank McGahern in which the protagonist is well aware of and invokes several types of responses to conflict.

> This old fella, he was fond of a drink, and I went down to see him with an old friend [in the hospital]. He used to be in Leggy Kelly's. He was an old friend of mine.
>
> I ran down a half pint [of poteen] and when I went to put it under the bed, there were four or five pints in the hospital, d' ye see.
>
> "If you're not so bad I'm going out tomorrow."
>
> This was a big ward he was in. There were about sixteen beds in it. And there was an old fella—he was about ninety-two—and he was talkin' about the good man he was. Says he, "But I'm dyin', I mean to die."
>
> "Right old fella."
>
> "And do you know what good is the whole damn thing when it's over? It's over now, and I have to die."
>
> This old fella ninety-two, and a big old shouting man—powerful old fella.
>
> The next day Dinny was going out, and he produced a half pint of whiskey. The old fellow was bad with his kidneys. He was all bad, d' ye see. He was breaking up, and he wasn't going to get anything. And then he [Dinny] gave him [the whiskey].
>
> "Damn but that's good whiskey. Give me another sup of that."

And then he give him a second glass d'ye see of the whiskey. Well, the old man sat up in bed, and he started to sing treason songs, "Kevin Barry" and "Lord Waterford" and anything that come into his head. And there were two or three Protestants down at the end of the ward and they objected, says that wasn't———, and him in the Queen's hospital, d'ye see. Always the Queen's down here. And a row got up.

"Indeed damn your souls," he says, "Was them not good songs?"

"No they were not. No gentleman would sing trash like that."

"One of them was [unintelligible] than the rest says, "I dare you sing a good Protestant song." Says he, "Could you sing The Sash?"

"Well," he says, "I can try it anyway."

And dammit, but he up and he sang The Sash. Now he says, "You rotten old Orange, old bastard," he says, "I'll sing you a good song."

And he sang "The Bold Fenian Men" or something. And then they pressed the bell again. Next thing, the nurses and all come in.

"O Holy God what's wrong?"

"He's trying to insult us singing old trash songs there to vex us."

"And sure Mr. So and So," the nurses called him, "You're in here, you're dyin'."

"Well sure what odds? I'm dyin' I suppose I am."

"O Holy God we thought you were dyin'.' "

"Well I'm supposed to be dyin'. Sure if I die now, I'm happy. I'm going straight to Heaven."

D'ye see, he was after getting that whiskey.

"Do you know where Heaven is?"

"Well," he says, "I don't. To tell the truth I don't know, but I know the very next station to it."

"Be God, if you know the next station you wouldn't be tellin'."

"It's just someplace about it now; the very last station to Heaven I know it."

"Where is it?"

"Newtownbutler," he says. He was just after getting the whiskey from the Newtownbutler men.

Conflict is acknowledged, but the protagonist invokes, when all is said and done, pride of place. Despite whatever problems may exist, he suggests, Newtownbutler is the next station to Heaven and all can sing proudly,

Newtown in sunshine or in rain
No matter when we leave it, sure we'll always come back again.

NOTES

1. Dennis P. Barritt and Charles F. Carter, *The Northern Ireland Problem: A Study of Group Relations* (London and New York: Oxford University Press, 1962).

2. Rosemary Harris, *Prejudice and Tolerance in Ulster: A Study of Neighbors and "Strangers" in a Border Community* (Manchester: Manchester University Press, 1972).

3. Henry Glassie, *All Silver and No Brass: An Irish Christmas Mumming* (Bloomington: Indiana University Press, 1975), and *Passing the Time in Ballymenone* (Philadelphia: University of Pennsylvania Press, 1982).

4. All quoted comments, narratives, dialogues, and song lyrics attributed to Newtownbutler residents were recorded or observed during my visits to that community in summer 1978, spring 1979, and summer 1983.

5. Peadar Livingstone, *The Fermanagh Story: A Documentary History of the County from the Earliest Times to the Present Day* (Enniskillen, Ire.: Cumann Seanchais Chlochair, 1969).

6. These are holidays recognizing the victory of William of Orange and the defeat of the Stuart cause: the 12 July battles of Boyne and Aughrim in 1690 and 1691, and the Apprentice Boys' Parade on 12 August.

7. Harris, *Prejudice and Tolerance.*

8. Victor W. Turner, *The Ritual Process: Structure and Anti-Structure* (Chicago: Aldine, 1969).

9. Roger D. Abrahams, "Toward an Enactment-Centered Theory of Folklore," in *Frontiers of Folklore,* ed. William R. Bascom (Boulder, Colo.: Westview Press, 1977), 79–120.

10. Glassie, *Passing the Time.*

11. George Dennis Zimmerman, "Irish Political Street Ballads and Rebel Songs" (Ph.D. diss., University of Geneva, 1966).

12. Harris, *Prejudice and Tolerance.*

Contributors

THOMAS FLANAGAN received the 1983 Gold Medal of the American Irish Historical Society and the National Book Critics' Circle Award for *The Year of the French*. At present he is finishing a second novel. He is Professor of English at the State University of New York at Stony Brook.

RICHARD MURPHY, one of Ireland's most notable contemporary poets, recently published *The Price of Stone*. He lives in Dublin and has frequently held visiting appointments at American universities. In the spring of this Tacoma conference he was Distinguished Writer in Residence at Pacific Lutheran University.

DECLAN KIBERD, Lecturer in English at University College, Dublin, has written *Synge and the Irish Language* and *Men and Feminism in Modern Literature*. One of the authors of the *Field Day* pamphlets, he directs a regular television show on Irish culture and writes regularly for Irish newspapers.

BONNIE KIME SCOTT is Professor of English at the University of Delaware. She has written numerous articles on Irish writers, modernist literature, and women writers, and is the author of *Joyce and Feminism*.

HAZARD ADAMS is Professor of English and Comparative Literature at the University of Washington and Senior Fellow of the School of Criticism and Theory at Dartmouth College. His most recent books are *Philosophy of the Literary Symbolic* and *Joyce Cary's Trilogies*.

ROBERT TRACY, Professor of English at the University of California, Berkeley, has edited Synge's *The Aran Islands and Other Writings* as well as translated the Russian poet Osip Mandelstram and written *Trollope's Later Novels*. His reviews appear frequently in *Eire-Ireland*, *Nineteenth-Century Fiction*, and the *Irish Literary Supplement*.

David Lloyd is Assistant Professor of English at the University of California, Berkeley. His *Nationalism and Minor Literature: James Clarence Mangan and the Emergence of Irish Cultural Nationalism* is forthcoming from the University of California Press. He is presently studying relations among political economy, political theory, and aesthetic culture in nineteenth-century Britain.

James S. Donnelly, Jr.'s publications include *Landlord and Tenant in Nineteenth-Century Ireland* and *The Land and the People of Nineteenth-Century Cork*, which won the American Historical Association's 1975 Herbert Baxter Adams Prize. His recent studies have focused on Irish agrarian rebellions in the late eighteenth and early nineteenth centuries. He is Professor of History at the University of Wisconsin, Madison.

Maryann Gialanella Valiulis is Assistant Professor of History at Lafayette College. She has written *Almost a Rebellion: The Irish Army Mutiny of 1924* and is now completing a political biography, *General Richard Mulcahy and the Establishment of the Irish Free State.*

Philip O'Leary has for fourteen years been affiliated with the Xavernian Brothers Highschool in Westwood, Massachusetts. In 1985 he was a Mellon Faculty Fellow in the Celtic Department at Harvard University. His essay here comes from work in progress on the creation of a modern prose literature in Irish between 1881 and 1916. He is the Irish Language Editor of the *Irish Literary Supplement* and chairs the Irish Language Committee of the ACIS.

Padraig O'Malley is Senior Associate at the John W. McCormack Institute of Public Affairs at the University of Massachusetts, Boston. He edits the *New England Journal of Public Policy,* and he is the author of *The Uncivil Wars: Ireland Today.*

Margaret Steiner expects the Ph.D. in folklore from Indiana University in 1987. Her works in progress include field research in the Mirimichi region of New Brunswick, a collection of folksongs from County Fermanagh, and a book on singing and sociability in Newtonbutler. An earlier version of the essay here appeared in Northeastern University's *Working Papers in Irish Studies,* 1985.

Index

Abbey Theatre, 147, 149, 150, 153. *See also* Irish Literary Theatre

Achebe, Chinua, 82; *Things Fall Apart*, 82

"Adam's Curse" (Yeats), 58

Æ. *See* Russell, George William

Aeneid, The (Virgil), 84

"Affirmative Capability," 71

Alexander the Great, 35

Alliance Party, 161, 163

All That Fall (Beckett), 93

Ambroses, 116, 124

American Conference on Irish Studies, 7, 9, 55, 62

Ante-Room, The (O'Brien), 61

Anxiety of Influence, The (Bloom), 33

Area of Darkness: An Experience of India, An (Naipaul), 42

Arendt, Hannah, 43–44

Autobiography (Mangan), 98, 101–2, 105–8

Awakening, The (Chopin), 59

Bakhtin, M. M., 75

Balliet, Conrad, 56, 57

Bards of the Gael and the Gall (Sigerson), 146

"Battle of Aughrim, The" (Murphy), 8, 15, 17, 19–23

BBC (British Broadcasting Company), 20, 85

Beckett, Samuel, 38, 39–40, 43, 88, 93–94. Works: *All That Fall*, 93; *Endgame*, 40; *Murphy*, 40, 93; *Play*, 85; *The Unnamable*, 39, 94; *Waiting for Godot*, 88

Belfast, 167, 173, 178

Berger, John, 36; "The Suit and the Photograph," 36

Beyle, Marie Henri [pseud. Stendhal], 81

"Biddy Mulligan," 179

Blackfeet, 117, 118–19, 124; and Shanavests, 117

Blake, William, 65, 68, 70, 71, 72, 73, 76–77

Bloom, Harold, 33; *The Anxiety of Influence*, 33

Blythe, Ernest, 136, 137, 140, 146; *Slán le hUltaibh (Farewell to Ulster)*, 146

Boland, Eavan, 60, 61; *In Her Own Image*, 60; *Night-feed*, 60

"Bold Fifteen, The," 179, 182

Books of Kells, The, 67

Botany Bay, 125

Boundary Commission, 140, 141

Brien, Paud, 115, 122

Brown, Norman O., 28

Browne, Ivor, 50; and Irish identity, 50

Browne, Joseph, 60

Brugha, Cathal, 43

Bruno, Giordano, 70, 74

Bryson, Mary, 58

Buber, Martin, 176

Bultmann, Rudolf, 27

Burgess, Anthony, 75

Caesar, Julius, 35

Campbell, Joseph, 66; (with Henry Morton Robinson) *A Skeleton Key to "Finnegans Wake,"* 66

Caravats, 114, 115, 117–18, 120; and faction fighting, 114; origin of name, 120; and Shanavests, 114–20

"Carey and O'Donnell," 184

Carmilla (Le Fanu), 86, 119

Carroll, Lewis. *See* Dodgson, Charles

Carte postale, La (Derrida), 68

Cathleen ni Houlihan (Yeats), 24

Chateaubriand, François, 81, 85; *Mémoires d'outre-tombe*, 85

Chekhov, Anton, 81, 85

Chopin, Kate, 59; *The Awakening*, 59

Churchill, Winston, 29

Churchyard Clay. See Cré na Cille